Religion and Law in India

Religion and Law in India

Third Edition

Mohammad Naseem

Saman Naseem

This book was originally published as a monograph in the International Encyclopaedia of Laws/Religion Law.

Founding Editor: Roger Blanpain
General Editor: Frank Hendrickx
Volume Editor: Wouter Druwé

Wolters Kluwer

Published by:
Kluwer Law International B.V.
PO Box 316
2400 AH Alphen aan den Rijn
The Netherlands
E-mail: lrs-sales@wolterskluwer.com
Website: www.wolterskluwer.com/en/solutions/kluwerlawinternational

Sold and distributed by:
Wolters Kluwer Legal & Regulatory U.S.
920 Links Avenue
Landisville, PA 17538
United States of America
E-mail: customer.service@wolterskluwer.com

ISBN 978-94-035-1179-5

e-Book: ISBN 978-94-035-1189-4
web-PDF: ISBN 978-94-035-1199-3

The Author

Mr Mohammad Naseem born and brought up in Sardarnagar, District Pilibhit, India, is a science graduate and has a Master of Laws with a specialization in Commercial Law from Aligarh Muslim University, India. He is an Energy Law Expert and ex-General Manager (Legal) of ONGC Limited, which he joined in 1985. He was also Vice President-Legal at ONGC-Videsh Limited for seven years. At present, he is the Chairman and Managing Partner of Global Law and Liaison Services, New Delhi. In his professional career spanning more than three decades, he has dealt with a large number of high-value commercial matters, domestic and international arbitration and litigation. He has been part of a large number of negotiation teams, having successfully negotiated various types of contracts worth billions of dollars including acquisitions of petroleum properties in a number of countries. He is the author of a monograph/book on energy law, environmental law, sports law, medical law of India, Islamic law of contracts, international energy law, international environmental law and international medical law for Wolters Kluwer, the Netherlands and has had to his credit a number of papers published in national and international journals of repute. He is the co-author of *Fuel and Energy II (Petroleum and Natural Gas)* of Halsbury's Laws of India Series (volume 21) published by LexisNexis Butterworths India Limited. Edward Elgar Publishing Limited has published a paper authored by him, by the title 'World Petroleum Regimes' in the Hand Book on *International Energy Law* and another article on 'Natural Gas Provisions in Host Government Contracts – Regulatory and Contractual Aspects in India' published by Oil, Gas and Energy Law Intelligence (OGEL), United Kingdom (UK). He is the visiting faculty and guest expert speaker of the Indian Academy of International Law and Diplomacy, University of Petroleum and Energy Studies, Dehradun and Indian School of Petroleum, New Delhi. He has travelled extensively throughout the world in relation to negotiation and delivering lectures. He has spoken in seminars organized by IBC Asia Limited in Singapore, Oil and Gas IQPC in Bangkok, Thailand, Kuala Lumpur, Malaysia and Tehran, Iran in a seminar conducted by OIPF, Iran. For conducting negotiations, he has visited Myanmar, Singapore, Vietnam, Japan, South Korea, Hong Kong, Thailand, Iran, UAE, Iraq, Jordan, Syria, Turkey, Egypt, Libya, Sudan, South Sudan, Italy, Russia, Kazakhstan, Denmark, the Netherlands, Switzerland, France, the UK, the United

The Author

States of America (USA), Canada, Ecuador, Venezuela, and Uzbekistan. He is a life member of the Indian Society of International Law and is a permanent member of the India International Law Foundation, a very prestigious body. With more than thirty years of varied practical and on-the-job legal experience in negotiation, drafting, interpretation and vetting of legal documents and dealing with arbitration and litigation on the one hand and acting as a trainer, speaker and author, on the other hand, Mr Naseem has been part of an exclusive team of trainers, negotiators, advisers, and strategists and is a legal luminary of international repute in his own right. Email: naseem_md@yahoo.com.

Co-author

Ms. Saman Naseem holds her post-graduation in Commercial Law from Aligarh Muslim University. She graduated in law from Symbiosis International University. She is a Founder Partner of Global Law and Liaison Services, a firm providing professional advice in the field of law. She is an active participant in seminars and conferences and has presented research papers on various topics. She is co-author of a monograph on energy law, international energy law, international environmental law, environmental law of India, international medical law, medical law of India, sports law of India and Islamic law of contracts for Wolters Kluwer, the Netherlands. Edward Elgar Publishing Limited has published an article co-authored by her, by the title, 'World Petroleum Regimes'. Another article on 'Natural Gas Provisions in Host Government Contracts –Regulatory and Contractual Aspects in India' has been published by OGEL, UK. She has been connected with Non-governmental Organizations (NGOs), namely the Madad Foundation Trust, and supports various social causes like the Leprosy Eradication Drive by the Indian Leprosy Foundation and collection of funds for HelpAge India for the poor, needy and blind, to name a few.

Email: saman1492@gmail.com.

Co-author

Table of Contents

List of Abbreviations

ADM	Additional District Magistrate
AIMPLB	All India Muslim Personal Law Board
BJP	Bhartiya Janta Party
BJS	Bharatiya Jana Sangh
Cr. P.C	Code of Criminal Procedure, 1973
Evidence Act	Indian Evidence Act, 1872
FCI	Food Corporation of India
G. O.	Government Order
HAMA	Hindu Adoption and Maintenance Act, 1956
HIV	Human Immunodeficiency Virus
HJF	Hindu Joint Family
HMA	Hindu Marriage Act
HRCE Act	Hindu Religious and Charitable Endowment Act
HUF	Hindu Undivided Family
ICCPR	International Covenant on Civil and Political Rights
IPC	Indian Penal Code
J&K	Jammu and Kashmir
LGBT	Lesbian, Gay, Bisexual, and Transgender
LTTE	Liberation Tigers of Tamil Eelam
NCDC	National Council of Dalit Christians
NCM	National Commission for Minorities
NCMEI	National Commission for Minority Educational Institution
NGOs	Non-governmental Organizations
NRI	Non-resident Indian
NRC	National Register of Citizens
OBC	Other Backward Castes
OSCE	Organization for Security and Co-operation in Europe

List of Abbreviations

PIL	Public Interest Litigation
POTA	Prevention of Terrorism Act, 2002
PUCL	People's Union for Civil Liberties
RP Act	Representation of Peoples Act
RPM	Respiratory Particulate Matter
RSS	Rashtriya Swayam Sewak Sangh
SAD	Shiromani Akali Dal
SAD-S	Simranjit Singh Mann
SARDA Act	Child Marriage Restraint Act is called SARDA Act as Mr Harbilas Sarda made all efforts and got it passed in the Legislative Assembly
SC/ST	Scheduled Caste/Scheduled Tribe
SPM	Suspended Particulate Matter
TN	Tamil Nadu
UCC	Uniform Civil Code
UDHR	Universal Declaration of Human Rights
UN	United Nations
UNCITRAL	United Nation Commission for International Trade Law
UNICEF	United Nations International Children Education Fund
UP	Uttar Pradesh
UPA	United Progressive Alliance
USA	United States of America
UT	Union Territory

Preface

This description of the Religion Law of India and views expressed herein are in the personal capacity of the authors and do not represent in any way their employer or other organizations with which they are associated in one capacity or another.

Mohammad Naseem & Saman Naseem
New Delhi, August 2024

General Introduction

§1. General Background of the Country

I. Basic Structure

A. Geography

1. India lies in the southern peninsula of the Asian Continent and has a triangular shape tapering southwards to the Indian Ocean. It has an area of approximately 3,287,580 sq. km. with the Bay of Bengal to the east, the Indian Ocean to the south and the Arabian Sea to the west. A mountain range, the Himalayas, lies to the north. India may be divided into four main regions, namely the great mountain zone, the Ganges and Indus Plains, the desert zone and the southern peninsula. Its neighbours are Myanmar and Bangladesh in the east, China, Nepal and Bhutan to the north and Afghanistan and Pakistan in the north-west. Sri Lanka lies to the south, separated from India by the Palk Straits. There are several varied ecological and climatic zones. India has the highest snowbound mountain range in the world, the Himalayas, and humid tropical forests on the south-west coast, the fertile Brahmaputra valley, low mangrove swamps of the Sundarbans and the Garo Hills of Meghalaya, which is the wettest spot on the universe, lying to the east.

2. India is a vast country endowed with diverse physical features of the land, ecological and climatic zones, fauna and flora, culture, religions, languages, climate, etc. The land consists of snowbound peaks, beautiful hills, fertile river valleys, lush and green plains, tropical rainforests, blistering deserts and breathtakingly beautiful long coastal areas. India lies entirely in the northern hemisphere, measuring about 3,214 km from north to south between the extreme latitudes and about 2,933 km from east to west between the extreme longitudes. With a land frontier of 15,200 km and a mainland coastal line of 6,100 km and those of the Lakshadweep group of islands and Andaman and Nicobar group of islands of about 1,516.5 km, India is rightly called a subcontinent.

3. The Ganga and Yamuna emerge from the mountains and flow into the Gangetic plain. These rivers cause constant erosion thereby building the vast alluvial Gangetic plains. The Brahmaputra river forms the world's largest and most fertile delta, the Brahmaputra valley, before flowing into the Bay of Bengal. A series of low mountain ranges lies between the Deccan Plateau and the Gangetic plain like the Aravallis and Vindhyas. The plateau has the Eastern and Western Ghats flanking its sides. The western coastal plain is uneven and rivers flow through it forming beautiful lagoons and backwaters. On the western side of India are the Lakshadweep Islands in the Arabian Sea and on the eastern side lie the Andaman and Nicobar Islands in the Bay of Bengal. Because of these islands, India shares its border with Indonesia.

4. India has three major seasons, namely summer, winter and rainy season (monsoon). Summer months are generally hot and humid in most parts of India. Summer is experienced between the months of March to May. Winter months fall between the months of mid-November to early March and are pleasantly cool for most parts of India but severe in the northern plains and the areas around the Himalayan range. India experiences two monsoon spells, the south-west monsoon from June to September and the north-west monsoon from October to early December. There is a wide variety of natural vegetation that ranges from the tropical to tundra regions. India can be divided into four major vegetation regions, namely: (a) the Himalayan region; (b) the tropical wet evergreen and semi-evergreen forests; (c) the tropical deciduous forests; and (d) the thorn forests and shrubs.

5. There are over 1,350 species of birds, (State of India's Birds, 2023) which include varieties of pheasants, quails and wildfowl, mostly found in the Himalayan region. Storks, cranes, flamingos and kingfishers can also be found in certain regions of the country. The most spectacular and exquisite of all the birds is the peacock, the national bird of India, which is found throughout the country. There are over five hundred species of mammals which include elephants, rhinoceros, bears, lions and tigers, just to name a few. A large variety of marine life is found in rivers and seas around it.

B. Cultural Composition

6. Indians belong to diverse ethnic groups and present the most diverse mixture of races. The five major racial types, Australoid, Caucasian, Europoid, Mongoloid and Negroid, find representation among the people of India. Various phases of Indian history show waves of invaders and settlers including the Aryans, Greeks and Central Asians coming into the country, intermingling religions, settling and merging with the local population. This historical process explains the racial, linguistic, and cultural variety and diversity of India.

C. Population

7. The population of India was 1,403,606,220 as of March 31, 2022, based on Worldometer elaboration of the latest United Nations data. This population is equivalent to 17.7% of the total world population. The population density in India is 464 per km^2. Yet, it is still lower than the population density in South Korea (526), Taiwan (669) and the Netherlands (507). The growth in population eats away the fruits of development, thereby keeping down the growth in per capita income and is considered not only contributing to but also accelerating environmental degradation. Reaching such densities of population presents monumental problems on the environment front. However, the rate of growth of the population has started steadily declining. India started its population control programme on a large scale early in the 1950s, but it relied only on publicity and persuasion except for a brief period in 1975–1977 during the emergency. An interesting development has taken place in Haryana, one of the States of India where any person having more than two children is disqualified from contesting local body elections and this has been upheld by the Supreme Court. Bihar, Assam, Himachal Pradesh, Madhya Pradesh, Rajasthan, Haryana, Andhra Pradesh, Odisha, Chhattisgarh, Gujarat, Maharashtra and Uttarakhand have also at some point implemented the two-child policy for state government employees.

8. Indians belong to diverse ethnic groups and India presents the most diverse mixture of races. The five major racial types, Australoid, Caucasian, Europoid, Mongoloid and Negroid, find representation among the people of India. Various phases of Indian history show waves of invaders and settlers including the Aryans, Greeks and Central Asians coming into the country, intermingling religions, settling and merging with the local population. This historical process explains the racial, linguistic, and cultural variety and diversity of India.

D. Environment

9. The growing population, high degree of mechanization and steep rise in energy use have led to activities that directly or indirectly affect the sustainability of the environment. Reduction in forest cover has resulted in a reduction of sink for the carbon dioxide and soil degradation, contamination of surface and groundwater and pollution of the air with Suspended Particulate Matter (SPM), Respiratory Particulate Matter (RPM), hydrocarbons and acid gases, all of which are causing health problems. There is dumping of poisonous waste on the ground. The water resources are polluted due to the discharge of untreated or partially treated wastes from industry, domestic sewage and fertilizer or pesticide runoff from agricultural fields into water bodies. The country faces serious threats to its rich and diverse natural resource environment from industrial and other pollution.

E. Economy

10. India is the fifth largest economy in the world and a prominent developing country. It launched a strategy of planned development in 1950, starting with a mixed economy and subsequently allowing moves towards a market economy. India is reasonably well endowed with a variety of natural resources. The economy is largely self-sufficient in spheres like agricultural produce. The quality and sophistication of Indian skills best illustrate the economic power of the country. A major part of income comes from the export of manpower. The Indian market is widely diversified and sophisticated, with considerable industrialization made possible by its own machine-building industry. India is a large emerging and open market for international trade.

11. India has the know-how and capacity to produce atomic energy from nuclear reactors designed indigenously. It has installed huge thermal power plants of 500 MW capacity. Industries like textiles, sugar and cement largely run on machinery made in the country. India has attained such sophistication and degree of skill that it can design and build large steel mills entirely on its own and has designed and put on the market its own supercomputer. Despite all these achievements, parts of the economy have not changed and still lag behind, while others are right at the forefront of technology.

II. General Legal System

12. After Independence, India adopted a parliamentary form of democracy. On 26 January 1950, the Constitution of India was enacted which is in force and in practice since then. It makes India a Union of States with a strong federal centre and declares India a Sovereign, Socialist, Secular, Democratic Republic. The Constitution closely follows the British Parliamentary model with the difference that in India the Constitution is supreme, whereas in England, Parliament is supreme. The laws in existence at the time of promulgation of the Constitution or passed thereafter must conform to the Constitution. In case any law is inconsistent with or derogates from the constitutional provisions, such law shall be void to the extent of such inconsistency or derogation. The Supreme Court and High Courts are vested with the authority to adjudicate on the constitutionality of laws. The Constitution guarantees fundamental rights to the citizens, e.g., the right to equality, the right to freedom, the right against exploitation, the right to freedom of religion, cultural and educational rights for minorities, etc. These rights are enforceable against the State. The right to enforce fundamental rights and to seek judicial remedies against the State through issuance of writs is also a fundamental right.

13. The Constitution also prescribes fundamental duties such as the duty to respect the Constitution, National Flag and National Anthem; to develop scientific awareness; to strive towards excellence in all spheres of individual and collective activity so that the nation constantly rises to higher levels of endeavour and achievement, etc. The Directive Principles of State Policy contain principles to be kept in view by the State while framing laws and policies of the State but these are not binding and enforceable against the State. However, courts have selected certain Directive Principles, which are identifiable with fundamental rights and have treated them as fundamental rights and enforced them as such.

14. The Parliament in New Delhi is the supreme and central legislative body. It comprises the President and the two Houses, namely Lok Sabha (House of the People) and Rajya Sabha (Council of States). The President is the Executive Head of the State and Supreme Commander of the Armed Forces (Article 53 of the Constitution). The President is elected from an Electoral College consisting of: (a) elected members of both Houses of Parliament; and (b) the elected members of the Legislative Assemblies of the states (Article 54). The President holds office for a period of five years and can be re-elected for a further period of five years (Articles 56 and 57 of the Constitution).

15. There is a demarcation of power between the Centre and states with respect to framing of laws and their implementation. The Constitution contains three lists, namely the Union List, the State List and the Concurrent List. The Union List contains matters on which the Central Government has the exclusive right to make laws. The State List includes items over which a state government has the power to make laws, and the Concurrent List contains items over which both the Centre and states have authority to make laws. States enact their own laws on education, public health and local taxes, while the Centre deals with income tax, defence, foreign policy, railway, postal department, telecommunication, etc. The subjects of police force, education, agriculture and industry fall under the State List and are reserved for the state.

16. The country is divided into twenty-eight States and nine centrally administered Union Territories (UT). Some Union Territories have assemblies whereas some do not have and are directly governed by the Central Government. The Central Government appoints a Lt. Governor for Union Territories. Each state has an elected legislature headed by a Chief Minister. The Governor is the Head of the state government, appointed by the President for a term of five years. The Chief Minister, assisted by a cabinet, looks after the day-to-day administration of the state government. The Parliament, state legislatures, local bodies and other legally constituted authorities enact the laws falling within their respective sphere. The states have been divided into districts, districts into subdivisions, and subdivisions into basic units called *taluks* or *tehsils.* Large cities have corporations led by a mayor with the authority to make rules on certain local matters.

§2. Social Facts about Religion

I. Religious Affiliation

17. Religion is associated with emotions, especially with fear, awe or reverence of some entity by an individual and society. There is a wide range of institutions connected with religion and a body of special officials, with forms of worship, ceremonies, pilgrimages, etc. Looking at the definition of religion by Ogburn, 'Religion is an attitude towards super human power, it may be submitted that religion explains the relation of man with god and also elaborate rules of conduct.' Max Muller defines religion as a 'mental faculty or disposition, which enables man to apprehend the infinite'. Max Muller has also attempted to define religion as a matter of belief in supernatural forces. Man believes that he is at the mercy of the supernatural forces and shows his subordination to them by means of prayers, hymns, and other acts. A follower believes that his disrespect and non-observance of religion would bring disaster to him, so he engages in a continuous endeavour to adjust himself with the supernatural. He attempts to do only those acts, which according to religious teachings, are righteous and sacred to please the supernatural.

18. There is no universally acceptable definition of 'religion'. Religion, generally, is a belief or faith in the existence of a Supernatural Being and the precepts, which people follow for attaining salvation. Religion may be regarded as a belief and patterns of behaviours by which humans try to deal with what they view as important problems that cannot be solved through the application of known technologies and techniques. To overcome these limitations, people turn to the manipulation of supernatural beings and powers. Religion consists of various rituals, prayers, songs, dances, offerings and sacrifices, through which people try to satisfy supernatural beings and powers to their advantage. These beings and powers may consist of Gods and Goddesses, ancestors and other spirits or impersonal power. In all societies, there are certain individuals especially skilled at dealing with these beings and powers and who assist other members of society in their ritual activities.

19. In India, many religions are followed like Hinduism, Islam, Christianity, Buddhism, Sikhism, etc. Except for Hinduism, the caste system, particularly untouchability, is not practised by followers of other religions. The Hindu society was divided into caste lines based on Manusmriti (an ancient text written by Manu). In this social system, some castes were considered untouchables. After independence, the Constitution specifically abolished untouchability and its practice was made a punishable offence. The constitutional provisions also signify that India is a socialist and secular state. The Preamble of the Constitution reflects the way of life adopted by Indian citizens for themselves after independence. Religion indicates the faith of human beings in values propagated by the religion one follows and a practical way of life to realize those values. Religious faith provides the passion for preserving the way of life, and if the essence of the religion is not understood, the value system declines, obedience degenerates into habit and habit slowly withers way. Therefore, along with laws, customs and conventions, religion and morality which form the inner core of conscience also formulate and shape human behaviour. Religion and morality are the forces of control besides the law and also guide human behaviour. Religion is a major factor in Indian society, and many moral values emanating from religion are followed as divine dictates out of fear of supernatural forces rather than because of fear of law.

A. *Varna (Colour) and Jati (Caste) System*

20. In the post-Vedic times, the caste-based social system occupied a predominant position in India. There are about three thousand castes with four varnas, namely the learned people (Brahmans), the warriors (Chattries), traders (Vaishyas) and the service class (Shudras). However, there have been several kings or soldiers who came up from non-warrior backgrounds but attained success due to self-effort. For example, Chandra Gupta was born into a non-ruling family but became the

Emperor through his valour. Valmiki who composed Ramayana and Vyas who composed Mahabharata came up from a lower caste.

21. The problem with the caste system is that it permanently fixes the status of an individual in society on the basis of birth and puts certain restrictions. With modernization taking over the way of thinking and changing the very basis of living, some of these restrictions are softened but still prevalent in society, particularly at the village level. Still, professions, services, and political affiliations are influenced by castes. For example, in the elections for the assembly or the Parliament, caste and community considerations come into focus and are considered an important and deciding factor.

22. Among the non-Hindu groups, castes are not based on or recognized in terms of doctrine but exist as ground reality. Particularly arranged marriages are generally solemnized within once own caste and not outside. Even the converts from upper castes to other religions prefer their own caste level, in choosing the marriage partners. However, in present-day India, castes are interacting in public places as never before and the old social isolation does not exist in its extreme form except in some isolated places. In public places, people move together and take food in hotels without reference to their caste background. But in villages still, some caste boundaries are followed even in sitting, interacting, taking food, marriages, etc.

B. Social Movements

23. The Bhakti movement and Sufiism were important and prominent social movements emanating from religion and influencing society in a big way. Bhakti was a devotional movement, which emphasized the common man's nearness to God through love, affection and goodwill. The poets and saints composed poetry in the language of the common man. This also led to the start of the modernization of Indian languages by the literary efforts of these saints. They were popular because common people could easily understand the message and relate to them. The movement contributed to the softening of the caste system and secularization of Indian society by opening up common channels of communication and leading to social interaction among the people without any restriction to the caste background. In religious assemblies, (Satsang) organized by these saints, men, women and children and people from different castes prayed together, ate the food served to them and also stayed in common shelters bringing elements of unity. Similarly, the Sufis rallied people around them irrespective of their caste, creed or religious background. Both Bhakti and Sufi social gatherings helped in developing and fostering a harmonious culture in India.

II. Religious Practice

24. After independence, sections of lower castes, including the Dalits, acquired a new sense of dignity and self-respect through political mobilization and access to resources so as to assert and promote their interests at all levels. There has been greater inclusion of the lower strata of the people at the local, state, and national levels in the transition of power from the upper castes to the lower castes with major political consequences. The democratic empowerment based on 'one man one vote' in free and fair elections has put power in the hands of the more numerous lower castes and other backward castes (OBC). The shift in political power is helping loosen the grip of the caste system.

A. Secularism

25. Secularism has become the main trend in the modern world, and in Europe after the industrial revolution, many countries separated the state from the church in the public domain. The state adopted secular policies independent of the religion, thus making religious affairs part of the private domain of individual life. In India, there is not a strict separation between the secular and the religious domain. The different rulers adopted different practices. Some based their policies on religion, whereas others did not use religion for running or ruling the state and also did not like the interference of religion in the affairs of the state. The noted rulers of the past such as Ashoka, Kanishka, the Imperial Guptas and Harsha who controlled most parts of north India had followed a policy of tolerance towards religions. They made grants and donations to Hindu, Buddhist and Jain temples and monasteries. During the Muslim rule (eleventh to seventeenth centuries A.D.) there were some mixed trends. However, the Muslim sultans and kings tolerated religious diversities because it ensured for them the loyalty of their subjects. One such ruler was Allauddin Khilji who did not allow any interference in the affairs of the state by clergy. Aurangzeb, the later Mughal ruler, not only imposed upon non-Muslims a tax known as Jizya as Muslims pay Zakat but also ordered grants (jagirs) to Hindu temples. The actions were more influenced by administrative, political and financial considerations rather than enforcement of religion. Akbar, a liberal ruler, brought together Hindus and Muslims through his amity and goodwill. He even started a new religion with the name of Deen-e Elahi by combining the good attributes of all religions. The British rulers of the early period of colonialism were not opposed to India's religious traditions. Warren Hastings, the Governor General, sent his offerings to the temple of kali in Kolkata worshipped by Hindus. He also gave grants to Max Muller to edit and translate the Rigveda from Sanskrit into English. They also respected family laws of different religions and applied them in the administration of justice.

26. As India is inhabited by a large number of castes, communities, and races practising different religions so after independence, it was felt necessary that the State should keep itself aloof from the religion in accordance with a specific constitutional scheme peculiar to Indian conditions. The Constitution of India contains provisions for both secular and religious pursuits. The individuals and groups are free to follow their chosen way of life without curtailing and infringing on each other's rights. Dr B.R. Ambedkar, the main architect of the Constitution and belonging to a Dalit community, became a Buddhist and launched a social movement for the improvement of underprivileged groups. Mohan Das Karam Chand Gandhi, the Father of the Nation who led India to political freedom, was a religious person. He drew his ideas from the Gita, Bible and Quran. In the 1950s, Vinoba Bhave, a follower of Gandhi launched the Sarvodaya Movement to redeem the plight of the landless peasants and other deprived sections. He too used ideas drawn from religious texts to awaken the people and draw them out of their backwardness.

§3. Historical Background

27. In India, various religions are being practised, so historical background can be better understood by studying it individually. Often the implication of religion for law is that religion cannot be altered, modified or reformed easily as the practices being followed for generations, may not be given up easily. Further, in some religions, the religious texts are considered the word of God which cannot be amended or legislated. However, a thorough and detailed legal system has been developed with respect to all communities through human elaboration and also changes with time as circumstances change. For instance, the Quran is the source of Muslim law, and it acts as a source of further legal development through interpretation, Qiyas (reasoning by analogy), Ijma (consensus) and precedent. This is mainly contained in a body of law and jurisprudence known as Sharia and Fiqh, respectively. Another example is the Torah or Old Testament, in the Pentateuch or Five Books of Moses, which contains the basic code of Jewish law, used by some Israeli communities. The Halakha is also a code of Jewish law, which summarizes some of the Talmud's interpretations. Nevertheless, Israeli law allows litigants to use religious laws only if they choose. Canon law is only in use by members of the Catholic Church, the Eastern Orthodox Church and the Anglican Communion. The historical perspective of religion law can be understood by explaining the history and development of Hindu law, Muslim law, Christian law, Jews law, Jain law, etc., in India.

I. Hindu Law

28. Hindu law is mainly based on the teachings of the dharmashastra (religious books) and the distinguished sources of dharma (religion) as pointed out by the learned in the Vedas (ancient texts). The law was primarily derived from Vedic knowledge, but in actual practice, the community norms and practices of particular social groups determined the actual rulings. In this manner, law was highly decentralized and quite particular in nature towards specific groups. The court's records in India are completely lacking and are not available for the classical and medieval periods. In lieu of such records, other kinds of evidence for legal practice are used as a source to understand the outline of classical law like inscriptions from this period record a variety of legal transactions, gifts, contracts, decrees, etc., associated with political rulers, temples, individuals, groups and others. Many aspects of law were likely under the jurisdiction of castes or other groups such as merchant guilds, military groups, traders, and religious orders.

29. Starting around the eighth century AD, Hindu legal traditions began to spread in Southeast Asia, e.g., Cambodia, Java, Bali, Malaysia, Thailand, and Burma. This was part of a larger cultural influence mediated by trade and diplomatic relations. In each of these regions, Hindu law fused with local norms and practices, developed in the form of legal texts (Agamas such as the Kuṭara-Manawa in Java, and the Buddhist-influenced Dhammasattas/Dhammathats of Burma and Thailand) as well as legal records embodied in stone and copper-plate inscriptions. There is little documented material and evidence in the modern sense for the practice of law in India prior to about the eighteenth century. In some regions, such as Maharashtra, a kind of hybrid Hindu and Islamic legal system was fashioned under the Maratha kings. In South India, temples were intimately involved in the administration of law.

II. Muslim Law

30. After the advent of Muslims in India, Islamic law started to be the law applicable to the administration of the affairs of the kingdoms held by Muslim rulers. It reflected in the dictates of the ruler or pronouncements of Qazi. The Muslim's personal law is based on the Sharia. The portion of the Fiqh (jurisprudence) applicable to Indian Muslims as personal law is termed Muslim law or Mohammedan law or Islamic law. Despite being largely uncodified, but based on main sources of Islamic law, Muslim law has the same legal status as other codified statutes. The development of the law is largely on the basis of judicial precedent, which is subject to review by the courts and legislation.

31. Until the eighteenth century, Sharia law was practised throughout the Muslim world in a non-codified form, with the Ottoman Empire's Micelle code in the nineteenth century being the first attempt at codifying elements of Sharia law. Since the mid-1940s, efforts were made, in country after country, to bring Sharia law more in line with modern conditions and conceptions. In modern times, the legal systems of many Muslim countries draw upon both civil and common-law traditions as well as Islamic law and customs. During the last few decades, one of the fundamental features of the movement of Islamic resurgence has been the call to restore the Sharia, which has generated a vast amount of literature and affected world politics.

32. In India, Muslim law, as administered, has undergone some changes and modifications. Though legislative modifications are few, yet not insignificant. The changes in Muslim law through judicial interpretation have been made, and in some areas of law, such pronouncements have modernized Muslim law. In India, the first enactment related to Muslims was the Kazis Act, 1880. Thereafter Muslim Personal Law (Shariat) Application Act, 1937 was enacted. The Muslim matrimonial law was statutorily modified by the Muslim Dissolution of Marriage Act, 1939, so as to permit the wife to have a judicial divorce. The Mussalman Waqf Validating Act, 1913 was brought in, and after independence, the Wakf Act, 1954 was enacted which has regulated and also made some changes in the traditional Muslim law relating to wakfs.

III. Christian Law

33. For Christians, a distinct set of laws known as Christian Law was enacted by the colonial British rulers through statutes. The Christian Law of Succession and Divorce in India has undergone changes. The Christian Marriage Act, 1872 and the Indian Divorce Act, 1869 form the basis of the matrimonial laws of Christians. The Indian Divorce (Amendment) Act of 2001 has brought considerable changes in the grounds available for divorce by a Christian. Christian Law covers the entire spectrum of family law and to a great extent is based on English law but there are certain laws that originated in India on the strength of customary practices and precedents and were made part of Statutes applicable to Christians.

IV. Parsi and Jew Laws

34. There are special rules for Parsi intestate provided under sections 50–56 of the Indian Succession Act, 1925. The Parsi matrimonial laws before its codification were based on Hindu customs and English common law. On the demand of the Parsi community for the reform of their matrimonial law, the Parsi Marriage and Divorce Act was passed in 1865. It was modified in 1936 and 1988 and is now almost at par with Hindu matrimonial law.

For Jews, there is no codified law in India and they are governed by their religious laws. The Jew matrimonial law is still based on customs. Among Jews, marriage is not a civil contract but a relationship based on sacred duties.

Part I. Legal Framework and Sources

35. India has a well-developed judicial system. There is a Supreme Court in New Delhi, the capital of India and High Courts in each of the capitals of the States barring a few exceptions. There are district courts in every district functioning under the administrative control of the concerned State High Courts. The court procedure is based on the Anglo-Saxon system, which is generally slow and cumbersome. There is separation of the judiciary from the executive and legislature. In commercial and labour matters, various recognized alternative modes of resolution of disputes are in use such as sole expert, mediation, conciliation and arbitration. Conciliation has been accepted and given legal recognition through the enactment of the Arbitration and Conciliation Act of 1996, which is largely based on the Model Law of the United Nations Commission for International Trade Law (UNCITRAL). It has brought arbitration law in India in conformity with international law on international commercial and arbitration practices.

36. The government has brought the Mediation Bill 2021 which is aimed at institutionalizing mediation to settle civil and commercial disputes quickly to ensure speedy justice. The bill provides institutional mediation for the resolution of disputes and encourages community mediation. Mediation will contribute to the realization of Judiciary Vision 2047 by being a catalyst for the development of a strong judicial environment. The Bill does away with out-dated laws and promotes dialogue and mediation to resolve disputes, which has been a tradition for centuries. The Bill provides a strong legal basis for the long-standing tradition of mediation, which will help resolve not only ordinary disputes but also complex and uncommon situations through mutual discussions. (Economic Times, 15 October 2022). The Mediation Bill 2021 has been passed by the Upper House (Rajya Sabha) of the Parliament (Press Trust of India, 1 August 2023).

37. To exclusively deal with family matters, the Parliament has enacted the Family Courts Act, 1984 with a view to promote conciliation in and to secure speedy settlement of disputes relating to marriage and family affairs. For enforcement and adjudication of all matrimonial and other related disputes of any person in any of the different religious or non-religious communities under the respective legislations, the designated judicial forum or court where such petition is to be lodged is prescribed in the relevant enactments itself. Despite the existence of an organized, well-regulated and established hierarchy of courts in India, there are still unrecognized parallel caste, community and religious courts in existence whose interference has been deprecated by the courts since such unauthorized and unwarranted bodies work without the authority of law and are not part of the judicial system established by law. But these forums can be treated as alternate dispute resolution forums which try to resolve issues with the consent of the parties in the same manner as conciliators and/or arbitrators, and in fact act as such, there may not be any problem. But if they indulge in mob justice based on some whims and fancies like community courts (khap panchayats), it is decried by the courts.

Chapter 1. Constitutional Position of Religion

38. The Constitution of India brought into force on 26 January 1950 is the basic law for the whole of the country and individual states or federal units do not have their separate constitutions. As per the Constitution, the Indian legal system is based on equality, freedom of conscience and secularism. The Supreme Court has observed that secularism is a basic feature of the Constitution as enshrined in Articles 25–30. In the cases of *Kesavananda Bharti v. State of Kerala* and *Indira v. Rajnarain*, the Supreme Court held that secularism meant that the State shall not discriminate against any citizen on the ground of religion only and that the State shall have no religion of its own and all persons shall be equally entitled to the freedom of conscience and right to profess, practise and propagate any religion.

§1. The Preamble

39. The Preamble of the Constitution resolves to constitute India as a Union of States and a Sovereign, Socialist, Secular, Democratic Republic. The basic principles of secularism were incorporated into various provisions of the Constitution when originally enacted. However, the Preamble did not include the word 'secular' in the short description of the country which was originally called a 'Sovereign Democratic Republic'. Twenty-five years later prompted by judicial decisions, the Preamble to the Constitution was amended by the Constitution (Forty-second Amendment) Act 1976 to include the word 'secular' along with 'socialist', to declare India to be a 'Sovereign Socialist Secular Democratic Republic'. India is a declared secular country, but neither in law nor in practice there exists any 'wall of separation' or clear line of separation or demarcation between religion and the State. The Constitution contains provisions which allow to depart from the principle of equality on the basis of reasonable classification and provide for special treatment to scheduled caste Hindus, Scheduled Tribes, other backward castes and economically weaker sections of the society.

40. In *Narayanan Namboodripad v. State of Madras*, the Madras High Court examined the US principle of the 'wall of separation' between religion and State and concluded that there are provisions in the Indian Constitution which are 'inconsistent with the theory that there should be a wall of separation between church and State'.[1]

41. In the case of *S.R. Bommai v. Union of India,*[2] the Supreme Court explained the significance and place of 'secularism' under the Constitution and held that the Constitution has chosen secularism as its vehicle to establish an egalitarian social order. Secularism is part of the fundamental law and basic structure of the Indian political system. Notwithstanding the fact that the words 'Socialist' and 'Secular' were added later in the Preamble of the Constitution, the concept of secularism was

1. AIR 1955 Mad 385.
2. (1994) 3 SCC 1.

very much embedded in the constitutional philosophy from the very beginning. By this amendment what was implicit has been made explicit. The constitutional provisions prohibit the establishment of a theocratic State and prevent the State from identifying itself with or otherwise favouring any particular religion. Secularism is more than a passive attitude of religious tolerance. It is a positive concept of equal treatment of all religions. When the State allows citizens to practise and profess their religion, it does not either explicitly or implicitly allow them to introduce religion into non-religious and secular activities of the State. The freedom and tolerance of religion are only to the extent of permitting the pursuit of spiritual life, which is different from secular life. The latter falls in the exclusive domain of the affairs of the State.

42. In *Dr. M. Ismail Faruqui etc. v. Union of India and Others* on 24 October 1994 (AIR 1995 SC 605), a Bench of Supreme Court consisting of Mr Justice M V Verma, Mr Justice G Ray and Mr Justice S Bharucha further clarified the constitutional position on theocratic state and held:

> '139. That secularism is a part of the basic features of the Constitution, was held in Kesavananda Bharati v. State of Kerala. It was unanimously reaffirmed by the nine-judge bench of this Court in S.R. Bommai v. Union of India. Sawant, J. analysed the Preamble of the Constitution and various articles therein and held that these provisions, by implication, prohibited the establishment of a theocratic State and prevented the State from either identifying itself with or favouring any particular religion. The State was enjoined to accord equal treatment to all religions.' K. Ramaswamy, J. quoted the words written by Gandhiji that are as apposite now as they were when he wrote them: 'The Allah of Muslims is the same as the God of Christians and Ishwara of Hindus'. B. P. Jeevan Reddy, J. said (at p. 3152 of AIR):
>
> 'While the citizens of this country are free to profess, practice and propagate – such religion, faith or belief as they choose, so far as the State is concerned, i.e., from the point of view of the State, the religion, faith or belief of a person is immaterial. To it, all are equal and all are entitled to be treated equally. How is this equal treatment possible, if the State were to prefer or promote a particular religion, race or caste, which necessarily means a less favourable treatment of all other religions, races and castes. How are the constitutional promises of social justice liberty of belief, faith or worship and equality of status and of opportunity to be attained unless the State eschews the religion, faith or belief of a person from its consideration altogether while dealing with him, his rights, his duties and his entitlements? Secularism is thus more than a passive attitude of religious tolerance. It is a positive concept of equal treatment of all religions. This attitude is described by some as one of neutrality towards religion or as one of benevolent neutrality. This may be a concept evolved by Western liberal thought or it may be, as some say, an abiding faith with the Indian people at all points of time. That is not material. What is material is that it is a, constitutional goal and a basic feature of the Constitution as affirmed in

Kesavananda Bharati v. State of Kerala and Indira N. Gandhi v. Raj Narain. Any step inconsistent with this constitutional policy is in plain words, unconstitutional.'

'The State has no religion. The State is bound to honour and to hold the scales even between all religions. It may not advance the cause of one religion to the detriment of another.'

I. Proposed Amendments Relating to Secularism

43. On two different occasions, attempts were made to amend the Constitution with a view to further strengthen and clarify its provisions on secularism, but the Bills moved for this purpose could not be passed for technical reasons. Among these Bills were the following:

(a) Constitution (Forty-fifth) Amendment Bill 1978 proposing to define the expression 'Secular Republic' as 'a Republic in which there is equal respect for all religions'.
(b) Constitution (Eightieth Amendment) Bill 1993 seeking to empower Parliament to ban parties and associations if they promote religious disharmony and disqualify members who indulge in spreading religious disharmony.

II. Religion: Not Defined in the Constitution

44. The words 'religion' and 'religious denomination' have been used but not defined in the Constitution and therefore the courts have to explain the meaning of these words. The Supreme Court in *SP Mittal v. Union of India* observed that in the background of the provisions of the Constitution and the light shed by judicial precedent, religion is a matter of faith, belief and doctrine. It concerns the conscience, i.e., the spirit of man. It must be capable of expression in word and deed, such as worship or ritual.[3] There is also no state religion mentioned in the Constitution of India. All the religions in India have, to some extent, their personal laws enacted by the legislature and some special laws, which can be opted by the concerned individuals.

§2. Power of Legislation

45. The power to legislate on religion has been conferred both on the centre and states by the Constitution. Article 246 of the Constitution read with Schedule VIII contains a provision as to which religious matter will fall in the jurisdiction of the State – and both Parliament and the state legislatures, or either of them:

3. AIR 1983 SC 1.

- Pilgrimage outside India – Union List, entry 20. Central Government has been given the power to legislate.
- Pilgrimage within India – State List, entry 7. States have got power to legislate.
- Burials and burial grounds, cremations and cremation grounds – State List, entry 10. States have got power to legislate.
- Family relations, succession and other personal law matters – Concurrent List, entry 5. Both States and Centre can legislate.
- Charities, charitable institutions and endowments; Religious endowments and religious institutions – Concurrent List, entry 28. Both States and Centre can legislate.

§3. Freedom of Religion or Belief

46. The Constitution of India embodies that all persons are equally entitled to freedom of conscience and the right freely to profess, practise and propagate religion (Article 25(1)). There shall be freedom as to payment of taxes for the promotion of any particular religion by virtue of which no person shall be compelled to pay any taxes the proceeds of which are specifically appropriated in payment of expenses for the promotion or maintenance of any particular religious denomination (Article 27). Constitutionally, India has no state religion and citizens are free to pursue any religion or belief. However, it has developed over the years its own unique system that is fundamentally different from the parallel American and Western concept of secularism requiring complete separation of church and state, as also from the French ideal of *lacite*. Secularism in India as practised by various governments is not based on a total banishment of religion from the societal or even State affairs. Different governments have different definitions and understanding of secularism. The essence of secularism, as generally understood, is that the State must treat religious creeds and their respective adherents equally and without any discrimination in all matters under its direct or indirect control.

47. Interpreting the constitutional provisions relating to freedom of religion the Supreme Court in the case of *AS Narayana Deeshitalyu v. State of Andhra Pradesh,*[4] observed that the right to religion guaranteed by the Constitution under Articles 25 and 26 is not an absolute or unfettered right. It is subject to reform on social welfare by appropriate legislation by the state. A careful balance is to be maintained between matters, which are essential and integral part of religion and those, which are not and also to look into the need for the State to regulate or control the interests of the welfare of the community. Articles 25–30 embody the principles of religious tolerance. They serve to emphasize the secular nature of Indian democracy, which the founding fathers considered should be the very basis of the Constitution.[5] Religious practices or performances of acts in pursuance of religious beliefs are as much a part of religion as faith or belief in particular doctrines. Freedom of conscience is a person's right to entertain beliefs and doctrines concerning

4. (1996) 9 SCC 548.
5. *Sardar Suedna Tahir Saifiiddin v. State of Bombay,* AIR 1962 SC 853.

matters which are regarded by him to be conducive to his spiritual well-being. A law, which takes away the right of administration from a denomination and instead vests it in a secular body would infringe upon the Constitution.[6] Further, to profess a religion means the right to declare freely and openly one's faith.[7]

48. What constitutes an integral or essential part of a religion or religious practice is to be decided by the courts with reference to the doctrine of a particular religion and includes practices regarded by the community as parts of its religion.[8] The right to profess, practise and propagate religion does not extend to the right of worship at any or every place of worship so any hindrance to worship at a particular place per se will infringe religious freedom.[9] As per Article 25, to 'propagate' religion means 'to propagate or disseminate ideas for the edification of others' and for the purpose of this right it is immaterial 'whether propagation takes place in a church or monastery or in a temple'.[10] To claim to be a religious denomination a group has to satisfy three conditions, namely common faith, common organization and designation by a distinctive name.[11] The expression 'matters of religion' in Article 26 extends to acts done in pursuance of religion and covers rituals, observances, ceremonies and modes of worship.[12] A religious denomination has the right to lay down the rites and ceremonies to be performed by its members.[13] A 'common burden' (e.g., land revenue) applicable to all does not violate the right of a religious denomination.[14] Property of a religious body violating the agrarian reform and land ceiling laws can be lawfully acquired by the State.[15] Since the State is secular and freedom of religion is guaranteed both to individuals and groups, it is against the constitutional policy to pay out of public funds any money for the promotion or maintenance of a particular religion.[16]

49. In *Dr. M. Ismail Faruqui etc. v. Union Of India And Others* decided on 24 October 1994 (AIR 1995 SC 605) a Bench of M V Verma, G Ray, S Bharucha held with respect to the position of mosque in Islam as follows:

> Under the Mahomedan Law applicable in India, title to a mosque can be lost by adverse possession (See Mulla's Principles of Mahomedan Law, 19th Edn. by M. Hidayatullah – Section 217 and AIR 1940 PC 1.16). If that is the position in law, there can be no reason to hold that a mosque has a unique or special status, higher than that of the places of worship of other religions in secular

---

6. *Ratilal Panachand Gandhi v. State of Bombay,* AIR 1954 SC 388.
7. *Punjab Rao v. DP Meshram,* AIR 1965 SC 1179.
8. *Seshammal v. State of Tamil Nadu,* AIR 1972 SC 1586.
9. *Ismail Faruqi v. Union of India* (1994) 6 SCC 360.
10. *Commissioner, Hindu Religious Endowments, Madras v. Lakshmindra Thirtha Swamiar of Sri Shirur Mutt,* AIR 1954 SC 282.
11. *SK Mittal v. Union of India,* AIR 1983 SC 1.
12. *Jagannath Ramanuj Das v. State of Orissa,* AIR 1954 SC 400; *Dargah Committee v. Husain* AH AIR 1961 SC 1402.
13. *Ramanuj v. Tamil Nadu State,* AIR 1972 SC 1586.
14. *Govt. of Tamil Nadu v. Ahobila,* AIR 1987 SC 245.
15. *Narendra v. State of Gujarat,* AIR 1974 SC 2098.
16. *Supra* n. 20.

India to make it immune from acquisition by exercise of the sovereign or prerogative power of the State. A mosque is not an essential part of the practice of the religion of Islam and Namaz (prayer) by Muslims can be offered anywhere, even in open. Accordingly, its acquisition is not prohibited by the provisions in the Constitution of India. Irrespective of the status of a mosque in an Islamic country for the purpose of immunity from acquisition by the State in exercise of the sovereign power, its status and immunity from acquisition in the secular ethos of India under the Constitution is the same and equal to that of the places of worship of the other religions, namely, church, temple, etc. It is neither more nor less than that of the places of worship of the other religions. Obviously, the acquisition of any religious place is to be made only in unusual and extraordinary situations for a larger national purpose keeping in view that such acquisition should not result in extinction of the right to practice the religion, if the significance of that place be such. Subject to this condition, the power of acquisition is available for a mosque like any other place of worship of any religion. The right to worship is not at any and every place, so long as it can be practiced effectively, unless the right to worship at a particular place is itself an integral part of that right.

I. Limits of Religious Freedom

50. The Fundamental Right to religious freedom cannot be enjoyed in an unrestricted way. Therefore, the Constitution contains limitations within which these rights can be exercised. The restrictions which can be imposed by the State on such rights are the following:

(a) The right to freedom of religion is, in general, subject to public order, morality, health and the other provisions of the Constitution (Article 25).

(b) The State can pass laws providing for social welfare and reform and also to regulate or restrict any secular activity – economic, financial, political, etc. – even though it may be traditionally associated with religion (Article 25 (2)).

(c) Despite the minorities' right to establish and maintain educational institutions, no citizen can be kept away from any State-aided or State-maintained educational institution only on religious grounds and only 50% of seats can be filled by the students of such minority communities and rest from others [*St. Stephen's College v. University of Delhi*, (1992) 1SCC588].

II. Positive Discrimination

51. The State can, by way of positive discrimination and affirmative action, make special provisions in certain cases, and making of such special provisions will not amount to detraction from the provisions relating to the rights of equality and non-discrimination in general:

(a) The State can provide special measures for women and children, and for the advancement of any socially and educationally backward class of citizens, or for the Scheduled Castes and Scheduled Tribes (Article 15(4)).
(b) The State can reserve appointments or posts for any backward class of citizens not adequately represented in State services (Article 16(4)).
(c) A law may require that the incumbent of a religious or denominational office, or member of such a committee, must be a person of the concerned religion (Article 16(5)).
(d) In pursuance of a Directive Principle of State Policy, the State can promote with special care the economic and educational interest of the weaker sections of the people, including the Schedules Castes and Scheduled Tribes, and protect them from social injustice and exploitation (Article 46).

III. Fundamental Duties

52. The Chapter on Fundamental Duties, inserted into the Constitution by the Constitution (Forty-second Amendment) Act 1976, includes the following among the basic obligations of all the citizens:

(a) To promote harmony and the spirit of common brotherhood among all the people of India transcending religious, linguistic and regional or sectional diversities (Article 51A(e)).
(b) To value and preserve the rich heritage of our composite culture – Article 51A(f).

§4. Institutional Guarantees

53. The Constitution created an institutional structure and laid down principles that allow diverse people to live together as citizens of India. The Indian state is based on a constitution whose secular character has been defined by apex court decisions and an amendment to its Preamble and provides for institutional guarantees. Every religious denomination or any section thereof has the right to manage its religious affairs; establish and maintain institutions for religious and charitable purposes; and own, acquire and administer properties of all kinds (Article 26). Any section of the citizen having a distinct language, script or culture of its own has the right to conserve the same (Article 29). Religious and linguistic minorities are free to establish and administer educational institutions of their choice, which shall not be discriminated against by the State in the matter of giving aid or compensation in the event of acquisition (Article 30).

I. Community-Specific Constitutional Provisions

54. The Constitution of India contains a number of religion-based and religion-related provisions for certain communities as follows:

(a) The Hindus, Buddhists, Jains and Sikhs, who are mentioned in the Constitution by their denominational names.
(b) Certain groups who are mostly Christian by religion but the special provisions do not mention them as denominational groups.

55. The Constitution includes the following specific provisions for the Hindu, Buddhist, Jain and Sikh communities:

(a) Declaration of the abolition of untouchability (mainly a Hindu religious custom) and prohibition of its practice in any form (Article 17).
(b) A Directive Principle of State Policy requiring the State to take steps to prohibit the slaughter of cows and calves (reverence for whom is customary among the Hindus) (Article 48).
(c) Declaration of the validity of pre-existing and future laws made to throw open Hindu places of worship to all sects and sections of the Hindus with a supplementary provision giving the power for the Buddhist, Jain and Sikh shrines (Article 25, Explanation I).
(d) A special provision for the grant of specified annual maintenance allowances to be given from the State exchequer for the upkeep of Hindu temples of a certain denomination in two South Indian states, Kerala and TN (Article 290A).
(e) Declaration of wearing and carrying a Kirpan (small sword) a Fundamental Right for the Sikhs (Article 25, Explanation II).

56. The following special provisions were included in the Constitution for certain communities, mainly Christian by religion:

- Some special provisions of a transitory nature for the representation of the Anglo-Indian community in Parliament and State Assemblies (Articles 331, 333, 336–337, 366(2)). These were first reduced by the Constitution (Twenty Third Amendment) Act, 1969 and discontinued through further non-extension, vide the Constitution (126th Amendment) Bill, 2019 and implemented as 104th Constitutional Amendment Act, 2019.
- A provision for the protection of the customary law and its administration among the Nagas in the Christian-dominated State of Nagaland (Article 370A).
- A similar provision for the Mizos in the Christian-dominated State of Mizoram (Article 370 G).

A. Scheduled Castes

57. The constitutional framework is based on the right to equality and freedom of conscience but there are certain exceptions like special treatment to Hindu scheduled castes. They continue to avail the special facilities only if they remain Hindu which appears like a bonus for keeping them as Hindus. The Constitution originally provided these measures for ten years only but was extended and continued thereafter as well. Now it may be difficult to withdraw these special facilities. In case of conversion to Islam or Christianity by a scheduled caste Hindu, the converts lose all benefits and rights, which are available to them as Scheduled Caste Hindu. There are also restrictions on conversion like conversion should not have been obtained or tainted by fraud, allurement, etc.

58. Article 25 of the Constitution, besides declaring freedom of religion, also directs the government to undertake 'social welfare and reform' for 'Hindu' institutions. The term Hindu is 'construed as including a reference to persons professing the Sikh, Jain or Buddhist religion'. This Hindu category excludes Muslims and Christians.

59. Article 341 of the Constitution provides for the scheduled caste category. In this respect, the Constitutional Order of 1950 says: 'No person who professes a religion different from the Hindu religion shall be deemed to be a member of a Scheduled Caste.' Muslims and Christians remain outside this 'Hindu' category. It is illogical; as both Sikhism and Buddhism (both of which have been included in the definition of Hindu) were significant anti-caste movements and do not practise a caste system, and like Islam and Christianity, believe in the equality of human beings. The landless Muslim castes who have been engaged in menial professions for generations have been denied this urgently needed 'depressed' status for seven decades, and have been pushed into further impoverishment, as they are hardly supported by any relevant programmes for affirmative action of like nature at the central or state level.

60. The Constitution of India contains special provisions for the betterment and upliftment of Scheduled Castes. The Constitution (Scheduled Castes) Order 1950 issued under this provision provided the first list of the Scheduled Castes but made the list religion-specific. Initially, the 1950 Order restricted the Scheduled Castes list to the Hindu religion, although the castes included in the list were shared by various other communities as well. Later, Sikhs and Buddhists were also included in the list by amendments introduced in 1956 and 1990, respectively. The other religious communities, namely the Christians and the Muslims who share many vocation-based castes with the Hindus, have been kept outside the ambit of Scheduled Castes. But as a matter of fact, the caste system is also found among the Christians and the Muslims, so demands have been made by these communities from time to time for the removal of the religion-related proviso from the Scheduled Castes Order of 1950 so that the same castes among them may also be included in the list so that they also benefit from the special measures introduced for their community professing Hindu religion. The issue has been agitated in courts, but the courts have not agreed to it due to the egalitarian nature of Christianity and Islam in their puritan form.

61. The Supreme Court has observed that Christianity and Islam are religions prevalent not only in India but also in other countries of the world. 'We know that in other countries these religions do not recognize a system of caste as an integral part of their creed or tenets … The general rule is that conversion operates as expulsion from the caste; in other words a convert ceases to have any caste.'[17]

62. A three-judge bench of the Supreme Court on 8 January 2020 admitted a petition filed by the National Council for Dalit Christians (NCDC) seeking the inclusion of Dalit Christians in the category of Scheduled Castes and issued notice to the government. This petition opposes the non-inclusion of Dalits professing religions other than Hinduism, Sikhism, or Buddhism and states that the consideration for scheduled caste (SC) status should be made 'religion neutral'. Exclusion of people from the scheduled caste category is discriminatory and in violation of Articles 14, 15, 16, and 25. The petition seeks that paragraph (3) of the Constitution (Scheduled Castes) Order, 1950 has to be declared unconstitutional and void. This Paragraph states that the Scheduled Caste status may not be granted to any person not belonging to any one of the three religions – Hinduism, Sikhism, and Buddhism. It has been pleaded that a change in religion does not take away the discrimination meted out to the people belonging to the Dalit community. The plea seeks for religion to be delinked from consideration for scheduled caste status and allow and extend the scheduled castes status to Christians of scheduled castes origin for availing the constitutional provisions under Articles 16, 46, 330, 332, 335, 338, 341, 366-24. It also prayed for availing the legal remedy/protection under the Scheduled Castes and Scheduled Tribes (Prevention of Atrocities) Act, 1989. A pending petition has also been clubbed with the present petition (The Hindu, 8 January 2020).

63. The Misra Commission for backward classes among religious and linguistic minorities, constituted in 2004 in its report of 2007 recommended delinking of Scheduled Caste status from religion. The Report was laid on the Table of both the Houses of Parliament on 18 December 2009. The recommendations have been endorsed by the National Commission for Scheduled Castes with certain conditions. The government did not take any action with respect to this recommendation but brought out a Prime Minister's 15-point programme for the overall upliftment of minorities.

B. Scheduled Tribes and OBC

64. In terms of the provisions of the Constitution relating to the Scheduled Tribes a Constitution (Scheduled Tribes) Order was issued in 1951. Unlike the Scheduled Castes Order of 1950, this Order is not religion-specific because the tribal groups in various parts of India profess different religions which may be established one or local. There are numerous Christians and Muslims among the Scheduled Tribes. The 'Other Backward Classes' (OBC) group is also not religion-specific. Many lower castes and backward sections of various religious faiths not finding a place in the Constitution (Scheduled Castes) Order 1950 have been accommodated in the OBC group. The OBC lists in some states include 'Scheduled Class

17. AIR 1976 SC 939.

converters of Christianity'. There is no parallel provision in any State of Scheduled Caste persons who convert to Islam. The Muslim groups are agitated over these anomalies but being in the minority cannot force the government to remove these anomalies, which are perceived as a violation of the right to equality.

II. Religious Establishments

65. There are in India various official establishments for religion, statutory and non-statutory, set up by both the Central and State Governments. Among these are the following:

- Departments of Religious Affairs in some States including Jammu and Kashmir and Uttar Pradesh (UP).
- Minority Welfare Departments in the States.
- Union Ministry of Minority Welfare.
- Special bodies to manage certain religious matters of particular communities like Hindu Religious Endowment Boards, Muslim Wakf Boards, Sikh Gurdwara Committees, State-appointed boards or committees to manage particular shrines, Central Haj Committee, etc.

66. Further, Minorities Commissions have been set up in a number of States and in most of them under State statutes. These are as follows:

(a) Bihar State Minorities Commission Act, 1991.
(b) Karnataka State Minorities Commission Act, 1994.
(c) UP State Minorities Commission Act, 1994.
(d) Madhya Pradesh State Minorities Commission Act, 1996.
(e) West Bengal State Minorities Commission Act, 1996.
(f) Andhra Pradesh State Minorities Commission Act, 1999.
(g) Delhi Minorities Commission Act, 1999.

Besides the above, State of Telangana, Assam, Chhattisgarh, Jharkhand, Kerala, Maharashtra, Manipur, Punjab, Rajasthan, TN and Uttarakhand have also enacted legislation and constituted State Minority Commissions. Ten States and seven Union Territories are yet to constitute State Minority Commissions.

67. The State Minorities Commissions Acts either provide that 'minorities' in the concerned States would mean the religious communities notified as such by the Central Government, or empower the State Government concerned to notify the minorities. Under both these kinds of provisions in the Minorities Commission Acts of the State, Muslims, Christians, Sikhs, Buddhists, Jains and Parsis are recognized as religious minorities.

III. Sunday as Weekly Holiday

68. Despite its association with the Christian religion, Sunday has been continued, even after independence, as the weekly holiday throughout India. In the US, this was challenged in the court on the grounds of violation of the non-establishment clause in the Constitution. However, in India, it has not been objected and has been continuing since the days of the British. Three national holidays are celebrated in India, namely Independence Day on 15 August, Republic Day on 26 January and Father of the Nation's birthday called Gandhi Jayanti on 2 October.

§5. Religious Instructions in Public Schools

69. No religious instruction is to be imparted in the schools wholly maintained by State funding. Further, those attending any State-recognized or State-aided school cannot be required to take part in any religious instruction or services without their, and if they are a minor, their guardian's consent (Article 28).[18] However, in the name of culture, Hindu religious scriptures have been added to the syllabus of government schools in many states.

§6. National Flag, National Anthem and Emblem

70. The National Flag of India with its saffron, green and white colours and the Buddhist wheel of dharma (faith) is seen by many as religious symbolism, though legal texts do not specify this implication. India's National Anthem is more conspicuously religious. Drawn from a Bengali-language song, it invokes the Supreme God. The National Emblem of India is an adaptation from Ashoka's pillar at Sarnath super scribed with the Vedic expression Satyameva Jayate (truth alone triumphs) in Devanagari script. The Emblem is used on all official stationery and seals of the government. It also appears on government publications, coins and currency notes.

§7. Equal Treatment

71. The Constitution in the chapter on Fundamental Rights emphasizes complete legal equality of its citizens irrespective of their religion and creed and prohibits any kind of discrimination between them. The State shall not deny to any person equality before the law or the equal protection of the laws within the territory of India (Article 14). The State shall not discriminate against any citizen on grounds only of religion, race, caste, sex, place of birth, or any of them, either in general or in the matter of access to or use of general and public places and conveniences (Article 15). There shall be equality of opportunity for all citizens in the matter of employment or appointments under the State, and no citizen shall on

18. For details *see* Part IX on Education.

grounds only of religion be ineligible for, or discriminated against, in respect of any employment or office under the State (Article 16). The traditional religious concept of 'untouchability' stands abolished and its practice in any form is strictly forbidden (Article 17 of the Constitution).[19] If the State imposes compulsory service on citizens for public purposes, no discrimination shall be made in this regard on the grounds of religion only (Article 23(2)).

I. Citizenship (Amendment) Act, 2019: A Departure from Equal Treatment

72. The Citizenship (Amendment) Act, 2019 has amended the Citizenship Act of 1955 to give eligibility for Indian citizenship to illegal migrants who are Hindus, Sikhs, Buddhists, Jains, Parsis and Christians from Afghanistan, Bangladesh and Pakistan, and who entered India on or before 31 December 2014. The Amendment Act does not include Muslims. The Amendment has been enacted under the Union List of the seventh Schedule of the Constitution.

73. Under the unamended Citizenship Act, one of the requirements for citizenship by naturalization is that the applicant must have resided in India during the last twelve months and for eleven of the previous fourteen years. The Bill relaxes this eleven-year requirement to five years for persons belonging to the same six religions and three countries. The Bill exempts the tribal areas of Assam, Meghalaya, and Tripura from its applicability. It also exempts the areas regulated through the Inner Line Permit, which include Arunachal Pradesh, Mizoram and Nagaland. The inclusion of Manipur in the Inner Line Permit was also announced on 9 December 2019.

74. Muslims from Pakistan, Bangladesh and Afghanistan are not offered citizenship under the amendment which has been questioned. The Amendment limits itself to the Muslim-majority neighbours of India and takes no cognizance of the persecuted Muslims of those countries. The government has stated that Pakistan, Afghanistan, and Bangladesh are Muslim-majority countries. They have modified their constitutions in recent decades to declare Islam as their official state religion, and therefore Muslims in these Islamic countries are 'unlikely to face religious persecution'. The government states that Muslims cannot be 'treated as persecuted minorities' in these Muslim-majority countries. The Amendment also does not include migrants from non-Muslim countries fleeing persecution to India, particularly Rohingya Muslim refugees from Myanmar, Hindu refugees from Sri Lanka, and Buddhist refugees from Tibet, China. The Act does not provide relief to Tibetan Buddhist refugees. They came to India in the 1950s and 1960s. Their status has been of refugees over the decades.

---

19. Parliament had enacted an Untouchability (Offenses) Act, 1955 which was later amended and in 1976 was renamed as the Protection of Civil Rights Act. The Act prescribes penalties for the practice of untouchability in various specified forms. A second law enacted in this respect is the Scheduled Castes and Scheduled Tribes (Prevention of Atrocities) Act 1989.

75. Concerns have also been expressed that people who are unable to produce the required documents to prove their citizenship and inclusion in the National Register of Citizens (NRC), will be accepted as migrants and given Indian citizenship under the Amendment provided they are 'of any identity except Muslim(s)' and Muslims would risk becoming stateless because they are not included under the Amendment.

76. The Amendment has been challenged in the Supreme Court. The first hearing by the court on sixty petitions challenging the Act was on 18 December 2019. During the first hearing, the court declined to stay the implementation of the Citizenship (Amendment) Act, 2019. The matter is pending in the court.

§8. Oath of Office

77. The third schedule of the Constitution of India contains forms of oaths or affirmations. For example, form of oath of office for a minister for the Union is that:

> 'I, A.B., do swear in the name of God / solemnly affirm that I will bear true faith and allegiance to the constitution of India as by law established … that I will uphold the sovereignty and integrity of India, that I will faithfully and conscientiously discharge my duties as a Minister for the Union and that I will do right to all manner of people in accordance with the Constitution and the law, without fear or favor, affection or ill-will.' So, it is clear that a person may swear in the name of God or may solemnly affirm and there are no limitations or individual is not bound to affirm in the name of God.

§9. UCC and Directive Principles of State Policy

78. Part IV of the Indian Constitution lays down 'Directive Principles of State Policy' which are not enforceable by court but are nevertheless fundamental in the governance of the country and the state to apply these principles while making laws. Article 44 of the Constitution (Part IV) provides that the state shall endeavour to secure for the citizens a uniform civil code (UCC) throughout the territory of India. The question for consideration is whether in the name of uniformity, religion or religious notions of the majority can be imposed on religious minorities. How to harmonize freedom of religion with interference by legislation in basic religious notions or percepts by a legislature composed of a majority of followers of one religion. Whether efforts to bring UCC can be like Deen-e-Ilahi as propagated by Akbar, the Mughal Emperor. In the Scheme of the Constitution, the freedom of Religion is a fundamental right enforceable by law whereas UCC is a Directive Principle, not enforceable by law. So, the Directive Principle must be seen and understood in the light of fundamental rights granted and guaranteed by the same Constitution. As a matter of fact, a Directive Principle may not be so interpreted and applied that it obliterates one of the universal fundamental freedoms, i.e., freedom of religion.

79. From the scheme of the Constitution as it exists, the Directive Principle for UCC is subordinate to freedom of religion and efforts to implement Directive Principles may interfere with freedom of religion and make this freedom subservient or redundant. Further, the yardstick and rationale for any uniformity must be based on and should emanate from the system of law itself and in consultation with those to whom this will apply; otherwise, a change may distort the whole system whether it is Hindu law, Muslim law or Christian Law. Any imposition of law on minorities may be taken as majoritarian dominance against the will of minority groups.

I. Law Commission Consultation Paper, 2018 on UCC

80. The Law Commission in the Consultation Paper, 2018 on Reform in Family Laws had urged the legislature to 'first consider equality within communities, between men and women rather than equality between communities'. The Commission dealt with laws that are discriminatory 'rather than providing a uniform civil code which is neither necessary nor desirable at this stage. The Commission emphasized that the best way forward may be to preserve the diversity of personal laws, but, at the same time, ensure that personal laws do not contradict fundamental rights guaranteed under the Constitution.

II. Notification by 22nd Law Commission

81. The 22nd Law Commission has released a notification on 14 June 2023 with the aim of gathering perspectives from diverse stakeholders, such as public and religious organizations, regarding the UCC. One of the main purposes is to bring out the inherent implications for women's rights. The Government holds the belief that personal laws rooted in religion are a challenge to the unity of the nation. However, it asserts that the implementation of a Uniform Civil Code (UCC) will promote the integration of India by establishing a shared platform for diverse communities.

Chapter 2. Other Legislation with Regard to Religion

82. In addition to constitutional provisions, there are a number of other legislations with regard to religions practised in India. The personal laws of different religions are recognized and practised in India, some of which are codified. There are certain laws of general application like section 125 of the Code of Criminal Procedure, 1973 (Cr. P.C.) which provides that irrespective of religion, any person belonging to any religion can approach a Magistrate to request maintenance from the person who is liable to maintain such aggrieved person. Therefore, apart from personal family law legislations, both Hindus and non-Hindus with certain exceptions, have an independent right of maintenance under the general law of the land.

83. The Indian Succession Act, 1925, consolidates the law applicable to intestate and testamentary succession unless parties opt out and choose to be governed by their respective codified law otherwise applicable to them. In respect of issues relating to guardianship, the Guardian and Wards Act, 1890 applies to non-Hindus.

84. The Special Marriage Act, 1954, provides a special form of marriage in certain cases, for the registration of such and certain other marriages, succession and divorces under the Act. This enactment of solemnizing marriage by registration can be resorted to by Indians professing any religion and foreigners marrying in India who want to opt out of the customary ceremonial marriages under their respective personal laws. Divorce can also be obtained by non-Hindus under this Act. This legislation governs, subject to certain exceptions, people of all religions and communities in India, irrespective of their personal faith. Likewise, under the Foreign Marriage Act, 1969, a person has only to be a citizen of India to have a marriage solemnized under this Act outside the territorial limits of India. Succession to the property of a person married under the Special Marriage Act or customary marriage registered under the Act and that of their children are governed by the Indian Succession Act. However, if the parties to the marriage are of Hindu, Buddhist, Sikh or Jain religion, then the Hindu Succession Act governs the succession to their property.

§1. Hindu Law-Sources and Legislation

I. Sources of Hindu Law

85. From ancient times, Hindus have been leading their lives by following the guidelines and concepts given in the Vedas. These guidelines have evolved into customs, rules, etc., and assumed the form of de facto law. These practices have been refined and evolved to suit present conditions and, in some instances, codified in the form of several acts of which the important ones are – the Hindu Marriage Act (HMA), 1955, Hindu Adoption and Maintenance Act, 1956 (HAMA), Hindu Minority and Guardianship Act, 1956, and Hindu Succession Act, 1956, etc.

86. There is no precise definition of who is a Hindu and what is Hinduism. So, a negative definition of 'who is not a Hindu' is used. In *Shastri v. Muldas,*[20] the Supreme Court has held that various subsects of Hindus such as Swaminarayan, Satsangis, and Arya Samajis are also Hindus by religion because they follow the same basic concept of Hindu Philosophy. A person can be a Hindu if after expressing the intention of becoming a Hindu, follows the customs of the caste, tribe, or community, and the community accepts him.[21] The Kerala High Court held that mere declaration and actions are enough for becoming a Hindu.[22] A person who is born of Hindu parents is a Hindu, and in case only one parent is a Hindu, the person can be a Hindu if he/she has been raised as a Hindu. The Kerala HC has held that a son of a Hindu father and a Christian mother will be a Christian.[23] Persons who are not Muslim, Christian, Jew, or Parsee by religion and persons who are not governed by any other religious law are also governed by Hindu law.

87. With respect to sources of Hindu law, it is believed that Hindu law is a divine law. It was revealed to the learned people by God through the Vedas. Various sages and ascetics have elaborated and refined the concepts of life and practices explained in the Vedas. Sources of Hindu law can be divided into two parts, namely Ancient and Modern.

A. Ancient Sources

88. Before the codification of Hindu law, the ancient literature was the only source of the Hindu law. The basic ancient sources can be further divided into four categories, namely Shruti, Smriti, Dharamasutras and Dharmashastras. There are also other important sources like commentaries and digests, customs, etc.

1. Basic Ancient Sources

a. Shruti

89. Shruti means, 'What is heard'. It is believed that rishis and munis at the height of their spirituality were revealed the knowledge of Vedas, which is in the form of shrutis. The shrutis include the four Vedas – rig, yajur, sama, and atharva along with their brahmanas. The brahmanas are like the appendices to the Vedas. The Vedas primarily contain theories about sacrifices, rituals, and customs. Vedas contain no specific laws and these have to be inferred from the complete text of the Vedas. Vedas deal with certain rights and duties, forms of marriage, requirement of a son, exclusion of women from inheritance, and partition but these are given in general language and not very clear to apply, and thus relevant applicable principles are required to be adduced.

---

20. AIR 1961 SC.
21. *Peerumal v. Poonuswami*, AIR 1971.
22. *Mohandas v. Dewaswan board*, AIR 1975.
23. *Sapna v. State of Kerala.*

90. The Vedic period is assumed to be between 4000 and 1000 BC. During this time, several pre-smriti sutras and gathas were composed. However, not much is known about them today. It is believed that various rishis and munis added local customs into dharma and multiple 'shakhas' came into existence. It was during this period that society was divided into varnas and life was divided into ashramas. The concept of karma was evolved and came into prominence under which a person was expected to be rewarded as per his karma. He can attain salvation through 'knowledge'. Since Vedas had a divine origin, the society was governed as per the theories given in Vedas and they were considered to be the fundamental source of Hindu law.

b. Smriti

91. Smriti means, 'What is remembered'. With smritis, a systematic study and teaching of Vedas started. Many sages, from time to time, have written down and explained the concepts given in Vedas; thus smritis are a written memoir of the knowledge of the sages. Immediately after the Vedic period, a need for the regulation of the society arose. Thus, the study of Vedas and the incorporation of local culture and customs became important. It is believed that many smritis were composed in this period and some were reduced into writing; however, not all are known. The smritis can be divided into two – early smritis (Dharmasutras) and later smritis (Dharmashastras).

c. Dharmasutras

92. It is believed that Dharmasutras were written during 800–200 BC. These are mostly in prose form but also contain some verses and were used as training manuals of sages for teaching students. They incorporate the teachings of Vedas with local customs and bear the names of their authors and sometimes also indicate the shakhas to which they belong. They explain the duties of men in different relationships. These are writings based on the teachings of Vedas and the legal decisions given by the learned acquainted with Vedas and local customs. Some of the important sages whose Dharmasutras are known are: Gautama, Baudhayan, Apastamba, Harita, Vashistha, and Vishnu. Gautama belonged to Sam Veda School and dealt exclusively with legal and religious matters. The sutra of Apastamba is most preserved by those who belonged to Krishna Yajurveda School from Andhra Pradesh. His language is very clear and forceful. Vashistha was from north India and followed the Rigveda School. He recognized the remarriage of virgin widows.

d. Dharmashastras

93. Dharmashastras were mostly in verses, based on Dharmasutras and more systematic and clear. They dealt with the subject matter in three parts, namely: (a) 'Aachara' containing the theories of religious observances; (b) Vyavahar: dealing with civil law; (c) Prayaschitta, dealing with penance and expiation. While early smritis dealt mainly with Aachara and Prayaschitta, later smritis mainly dealt with Vyavahar. Out of the many Dharmashastras, the following three, namely Manusmriti, Yajnavalkaya and Narada, are the most important.

i. Manusmriti

94. Manusmriti, which was composed in 200 BC, is the earliest and most important Dharmashastra which defined the way of life for Hindus not only in India but also in other countries like Indonesia (Java, Bali, and Sumatra). The name of the real author is not known because these have been written under the mythical name of Manu, who is considered to be the first human. This was probably done to increase its importance so as to be taken as from divine origin. Manusmriti compiles all the laws that were scattered in pre-smriti sutras and gathas. Manu was harsh on women and sudras and held local customs to be most important and advised the king to obey the customs but tried to cloak the king with divinity. There have been several commentaries on this smriti; the main are: Kalluka's Manavarthmuktavali, Meghthithi's Manubhashya, and Govindraja's Manutika.

ii. Yajnavalkya Smriti

95. This was written after Manusmriti and is a very important smriti as its language is direct and clear and a lot more logical. It gives importance to customs but holds the king to be below the law. He considers law to be the king of kings and the king to be only an enforcer of the law. He did not deal much with religion and morality but mostly with civil law. It includes most of the points given in Manusmriti but also differs on many points such as the position of women and sudras. He was more liberal than Manu. Vijnaneshwar's commentary titled 'Mitakshara' on this smriti is the most important legal treatise followed almost everywhere in India except in West Bengal and Orissa. Mitakshara literally means 'New Word' and is a paramount source of law all over India. It is also considered important in Bengal and Orissa where it relents only where it differs from Dayabhaga. It is a very exhaustive treatise and an important source of Hindu law.

iii. Narada Smriti

96. Narada Muni (sage) was from Nepal and composed Smriti in AD 200. The Narada Smriti is well-preserved, logical, precise and complete text is available. This is the only smriti that does not deal with religion and morality at all but concentrates only on civil law. In general, it is based on Manusmriti and Yajnavalkya smriti but differs in many aspects due to changes in social structure.

B. Other Sources

1. Commentaries and Digests

97. After AD 200, most of the work was done only on the existing material given in smritis. The explanation of smriti was called a commentary. Some of the commentaries were manubhashya, manutika, and mitakshara. Mitakshara is followed throughout India except where Dayabhaga is followed. Thus, another most important digest is Jimutvahan's Dayabhaga that is applicable in areas of Bengal and Orissa.

2. Customs

98. The customs are a very important source of Hindu law as the large body of Hindu law is based on customs and practices followed by the people throughout the country. Even smritis have given importance to customs. They have held customs as transcendent law and have advised the king to give decisions based on customs after due religious considerations. Customs can be of three types:

(a) *Local Customs* – These customs are followed in a given geographical area. A custom gets its force from the fact that due to its observation for a long time in a locality, it has obtained the force of law.
(b) *Family Customs* – These are customs followed by a family consistently for a long time. These are applicable to families where ever they live. They can be more easily abandoned then other customs. The customs followed by a family have long been recognized as the source of Hindu law.
(c) *Caste and Community Customs* – These are some customs that are followed by a particular caste or community and such customs are considered binding on the members of that community or caste. For example, most of the law in Punjab belongs to this type. The custom to marry a brother's widow among the Jats is also of this type.

3. Requirements for a Valid Custom

99. For a custom to be applicable as law or criteria which is to be passed by a custom to be considered having binding force is that it must be ancient, continuous, certain, reasonable, not against public policy and not against law.

a. Ancient

100. A custom is valid when it is continuously and or persistently without interruption followed for hundreds of years. There are no precise criteria to determine how old or ancient it should be. For example, forty years have been determined to be ancient enough. A custom cannot come into existence by agreement. Therefore, a new form of Hindu marriage was not recognized in Tamil Nadu (TN) falling under custom. In the case of *Rajothi v. Selliah*,[24] a Self-Respecter's Cult started a movement under which traditional ceremonies were substituted with simple ceremonies for marriage that did not involve Shastric rites. The Madras High Court held that in modern times, no one is free to create a law or custom, since that is a function of legislature.

24. (1966)2 MLJ 40.

b. Continuous

101. It is important that the custom is being followed continuously and has not been abandoned. Thus, a custom may be 400 years old but once abandoned, it cannot be revived again.

c. Certain

102. The custom should be very clear in terms of what it entails and must be certain. In case custom is vague and may cause confusion, such custom will be invalid and will not be legally enforced. It is the duty of the individual who asserts a custom to prove the exact details and ambit of the custom.

d. Reasonable

103. There must be reasonableness and fairness in the custom. Though what is reasonable and fair depends on the time and existing social values but still custom should not be unreasonable.

e. Not Against Morality

104. The custom should not be morally wrong or repugnant. For example, a custom to marry one's granddaughter has been held invalid because it would have been against normal morality. In the case of *Gopikrishna v. Mst. Jagoo,*[25] a custom that dissolves the marriage and permits a wife to remarry upon abandonment and desertion of husband was held to be not immoral.

f. Not Against Public Policy

105. A custom against the general good of society or against public policy will be invalid. For example, the adoption of a girl child by dancing women is invalid. In the case of *Mathur v. Esa*, a custom among dancing women permitting them to adopt one or more girls was held to be void because it was against public policy.

g. Not Against Law

106. A custom against any statutory law is invalid and cannot be enforced. Codification of Hindu law has incorporated a number of customs and given them statutory status and at the same time abrogated those that are expressly not saved.

4. Proof of Custom

107. The burden of proving a custom is on the person who asserts it. Only one instance does not prove a custom. However, in another case of *Ujagar v. Jeo*,[26] it

25. (1936) 38 BOMLR 751.
26. AIR 1959 SC 1041.

was held that if a custom has been brought to the notice of the court repeatedly, no further proof is required. Besides, the existence of a custom can also be proved through documentary evidence such being a public custom/habit (rivaj-e-aam).

5. Usage and Custom

108. The terms 'custom' and 'usage' are commonly used together, but these are not the same. A usage is a repetition of an act whereas custom is the law or general rule that arises from such repetition. A usage may exist without a custom, but a custom cannot arise without a usage accompanying it or preceding it. Usage derives its authority from the assent of the parties to a transaction and is applicable only to consensual arrangements whereas custom derives its authority from its adoption into the law and is binding regardless of any acts of assent by the parties concerned.

C. Modern Sources of Hindu Law and Legislation

109. The present Hindu law has mainly developed during the British period by application of principles of equity, justice and good conscience. The concepts of equity and justice existed even in Dharmashastras but in a different form. Narada and Katyayana have mentioned the importance of dharma (righteousness) in delivering justice.

1. Equity, Justice, and Good Conscience

110. Equity means fairness in dealing through applying a uniform procedure without any distinction. The present-day judicial systems greatly rely on being uniform and impartial. Justice can only be delivered through equity and good conscience. In a situation where no rule is given, a sense of 'reasonableness' and justice must prevail. According to Gautam Buddha, the decision should be given that is acceptable to at least ten people who are knowledgeable in shastras. Yagyavalkya has said that wherever there are conflicting rules, the decision must be based on 'Nyaya' (justice). This principle has been even followed by the Privy Council while deciding cases.

2. Precedents

111. In India, there was no system of recording and preserving decisions of the court, till the introduction of the doctrine of *stare decisis* by the British. Thereafter, cases were recorded and new cases were decided on the basis of existing case laws. The Constitution of India contains provisions according to which the judgment of the Supreme Court is binding on all courts across India, and the judgments of the

High Court are binding on all courts in the concerned state and have persuasive value in other states in case there is no judgment of such other High Courts on the point to be decided.

3. Legislation

112. Presently legislation is the main source to bring in new laws. The Parliament, in accordance with the needs of society, brings in and enforces new laws. For example, a new way of performing Hindu marriages in TN that got rid of rituals and priests was rejected by the Supreme Court on the basis that new customs cannot be invented. However, TN later on passed an Act that recognized these marriages. At present, most of the Hindu laws have been codified through legislation.

113. During the British regime, the country became politically and socially integrated, but the government did not venture to interfere with the personal laws of any community and it was the social reform movements which raised the issue of amelioration of the woman's position in society. The earliest legislation bringing Hindu females into the scheme of inheritance was the Hindu Inheritance Act, 1929. This Act conferred inheritance rights on three female heirs, i.e., son's daughter, daughter's daughter and sister. Another landmark legislation conferring ownership rights on women was the Hindu Women's Right to Property Act, 1937 (Act No. XVIII of 1937). This Act brought revolutionary changes in the Hindu law of all schools, including the law of coparcenary, partition, alienation of property, inheritance and adoption.

114. The Act of 1937 enabled the Hindu widow to succeed along with the son and to take a share equal to that of the son. But, the widow did not become a coparcener even though she possessed a right akin to a coparcenary interest in the property and was a member of the joint family. The widow was entitled only to a limited estate in the property of the deceased with a right to claim partition. A daughter had virtually no inheritance rights. These enactments now stand repealed.

a. Status of Woman

115. The framers of the Constitution took note of the adverse and discriminatory position of women in society and ensured that the State took positive steps to give women belonging to different religions equal status. Articles 14,15 (2), (3) and 16 of the Constitution of India, thus not only inhibited discrimination against women but in certain circumstances also provided a free hand to the State to take steps for protective discrimination in favour of women. These provisions are part of the Fundamental Rights guaranteed by the Constitution. However, in Part IV of the Constitution, the Directive Principles provide that the State shall endeavour to ensure equality between man and woman.

b. Hindu Succession Act, 1956

116. The Hindu Succession Act, 1956 came into force on 17 June 1956. It amended and codified the law relating to intestate succession among Hindus and brought some fundamental and radical changes in the law of succession. The Act lays down a uniform and comprehensive system of inheritance and applies to all systems of Hindu law. The Act reformed the Hindu personal law and gave woman greater property rights, allowing her full ownership rights instead of limited rights in property. The daughters were also granted property rights in their father's estate. In the matter of succession to the property of a Hindu male dying intestate, the Act lays down a set of general rules in sections 8–13. Sections 15 and 16 of the Act contain separate general rules affecting succession to the property of a female intestate.

117. The Act was amended in 2005, introducing major changes in the classical concept of coparcenary as also in the class I heirs to the property of a Hindu male intestate. The Karta (Manager) of a Hindu Joint Family (HJF) is the senior-most member of the family entitled to manage family affairs, in his absence the next eldest male member after him is entitled to be the Karta. A Karta is the caretaker of the whole family and looks after the welfare of all the members of the family. His relationship with other members is a relationship of trust and confidence. At least one male member is necessary to constitute a coparcenary.

118. The Law Commission was concerned with the discrimination inherent in the Mitakshara coparcenary under section 6 of the Hindu Succession Act, as it only consists of male members. The Commission ascertained the opinion of a cross-section of society to find out, whether the Mitakshara coparcenary should be retained as provided in section 6 of the Hindu Succession Act, 1956, in an altered form, or it should be totally abolished. There also were other questions involved like, should women be the Karta in the absence of male members or not? The Commission's main aim was to end gender discrimination, which is apparent in section 6 of the Hindu Succession Act, 1956, by suggesting appropriate amendments to the Act. Accordingly, the amendments were carried out in 2005 conferring equal property share from the ancestral property to the daughter. By birth, a daughter now acquires property rights and is like any other coparcenary. This right is by birth and it is not necessary that the father should be alive on 9 September 2005, the effective date of the Hindu Succession (Amendment) Act, 2005. Thus, the Amendment Act shall have a retrospective operation [*Vineeta Sharma v. Rakesh Sharma*, (2020) 9 SCC1]

§2. Muslim Law-Sources and Legislation

I. Sources of Muslim Law

119. The basic sources of the Muslim law can be divided into two categories: (i) Primary Sources; and (ii) Secondary Sources.

A. *Primary Sources*

120. As per Sunni Law, the primary sources of Islamic law are: the Quran, Sunna or Ahadis (Tradition of the Prophet), Ijma (Unanimous Decision of the Jurists) and Qiyas (analogical deduction). As per Shia Law, the primary sources are: the Quran, Tradition (only those that have come from the family of the Prophet), and Ijma (only that confirmed by Imams).

121. It is believed that the Quran is of divine origin and was revealed to the Prophet for the benefit of mankind. The Quran has an overriding effect. Any custom or practice which is repugnant or in contradiction with or in derogation of the Quran is invalid even if it is a custom or proved by Sunna, Ijma or Qiyas. So, notwithstanding anything contained in Sunna, Ijma and Qiyas, the Quran has a predominant effect and prevails over any other primary source.

122. Ahadees contain what was said by the Prophet and Sunna is what he practised and his actions. Sunnas are the traditions of the Prophet. After the death of the Prophet, the original law making process came to an end. Ijma means the opinion of the learned. When persons knowledgeable in law would agree upon a point, such consensual opinion or unanimous decision of jurists on a particular question is called Ijma. It is through the tradition of the Prophet that Ijma derives its validity and authority as a source of law. The Prophet is believed to have said that, 'God will not allow his people to agree on an error.' The Hanafi doctrine of law changing along with times found support in the Maliki view that new facts require new decisions. Whenever law needed a new principle, the jurists used to give a consensual opinion so as to enable a solution. To be a jurist or Mujtahid, it was essential that a person was a Muslim with adequate knowledge of law and was competent to form logical deducements. Ijtihad refers to the process of creating law through consensus on the basis of 'exercise of one's reasoning so as to create a new rule of law'. The Ijma had to be justified with references to the principles given in the Quran or the tradition as well as public policy, the interest of the community and equity.

123. Qiyas refers to comparing a thing in relation to a standard or 'to establish an analogy'. Some have described it as the analogical deduction from the reason of a text to a case not actually covered by its language. In simple words, it is a method of comparing a problem in present times to a similar problem for which the solution is provided in the texts. First, a similar problem with a solution is found and the reasoning behind it was taken so as to establish a common cause. Then solution to the present problem is directly deduced from the texts in the form of a law derived. Here, the spirit or the implied meaning of the text is taken into consideration.

B. *Secondary Sources*

124. Custom, Judicial Decisions and Legislation are secondary sources of Islamic law. These sources are subservient to primary sources of law.

1. Custom

125. Before the advent of Islam, customary law governed Arabia. Most of the customs were abolished, as they were found to be un-Islamic. Some customs, however, were continued owing to the Prophet's (PBUH) silent approval. Some were even included in his traditions. Some customs survived due to their incorporation into the Ijma. Custom is not a formal source, yet, in the absence of the rule of law in the texts of the primary sources, customary practices are regarded as law. The British Courts in India held that a custom would prevail over a written text provided that the custom was ancient and invariable. The Shariat Act, 1937 noted this and abolished most of the customs. Section 2 of the Act lists ten matters including inheritance, marriage, divorce, wakf and maintenance wherein customs and usages cannot be applied anymore. Customs are still applicable to Muslims with regard to agricultural lands, charities and religious endowments. Even in matters of wills, adoption and legacies, the customary law will apply unless a Muslim expressly states that the Shariat should regulate them.

2. Judicial Decisions

126. Before independence, the Privy Council decided many cases related to Muslim law. In the absence of a judgment of the Supreme Court on an issue, the cases decided by the Privy Council continue to have a binding force on all the High Courts and the lower courts of India and a persuasive value in the Supreme Court of India. However, these precedents lose their binding force if the Supreme Court overrules a particular decision.

3. Legislation

127. God is the Supreme legislator as per Islam. Thus, sometimes, legislative modifications are also treated as an encroachment on religion. Still, there are a few acts that lay down principles of Muslim law and serve as a source of law for the courts with respect to the content covered by them:

(a) The Mussalman Waqf Validating Act, 1913 – It merely re-established the validity of family-wakfs.
(b) The Child Marriage Restraint Act – It makes the marriage of a boy under 21 years of age and a girl under 18 years a 'child marriage' and punishable without affecting the validity of it.
(c) The Muslim Personal Law (Shariat) Application Act, 1937 – It reiterated the Muslim stand that custom could not be an independent source of Muslim law all the time.
(d) Dissolution of Muslim Marriage Act, 1939 – It provided rights to judicial divorce under the grounds mentioned in it to women who traditionally had no independent right to seek divorce.

(e) Muslim Women (Protection of Rights on Divorce) Act, 1986 – The issues of maintenance after divorce and maintenance during Iddat are dealt with comprehensively in this enactment.
(f) Music in Muslim Shrine's Act, 1942 (Punjab and Haryana).
(g) Muslim Women (Protection of Rights on Marriage) Act, 2019, implemented retrospectively from 19 September 2018.

128. There are other Acts too which deal with Muslims. Some lay down the procedure rather than altering substantive rules of Muslim personal law. Acts like the following, replaced or restricted the application of those personal law principles with reference to the Act's objectives and aims:

(a) The Caste Disabilities Removal Act, 1850 changed the laws of the pre-existing rights of converts.
(b) The Indian Evidence Act, 1872 changes the traditional outlook on legitimacy via section 112.
(c) The Indian Majority Act, 1875 differed in its definition of age of majority.
(d) The Dowry Prohibition Act, 1961 prohibited dowry irrespective of religion.

129. Similarly, alternate legislation available to the people of all religions has its impact on Muslim personal laws. For example, a couple that marries under the Special Marriage Act, 1954 will be regulated by this Act for matters concerning the martial life, succession, etc., and not by their personal laws. The inheritance and intestate succession of the spouse or heirs will also be governed under the Indian Succession Act, 1925. It does not matter whether the persons getting married under this law are from the same religion or sect or not.

§3. Christian Law-Sources and Legislation

I. Sources of Christian Law

130. Christian law deals with matters such as marriage, divorce, succession, adoption, etc., and is mainly legislation-based. The Christians are governed by the provisions of the Indian Christian Marriage Act, 1872, the Indian Divorce Act, 1869, and the Marriage Dissolution Act, 1936. According to Christian law, a marriage is a permanent union of man and woman to the exclusion of others. Marriage, as is seen in Christian tradition, is not merely a civil contract nor is it purely a religious act. Roman Catholic Church regarded marriage as one of the sacraments.

131. The Christian Marriage Act of 1872 extends to the whole of India except in the states of Travancore Cochin, Manipur, and Jammu and Kashmir. In the Malabar area, the Act of 1872 was applicable but the Christians of the former Travancore area were governed by the customary law (canon law-personal law of Christians) only and not by any statute. Matrimonial reliefs like divorce, judicial separation, etc., were not allowed in Travancore Cochin till the Indian Divorce Act, 1869 came into force which provides matrimonial relieves among Christians in the whole of India including the former Travancore Cochin.

132. Under the Christian Marriage Act, 1872, a marriage can be solemnized by a minister/priest in a church. After the marriage, the priest registers the marriage and issues a marriage certificate. A marriage, which has already been solemnized by a priest in the church can also be registered by a registrar of marriages. The parties for registration of marriage have to apply to the concerned authority in whose Jurisdiction either party has been residing. The application form is to be accompanied by two attached passport-size photographs of the marriage ceremony, invitation card of marriage, age and address proof of both bride and bridegroom, affidavit with regard to these as well marital status, fit mental condition and the marriage certificate issued by the priest.

133. Christian Law of Succession and Divorce has undergone changes in recent years. The Indian Divorce (Amendment) Act of 2001 has brought in considerable changes in the grounds available for divorce. In 2019, through a combined amendment leprosy has been deleted as a ground for divorce. Christian Law, to a great extent, is based on English law but there are certain aspects and laws that originated on the strength of customary practices and precedents followed by Christians in India. Christian family law has now distinct sub-branches like laws on divorce, restitution, judicial separation, succession, maintenance, custody of minor children and relevance of canon law and all that which regulates familial relationships.

§4. Sikh Law: Sources and Legislation

134. Guru Nanak was the founder of Sikhism and the first Sikh Guru. The last Guru, Govind Singh passed the Guruship of the Sikhs to the Eleventh and Eternal Guru of the Sikhs, the Guru Granth Sahib (the sacred text of Sikhism). Guru Granth Sahib includes the writings of the Sikh Gurus and the writings of Hindu and Muslim saints because all are equal in front of Waheguru. Sikhs do not believe in idols and other rituals, they only believe in one God, i.e., Waheguru. The legislation pertaining to Sikhs are Sikh Gurudwara Act, 1925, Anand Marriage Act, 1909 both brought by the British and Delhi Sikh Gurdwara Act, 1971.

135. There are about twenty million Sikhs in India but they have no separate personal laws except the Anand Marriage Act, 1909. So, Sikhs are subjected to Hindu law, applied to them by including them in the definition of Hindu. Sikhs consider themselves a separate, distinct community and not Hindus, though originated from Hindus, as Christians are not Jews, though originated from Jews. Sikhs are monotheistic, guided by Guru Granth Sahib as a living Guru on all aspects of life from birth to death.

136. The Guru Granth Sahib is the principal source of Sikh laws. It accords sanctity and sanction to all Sikh institutions. Other sources are the gurus' teachings as documented in Guru Maryada or Sikh Code of Conduct. But notwithstanding these sources, Sikhs are governed by Hindu law in practical matters. Sikhs are monotheistic and casteless, whereas Hindus are polytheistic and caste-conscious, guided by Vedas, Smritis or Commentaries, Manu and others, which have been framed thousands of years back whereas Sikhism is the youngest religion.

§5. Jain Laws: Sources and Legislation

137. Jainism has an origin and history much anterior to the smritis (*Boddaladi v. Boddaladi*, Per Kumaraswami Sastri, J).[27] It rejects the authority of the Vedas and discards all ceremonies and rituals. Jainism does not believe in the existence of God. It holds that by tapasya (worship), by discarding worldly life and its worldly manifestation, atma (soul) can become paramatma (God) and thus one can attain salvation (moksha).

138. The excavations made at Mohenjo-Daro and Harappa show that Jainism existed in India five thousand years ago, it is so because the pose of the standing deities on the Indus seals resembles the pose of the standing image of Rushabhadeo obtained from Mathura. The Indus valley excavated material is said to establish that the founder of Jainism belonged to the pre-Vedic period. The nude Jain idol of 320 BC in the Patna Museum of Lohanipur also supports this proposition. Therefore, Jains have their own distinct history, sources and origins of laws. Jains differ from the Hindus in their conduct and practices towards the dead and rejection of the scriptural character of the Vedas.

139. There have been some mistakes and misconceptions in not considering Jainism as a distinct and separate religion. In 1926, the reformer Hem Chandra Rai noted in the Jain Gazette that a 'dark gloom of ignorance is stunting the growth of our community to a fearful extent all around … '. Thus, it is a misplaced notion that Jainism is part and parcel of Hinduism and therefore fits into Hindu laws. In the Buddhist scripture Majjima Nikaya, Buddha himself tells about his ascetic life and its ordinances, which are in conformity with the Jain monk's code of conduct.

140. The respectable, reliable and sacred book of the Hindus the Rigveda also establishes the most ancient nature of Jain thoughts. Rigveda, the oldest Hindu scripture refers to Lord Rishabha Deo, the founder of Jainism. It also talks about Vaman Avtar-incarnation, who is the fifteenth among the twenty-four incarnations. Rishabha's name comes as the ninth incarnation of Vishnu. Rishabha's name occurs before Vaman, Krishna, and Buddha incarnations. Therefore, Rishabha must have flourished long before the composition of even Rigveda. The great scholar Dr S. Radhakrishnan, ex-Vice President of India, in his book 'Indian Philosophy' had observed, 'Jain tradition ascribes the origin of the system to Rishabhadeva, the first Tirthankara. The Yajurveda mentions the name of three Tirthankaras-Rishabha, Ajitnath and Arshtanemi. The Bhagwat Puran endorses the view that Rishabhadeva was the founder of Jainism.'

---

27. 50 Mad 228, 1927.

141. Prime Minister Jawahar Lal Nehru made it clear that Jainism is not an off-shoot of Hinduism. He was of the view that 'Buddhist or a Jain in India is hundred percent of Indian thought and culture, yet neither is a Hindu by faith. It is entirely misleading to refer to Indian culture, as Hindu culture … Buddhism or even Vedic Dharma.'

142. Considering the Jain as a separate community, the President of the Constituent Assembly, Dr Rajendra Prasad nominated a Jain representative to the Minister Advisory Committee. The Position was officially recognized in a letter from the Principal Private Secretary of the Prime Minister to Shri S.G. Patil representative of the Jain deputation, which waited on the Prime Minister Sh. Nehru on 25 January 1950.[28] It says, 'With reference to the deputation of certain representatives of the Jain who met the Prime Minister on the 25 January 1950, I am desired to say that there is no cause whatever for Jains to have any apprehension regarding the future of their religion and community. Your deputation drew attention to the Article 25 of constitution. The constitution only lays down a rule for limited purpose of the provision in the Article and as you will notice, it mentions not only Jains but also Buddhists and Sikhs. It is clear that Buddhists are not Hindus. There is therefore no reason for considering Jains as Hindus. It is true that Jains are in some ways similar to Hindus and have many customs in common but there is no doubt that they are a distinct religious community and the Constitution does not in any way effect this well recognized position.'

143. Medieval Digambara texts with chapters on 'personal law' are the Bhadrabahu Sạhita (ca. eighth-fifteenth century CE), the Vardhamananiti of Amitagati (ca. 1011 CE), the Jina Sạhita of Vasunandi Indranandi (tenth century CE), and the Traivaṛikacara of Somasena (1610 CE). The pioneering Bhadrabahu Saṃhita was cited by all later texts, even by treatises of Svetambara authors such as the Arhanniti of Hemacarya (twelfth-fourteenth century CE). They usually follow the example of Brahmanical works such as the Manusṃti, which in part was influenced by earlier Jain teachings. The Jain texts also contain many original conceptions, especially on the rights of widows to inherit and to adopt a son, coloured throughout by the Jain value of non-violence.

144. Jainism has a great relation with the Prakrit language. Sanskrit was spoken only by Vedic Brahmins, while common people's language was Prakrit. Jains always promoted their religion through people's languages. So, most of the ancient Jain literature was written in Prakrit language. The principal sources of Jain law are the Prakrit Svetambara and Digambara scriptures, known as agama or siddhant, and their commentaries. The majority of the texts were authored by monks of the Digambara tradition, which had an influence on the ruling dynasties in the Deccan between the eighth and twelfth centuries. The most significant Jain works on statecraft are the Adipurạa of Acarya Jinasena (ca. 770–850 CE) and the Nitivakyaṃtam (ca. 950 CE) and the Yasastilaka (959 CE) of Acarya Somadeva Suri. It tells the life story of the first Jina, the legendary first king and lawgiveṛ ịabha, in the manner of

28. No. 23/94/50 P. M.S. New Delhi dated /3/50.

a Jain Mahabharata, and offers blueprints for Jain social rituals and Jain kingship. The Nitivakyaṃtam is an entirely secular text on statecraft modelled on the Arthasastra of Kaụilya (ca. third century BCE – first century CE).

145. The Compilations of 'Jain law' texts produced by modern Jain reformers in the nineteenth and early twentieth centuries focused exclusively on the rules of Jain 'personal law' concerning the role of property in contexts of marriage, adoption, succession, inheritance, and partition. At the centre of concern was the division of property, or daya-vibhagam. Reform-oriented 'liberal' Jain lawyers resisted the imposition of Anglo-Hindu law, which from 1858 was extensively codified, and the progressive juridical demotion of the notion of a scripture-based uniform 'Jain law', mirroring sastric 'Hindu law', and its replacement with local 'customs' of caste.

146. 'It is recognized that the Jains are not a bagful of castes and sects with diversified cultures, conceptions and creeds. There is one doctrine, one religion, one culture, one community of the Jains, and also one Law.'[29] Because no textual evidence was accessible to the courts during the period of codification of Hindu law and Jain law was treated merely as a 'deviation' from standard 'Hindu law'. 'Jainism' was not even recognized as an independent 'religion' until 1879 when Hermann Jacobi in the introduction of his edition of the Kalpa Sutra of Bhadrabahu furnished for the first-time textual proof that the ancient Buddhist scriptures already depicted the nirgranthas as a separate 'heretical' (tirthya) group. Officially, the category 'Jain' was used for the first time in the 1881 Census of India. In 1955–1956, Jain personal law was submerged under the statutory 'Hindu Code', and is even now only indirectly recognized by the legal system in the form of residual Jain 'customs' which are required to be proved in the court.

147. The present-day Jain law is the result of colonial legal intervention. 'Jain law' suggests uniformity where in reality there is a plurality of scriptures, ethical and legal codes, and customs of sect, caste, family and region. Attempts have been made to restate traditional Jain concepts by legal luminaries in the light of the modern Indian legal system and by Jain reformers. Thus, three interpretations of the term 'Jain law' can be distinguished[30] as follows:

- 'Jain law' in the widest sense signifies the doctrine and practice of Jain dharma, or Jain religion.
- It points to the totality of conventions (vyavahara) and law codes (vyavastha) in Jain traditions. Sanskrit vyavastha and its Arabic and Urdu equivalent 'qaanun' both designate a specific code of law or legal opinion/decision, whereas Sanskrit dharma can mean religion, morality, custom and law.
- The modern Indian legal system is primarily concerned with the 'personal law' of the ordinary Jains. In Anglo-Indian case law, the term 'Jain law' was used both

29. C.R. Jain, *A Complete Digest of Cases with the Jaina Law Supplement* (Delhi S B Jain Academy 1941).
30. Flugel Peter, *A Short History of Jain Law*, 3(4) Int'l J. Jain Stud. 1–15 (2007).

as a designation for 'Jain scriptures' (sastra) on personal law, and for the unwritten 'customary laws' of the Jains, that is the social norms of Jain castes (jati) and clans (gotra).

§6. Parsi Law: Sources and Legislation

148. Parsis follow the religion of Zoroaster, a prophet of the seventh century B.C. from the region between the Hindu Kush and Seistan. Their belief system includes ideas about a creator God, good and evil forces, individual choice, heaven and hell, the Last Judgment, and eternal life. These ideas are found in sacred texts that are fragmentary, including the Avesta dating from the fourth or sixth century A.D. and attributed to the Prophet himself. This is supplemented by later Pahlavi texts written in Middle Persian, from around the ninth century A.D., which consist mostly of commentaries, interpretations, and selections.

149. More modern sources of Parsi laws are from India, written in Gujarati and English, beginning around the middle of the nineteenth century. Zoroastrianism may be viewed as one of the earliest monotheisms since it postulates as First Cause Ahura Mazda, the Creator. It then introduces a radical dualism in the form of two opposing spirits who are both the offspring of Ahura Mazda. The presence of Spenta Mainyu, the beneficent spirit, and Angra Mainyu, the hostile spirit, explains the origins of good and evil; they are the prototypes of the choices between truth and lies that each individual must face in his or her own life. Humans aid the victory of good over evil by the pursuit of good thoughts, good words, and good deeds. At the end of temporal existence, evil will be completely vanquished, and only truth and happiness will prevail.

150. Besides the Creator and his two offspring, there are seven beneficent immortals, which are entities as well as representations of Ahura Mazda's virtues, such as 'best truth' and 'immortality'. Zoroastrianism also absorbed some of the earlier Indo-Iranian Gods who became Yazatas. The more important of these preside over aspects of the material world. Others worthy of reverence are the Fravashis or spirits of the soul, together with deceased mortals who led exemplary lives. Fire is the main symbol of Zoroastrianism which receives the offerings of the priests and the prayers of individuals. Every ritual and ceremony involves the presence of the sacred fire. The fire in the place of worship called the fire temple is ritually consecrated and installed. Non-Zoroastrians are not permitted to set eyes on this sacred fire. Offerings of sandalwood and frankincense are made to it at least five times a day by ordained priests. It represents God's splendour and divine grace. A smaller ritual fire is also found in every Zoroastrian's home.

151. The hereditary clergy is divided into Dasturs (high priests) and Mobeds. There are no monastic orders, nor are there women functionaries. Priests are allowed to marry. Becoming a priest is a long and arduous process involving several purification rituals and the memorization of texts. Sons of priests nowadays prefer to enter the modern professions, and the community is facing a critical shortage of qualified functionaries.

152. The Parsi Marriage and Divorce Act, 1936 governs the matrimonial relations of Parsis. The word 'Parsi' is defined in the Act as a Parsi Zoroastrian. A Zoroastrian is a person who professes the Zoroastrian religion. It has a racial significance. The Act provides only for monogamy. The Parsi Marriage and Divorce (Amendment) Act, 1988 enlarged the scope of certain provisions of the Parsi Marriage and Divorce Act, 1936 so as to bring them in line with the HMA, 1955. Sections 39 and 49 of the Parsi Marriage and Divorce Act, 1936 were amended by the Marriage Laws (Amendment) Act, 2001 to provide for alimony pendent lite or the maintenance and education of minor children to be disposed of within sixty days from the date of service of notice on the wife or the husband as the case may be.

§7. Jew Law: Sources and Legislation

153. Any person who professes or practises Jewish religion is a Jew. The legal position is that whether a man was or was not Jewish is a question of fact to be determined by evidence. All those persons who accept every tenet of, and observe every rule and practice and conduct prescribed by the Jewish religion, are obviously Jews. But there are others who do not accept all those tenets and are lax in the observance of some practices, rules and conducts. The extent to which the tenets are accepted and rules and practices are observed vary from individual to individual, But, if one asserts that he is Jew, and, it seems, he will be Jew unless the contrary is proved, such person shall be accepted as Jew. It is always a question of degree and if a person is Jew in any degree, he is a Jew. However, if a person is not a Jew to any degree, he is not a Jew. This means if a person can show some traits of a Jew, he is a Jew otherwise not.

154. The vast majority of Indian Jews live in the city of Mumbai, though several hundred live in other cities such as Pune, Ahmadabad, and Cochin, each of which has two synagogues. Some of the native Bene Israel villages along the Konkan coast of India still contain synagogues. There are four small but distinct groups of Jews in India, each with a unique history. The largest is the Bene Israel. According to the Bene Israel's ancient tradition, they descend from seven families who were shipwrecked over two thousand years ago on the Konkan coast (south Mumbai) in a village known as Nawgaon, which is home to their ancient burial ground and regularly visited by Jews.

155. Another aspect of Judaism in India is the nature of oral tradition. Though not all are fully Sabbath observants, the Jews of India are very pious. Since theirs is an oral tradition and not a written one, they do not have a written book in which to precisely place the various traditions. So, the Jews of India do not look up their traditions or ritual laws in books; they just know what to do and know how and when to do it.

156. Knowledge of how to follow the Torah and how to live as a Jew is embedded in the Jewish culture. The oral Jewish culture was not so much a reciting and teaching of structured legal knowledge but the practising of Jewish tradition organically passed from one generation into another. What is done is assumed to have always been done and is perceived to continue in its current state in future as well. There is a religious ceremony, which is unique to the Jews of India, the Melida. In celebration of Jewish semahot, five kinds of fruits and a large mound of sweet rice are placed on a decorative plate, the Melida. Blessings are made on the fruits which are then consumed by the participants, and finally, prayers are said which centre on Eliyahu haNavi, Elijah the prophet, who is perhaps the most important Jewish figure for the Bene Israel.

Chapter 3. Typology of the System

157. The term 'typology of religion' refers to studying, examining and classifying, things or concepts regarding religion according to different types or categories. Typology is used across all disciplines including theology. The typology of religion classifies religions according to shared features and studies religions in their totality to determine common features. However, phenomenology of religion studies variations of particular phenomena in religions. Thus, a typology in simple language means classifying items, people or concepts by general types. The word typology is simply a scientific term for grouping things together based on similarities. Typology is used to classify people, things or ideas into categories based on commonalities that they share. Using typology helps to better understand certain conditions or factors by grouping things with similar characteristics together.

158. Throughout history, religion has been an important part of the cultural life in India. The Indian subcontinent is the birthplace of four of the world's major religions, namely, Hinduism, Buddhism, Jainism, and Sikhism which are collectively known as native Indian religions. Besides, there are other religions in India namely, Islam, Christianity, Jews, etc. Polytheism refers to the worship of 'many gods'. Jews, Christians and Muslims are referred to as the 'People of the Book' in the Koran. Known as the Abrahamic religions because they recognize Abraham as a founding prophet, all three are said to be monotheistic religions that strictly endorse worship of the 'God of Abraham' – Jehovah to the Jews and Christians and Allah to the Muslims. They have distinguished themselves from 'pagans' or 'infidels' because they worship 'The One God', as opposed to those who worship many gods or no God at all.

159. There are many ways of classifying religious beliefs into typologies. For example, some religions are monotheistic as they believe in one God while others are polytheistic, believing in multiple gods. Atheists do not believe in any God. The Jains in India do not believe in God. Their concept is that a man by doing his duty (karma) attains ultimate salvation. So, Jainism is individual-centric rather than God-centric.

§1. Typology with Focus on God

I. Monotheism

160. The term 'monotheism' comes from the Greek word 'monos' which means 'one' and 'theos' means 'God'. Thus, monotheism is the belief in the existence of a single God Who is omnipotent, omniscient, omnipresent, created all of reality and is totally self- sufficient without any dependency upon any other being. The largest monotheistic religions are Judaism, Christianity, Islam and Sikhism. Monotheism is typically contrasted with polytheism which is a belief in many Gods, and atheism which is an absence of belief in any God. In Islam, God is one and has no partners to share His divine glory. Christianity goes slightly away from the traditional monotheism of Judaism and Islam because of the concept of the Trinity, in which the Christians see One God in Three personalities.

A distinction can be made in monotheism:

(i) Inclusive monotheism – the belief that there is only one deity and that all other claimed deities are just different names, merely different aspects or incarnations of their one supreme God. The Hinduism is an example of inclusive monotheism.
(ii) Exclusive monotheism – which refers to the belief that there is only one deity and that all other claimed deities are false and distinct from it, either the product of invention, evil, or human error; they deny the existence of the Gods of any other religious faiths. Most Abrahamic religions are examples of exclusive monotheism. Most monotheistic systems tend to be exclusive in nature. Due to this exclusivity, monotheistic religions have historically displayed less religious tolerance than polytheistic religions.

II. Polytheism

161. The term polytheism is derived from the Greek words 'poly' which means 'many' and 'theos' means 'God'. Thus, polytheism is used where plurality of Gods is acknowledged and worshipped. Any individual God in a polytheistic system is considered a member of a larger, coherent group called a pantheon rather than being totally separate and unrelated. Generally, each individual God represents a unique value, personifies some aspect of humanity, and controls some facet of nature. Thus, there are Gods of fertility, rivers, health, anger, sun, vegetation, life and death. Within polytheism, an adherent wishing to obtain something is expected to pray to that particular God rather than to others who do not have dominion in that area. In some polytheistic systems the Gods themselves may be subordinate to other forces of nature or fate – just because they are Gods doesn't mean that they are supernatural or transcendent. Thus, polytheism believes in a division of responsibility within the divine realm similar to that which is observed in the human world. The polytheistic notion of Gods is traced in the Vedic lore of India. Although polytheistic systems postulate a coherent group, they also acknowledge the existence of Gods outside the religion's pantheon.

162. There are usually three different responses regarding acceptance of Gods from other cultures and religions:

(1) Same with different names: It is believed that some or all of the outside Gods are really the same as the Gods currently worshipped, just with different names. Any new aspects or powers are simply incorporated into the older Gods.
(2) New additions: One approach is taking some of the new Gods and adopting them as new members of the pantheon. In this manner, the pantheon gradually grows.

(3) Acceptance but not worshipping: In this approach, one accepts that the other Gods exist, but does not worship them in any active manner.

163. As polytheistic systems accept the existence of Gods from other religions and cultures, polytheism offers more religious freedom than monotheism. Polytheistic belief promotes and assimilates all the indigenous and popular narratives.

164. Modern scientific thinking tends to reject polytheism because of its incompatibility with the understanding of natural laws. If there were different, independent Gods in charge of all the different aspects of reality, then there cannot be a set of natural laws which are common to all parts of reality. The laws of physics would not apply to chemistry and the laws of chemistry would not apply to biology, and so on. Scientific order would find no basis if multiple Gods were working for potentially contrary purposes.

165. Polytheism, with all its weaknesses and failures, is admittedly the embryonic stage in the evolution of religious thoughts. In the later part of the Vedic era, there is a tendency towards One Divine Being. It seems that the frantic competition among the Gods to gain supremacy over the other gradually developed into the idea of one single God – or the Supreme Being, which subsequently constitutes the central theme of religion.

III. Animism

166. Animism refers to the belief that non-human entities are spiritual beings, either intrinsically or because spirits inhabit them for a period of time. Unlike supernatural forces, animist spirits may be inherently good or evil. Often, these spirits are thought to be the souls of deceased relatives, and they are not worshipped as deities. Animism puts more emphasis on the uniqueness of each individual soul. In pantheism, everything shares the same spiritual essence – there are no distinct spirits and/or souls. Because humans are considered a part of nature, rather than superior to, or separate from it, animists see themselves on roughly equal footing with other animals, plants, and natural forces, and subsequently have a moral imperative to treat these agents with respect.

167. In animist societies, ritual is considered essential to win the favour of the spirits that ward off other malevolent spirits and provide food, shelter, and fertility. Shamans, also sometimes called medicine men or women, serve as mediums between the physical world and the world of spirits. Animism is thought to be the belief system that laid the groundwork for the notion of a soul and the animation of traditionally inanimate objects, allowing every world religion to take those basic principles in other directions. Examples of Animism can be seen in the forms of Shinto, Hinduism, Buddhism, pantheism, Paganism, and Neopaganism.

IV. Panthism

168. Pantheism considers that God and the universe are identical. The term 'Pantheism' is derived from the Greek pan, meaning 'all or everything' and theos, meaning 'god or divine' – 'everything is god, everything is divine'. Thus, pantheists believe that nature is God and that everyday reality is identical to the divine. Pantheist belief does not recognize a distinct personal god, but instead characterizes a broad range of doctrines which describe various types of relationships between material 'reality' and divinity. Pantheism is often viewed as a non-religious or atheistic philosophical position. By equating the universe – which is seen as the totality of all existence – and God as being identical, they deny the existence of God. In the Bhagavad Gita, Krishna makes a clear distinction between, material nature, the living entities, and the Supreme Lord who is the controller of both the inferior and superior energies.

V. Monism

169. Monism is the idea that 'it's all one' – everyone and everything is God. Monism is ultimately no different to polytheism – if everyone and everything is ultimately God, then there is no one supreme being to be worshipped by all others. The monist doesn't need to worship anybody else – he is the one and only god. In Kali-yuga, the Supreme Lord instructed Lord Shiva, in his role as Sankaracharya, to teach monism, also called mayavada philosophy or impersonalism.

VI. Dualism

170. Zoroastrianism of ancient Persia is based on Dualism where Ahriman is the bad god, the leader of the enemies who oppose the good god Ahura Mazda. In this dualistic doctrine, Ahriman is the first personification of the force of evil, a forerunner of the Devil or Satan. Founded by the Iranian prophet Zoroaster (or Zarathustra), Zoroastrianism presented the concept of an ever-lasting struggle between Good and Evil, where hopefully the Good will eventually prevail. In the Zoroastrian religious texts, the Gathas, the two opposing spirits – the Beneficent Spirit Ahura Mazda and the Destructive Spirit Ahriman – are complete and equal opposites in all respects. The Destructive Spirit is said to be the 'twin brother' of the Beneficent One, and the two spirits are said to be 'symmetrical' or equal in power, but contrary in their character and activities.

§2. Typology Based on Impact of Religion on Lives

171. The Pew Research Centre presented a seven-part typology grouping people into types based on how religion impacts their lives. Their types are: Sunday Stalwarts, God-and Country Believers, Diversely Devout, Relaxed Religious, Spiritually Awake, Solidly Secular, and Religion Resisters. Religious typology cannot be accurate as generalization may sometimes lead to misunderstanding. The range by which one can claim to be religious depends on the degree and level of devotion.

172. The Pew Research Centre created a 16-question survey about the participant's level of practice and belief. This process has resulted in a new typology of seven religious styles that will serve as the organization's classification system for a better understanding of how one practices faith.

173. The survey did not replace traditional religious categories but instead created categories built around personal religious and spiritual beliefs, as well as behaviours and experiences that are broadly shared by people of different faiths. The Seven Types are as follows:

I. Sunday Stalwarts

174. These believers are actively involved in their communities and their faith. Sunday morning is only for one thing for 80% of this group. Their level of belief in their doctrines and texts is unquestioned, even though 30% believe in psychics and the energetic importance of crystals and trees. Their identity is intimately tied to their faith. This is the oldest of any group, with 32% over age 65. Stalwarts are predominately Protestant but also include Hindus, Muslims, Jews, and many others.

II. God-and-Country Believers

175. This group's level of faith rivals the stalwarts, but they are much more politically focused. These are the nationalists and populists. They are also more intolerant of immigrants and those of other faiths. Evangelical Protestants are the largest contingent of this group, though Catholics, Mormons, and even religiously unaffiliated are included.

III. Diversely Devout

176. A majority of this group believes in crystals and reincarnation. Being a good person, as in the two previous groups, requires a belief in God. Interestingly, a percentage of this population includes those who claim their religion is 'nothing in particular'. This is the only group that is not majority white.

IV. Solidly Secular

177. This group is comprised predominantly of white men who are relatively affluent and highly educated. This is where atheists and agnostics conspire, relying more on science and provable facts over speculation and blind faith. Twenty per cent of this group describes themselves as agnostic, while it boasts the largest collection of atheists of any group.

V. Religion Resisters

178. This group resists traditional religious assumptions and places emphasis on energies and spiritual awakenings. These people are 'spiritual, not religious'. This group is more likely to be liberal.

VI. Relaxed Religious

179. This interesting collection features those who believe in God and who pray daily, yet they rarely attend services and do not feel a higher power is necessary to be a good person. Faith is more ambiguous and less proactive. The two top sources of meaning for those in this group are spending time with family and spending time with friends.

VII. Spiritually Awake

180. Every member of this group holds some New Age beliefs. Some form of higher power is involved in the daily orchestration of events. This group features the highest percentage of women of any group.

Part II. Religious Freedom in General

181. The role of religion begins from birth and continues to influence the life of an individual in India till the last moments and even after death. It is so because in what manner the mortal remains of an individual will be disposed of depends on which religion he belongs to. Freedom of religion or freedom of belief is a principle that supports the freedom of an individual or community, in public or private, to manifest religion or belief in teaching, practice, worship, and observance. This freedom also includes the freedom to change one's religion or not to follow any religion. Even in a country with a declared state religion, freedom of religion will mean that the government permits religious practices of other religious groups besides the state religion, and does not discriminate or persecute believers in other faiths.

182. The freedom of religion and freedom of conscience has been recognized under international law. The General Assembly of the United Nations adopted without dissenting vote on 10 December 1948, the Universal Declaration on Human Rights recognizing the fact that the entire humanity enjoys certain alienable rights, which constitute the foundation of freedom, justice and peace in the world. In order to give effect to the Universal Declaration of human rights (UDHR) the members of the United Nations (UN) also adopted the two conventions in 1966, namely the International Covenant on Economic, Social and Cultural Rights and the International Covenant on Civil and Political Rights (ICCPR). On 10 April 1979, the Government of India accepted UDHR and the two international covenants with certain reservations.

183. Right to freedom of religion is not a conferred right but a natural entitlement of every human being. In fact, law does not assign it but it asserts, protects and insures its entitlement. Every human being has a natural entitlement to religious faith and freedom of conscience and the right to adopt or abandon any faith of his/her own choice. Thus, the freedom of conscience has been recognized as a basic human right, both constitutionally and conventionally. The Constitution of India aims at securing freedom of religion and freedom of conscience under Articles 25, 26, 27, 28, and 30, and at the same time, it seeks to create harmony among all religions. Being suitable to the pluralistic society and historical lineage, such freedom should continue. Any other policy will be not only unconstitutional but also extremely harmful and suffocative for the public.

184. The ideas, faith, psyche, behaviour and attitude of people have always been subject to change, though the factors of change are spatial and temporal. An important aspect with respect to change of faith is the state of one's awareness and ignorance. More awareness and enlightenment definitely have an impact on the thoughts, beliefs and actions of a person, faith and elements of conscience. The right to freedom of religion also includes the right to propagate one's religion which means the right to communicate the person's beliefs to people of other faiths or to expose and introduce others to the tenets of faith. The freedom to leave or discontinue membership in a religion known as 'apostasy' is also a fundamental part of religious freedom, covered by Article 18 of the UDHR. Thus, freedom of religion is considered a fundamental human right. Article 25(1) of the Constitution of India guarantees to every person not only the right to entertain such religious beliefs as may appeal to his conscience but also the right to exhibit his belief in his conduct by such outward acts as may appear to him proper in order to spread his ideas for the benefit of others.

Chapter 1. Individual Religious Freedom

185. The Constitution of India in the chapter on Fundamental Rights contains several provisions that emphasize legal equality of citizens irrespective of their religion and creed and prohibit any kind of religion-based discrimination between them. According to these provisions, the State shall not deny to any person equality before the law or the equal protection of the laws within the territory of India (Article 14). The State shall not discriminate against any citizen on grounds only of religion, race, caste, sex, place, or any of them either in general or in the matter of access to or use of general and public places and conveniences (Article 15). There shall be equality of opportunity for all citizens in the matter of employment or appointment under the state, and no citizen shall on grounds only of religion be ineligible for or discriminated against in respect of any employment or office under the state (Article 16). In the event of the State imposing compulsory service on citizens for public purposes, no discrimination shall be made on the grounds of religion only (Article 23(2)).

186. The traditional religious concept of 'untouchability' stands abolished and its practice in any form is strictly forbidden (Article 17). To meet the demands of Article 17, after the commencement of the Constitution, Parliament enacted the Untouchability (Offenses) Act, which was later amended and renamed as the Protection of Civil Rights Act. A second law enacted as a safeguard is the Scheduled Castes and Scheduled Tribes (Prevention of Atrocities) Act, 1989.

187. Religious freedom as an individual's right is guaranteed by the Constitution to 'all persons' within certain parameters in Article 25 as follows:

(1) Subject to public order, morality and health and to the other provisions of this Part, all persons are equally entitled to freedom of conscience and the right freely to profess, practice and propagate religion.
(2) Nothing in this article shall affect the operation of any existing law or prevent the State from making any law:
   (a) regulating or restricting any economic, financial, political or other secular activity which may be associated with religious practice;
   (b) Providing for social welfare and reform or the throwing open of Hindu religious institutions of a public character to all classes and sections of Hindus.

   Explanation I. The wearing and carrying of Kirpan (dagger) shall be deemed to be included in the profession of the Sikh religion.

   Explanation II. In sub-clause (b) of clause (2), the reference to Hindus shall be construed as including a reference to persons professing the Sikh, Jain or Buddhist religion, and the reference to Hindu religious institutions shall be construed accordingly.

188. Therefore, Article 25(1) guarantees to every person the freedom of conscience and right to profess, practise and propagate religion. This right is, however, subject to public order, morality and health and to the other provisions of Part III of the Constitution. Under sub-clauses (a) and (b) of clause (2) of Article 25, the State is empowered by law:

(a) to regulate or restrict any economic, financial, political or other secular activity which may be associated with religious practice;
(b) to provide for (i) social welfare and reform, and (ii) to throw open Hindu religious institutions of a public character to all classes and sections of Hindus.

There shall be freedom as to payment of taxes for the promotion of any particular religion by virtue of which no person shall be compelled to pay any taxes the proceeds of which are specifically appropriated in payment of expenses for the promotion or maintenance of any particular religious denomination (Article 27).

189. The freedom of religion so available is not confined to citizens alone but also extends to all persons, including aliens and individuals exercising their rights either in their individual capacity or on behalf of some institution. This point was underlined by the Supreme Court in the case of *Rati Lal Panchand v. State of Bombay.*[31] Freedom of conscience connotes a person's right to entertain beliefs and doctrines concerning matters, which are regarded by him to be conducive to his spiritual well-being. A person has the freedom to believe in the religious tenets of any sect or community of his choice. The right is confined not only to entertain such religious beliefs as may be approved by one's conscience but also to exhibit them in overt acts and carry on practices as provided by the religion.

190. Article 25(1) does not give the right to convert any person to one's own religion; it only allows to transmit or spread one's religion by an exposition of its tenets. Thus, there is no fundamental right to convert another person to one's own religion because if a person purposely undertakes the conversion of another person to his religion, as distinguished from his effort to transmit or spread the tenets of his religion that would impinge on the 'freedom of conscience' guaranteed to all the citizens alike. The protection of Articles 25 and 26 is thus not limited to matters of belief. It extends also to acts done in pursuance of 'religion' and, therefore, contains a guarantee for rituals and observances, ceremonies and modes of worship, which are integral parts of religion. What constitutes an essential part of religion or religious practice has to be decided by the courts with reference to a doctrine of a particular religion and includes practices, which are regarded by the community as a part of its religion.

§1. Conversion and Freedom of Religion

191. Any ban on religious conversion may interfere with one's right to propagate one's religion under Article 25(1), apart from infringing the right to freedom of

31. 1954 AIR 388

speech guaranteed under Article 19(1) of the Constitution. The Supreme Court has held that there is no fundamental right to convert another person to one's religion as such a right would infringe on the right to freedom of conscience guaranteed to all citizens of the country alike. In this context, the Supreme Court has upheld the validity of the anti-conversion legislation passed by the States of Madhya Pradesh and Orissa, which prohibited forcible conversion from one religion to another in a manner reprehensible to the conscience of the community and which made conversions by force, fraud or allurement an offence.[32] Therefore, Article 25(1) of the Constitution does not guarantee the right to convert but only the right freely to profess, practise and propagate one's religion. Forcible conversions that are likely to give rise to an apprehension of a breach of public order are not permissible.

192. Indian society is a pluralist and heterogeneous society with a multiplicity of races, religions, cultures, castes, languages, etc. The incident of conversion causes a lot of hue and cry in society particularly feelings of suspicion in certain organizations because of its inherent socio-political impact. Rigid and stringent caste system is one of the factors behind the religious conversion. It is because of caste system that Dalits (the word Dalit includes Untouchables, Shudras and Adivasis) are considered the most susceptible section of the society to religious conversion.

I. The Impact of Religious Conversion

193. The religious conversion into Islam by a person from a non-Islamic faith is not valid if the conversion is done for availing the benefit of polygamy or for monetary benefits. Neither Islam nor the law of the land recognizes any such conversions. In the case of *Sarla Mudgal v. Union of India,*[33] a married Hindu male converted to Islam for the sake of solemnizing another marriage as polygamy is permitted in Islam. The Hon'ble SC held that conversion into another faith *ipso facto* does not dissolve the first marriage because no one is allowed to take the benefit of his own wrong. Moreover, the court held that the married person converting to Islam is not entitled to marry another woman after conversion. It was held to be an act of bigamy prohibited under section 17 of HMA, 1955 and punishable under section 494 of IPC (Indian Penal Code) and it was further observed that the second marriage so solemnized is void. In *Vilayat Raj v. Smt. Sunita,*[34] it was observed by the court that if both the parties to the marriage were Hindu at the time of marriage, prenuptial law, i.e., HMA, applied even after conversion to Islam.

194. In *Lilly Thomas v. Union of India,*[35] it was observed that an apostate husband is guilty of bigamy under section 494 of IPC if he marries another woman after converting to Islam. It was observed that holding such a person guilty of bigamy is

32. *Rev Stainislaus v. State of M.P.*, AIR 1997 SC 908.
33. AIR 1995 SC 1531.
34. AIR 1983 SC 6.
35. JT 2000 (5) SC 617.

not a violation of freedom of religion under Article 25 of the Constitution and section 17 of HMA 1955 is applicable. It is clear that after the aforementioned judicial verdicts, polygamy is no longer a valued reason for religious conversion to Islam.

195. A Hindu will not cease to be a Hindu merely because he declares that he has no faith in his religion or he does not practise his religion, till he renounces his religion or starts living and behaving like an atheist or agnostic or starts eating beef or insulting God or Goddesses. If a person converts from the Hindu religion to Sikh, Buddhism or Jainism, he does not cease to be a Hindu since all these religions fall within the definition of 'Hindu' for the purpose of application of law. He ceases to be a Hindu if he converts to Islam, Christianity, Jewish or Zoroastrian. Further, conversion into another religion is a ground for dissolution of marriage for the other spouse and not for the spouse who converts to any such religion (section 13 of HMA).

196. Under section 80 of the HMA if the husband converts to a non-Hindu faith, the wife is entitled to live separately and her right of maintenance will not be forfeited, but if she herself also ceases to be Hindu, she loses her claim of maintenance under the section but shall be entitled under section 24 of HM Act 1955 for pendente lite and permanent alimony.

197. Under the Indian Divorce Act, 1869, if the husband gets converted to non-Christian faith, the wife is entitled to divorce but vice versa is not possible. If the wife gets converted to a non-Christian faith, then the husband cannot apply for divorce. As per section 4 of the Dissolution of Muslim Marriage Act, 1939, if a wife renounces Islam, the marriage does not *ipso facto* dissolve unless the circumstances warrant otherwise. However, under the Special Marriage Act, 1954, conversion does not have any effect on matrimonial ties.

198. An aspect of freedom of conscience, which is problematic and controversial, is the right to propagate one's faith. The meaning of propagation is to promote, spread and publicize one's own faith for the edification of others. The term propagation implies persuasion and exposition without any element of fraud, coercion and allurement.

A. *Love Jihad*

199. Love Jihad is the alleged effort by Muslim men to target women belonging to non-Muslim communities for conversion to Islam by feigning love and marriage. The concept rose to national attention in 2009 with alleged conversions first in Kerala and subsequently in Karnataka. With widespread publicity, the allegations of love jihad have raised concerns in various Hindu, Sikh and Christian organizations, while Muslim organizations have denied the allegations. This has been a subject of political contention and social concern. But independent investigations have failed to find evidence of any organized plan of conversion and exposed claims of love jihad as fantasies and sometimes deliberate election-time inventions for polarization.

200. Hadiya (formerly Akhila Ashokan), a 24-year-old homoeopathic medical student from Kerala in early 2016 was reported to be missing by her father, who initially filed a police case and then a habeas corpus petition in the Kerala High Court. Hadiya came out with the version that she had converted to Islam and married a Muslim man, Shafin Jahan. Her family alleged she was brainwashed and her marriage was forced, but Hadiya contradicted it and said she did of her own volition. In May 2017, Hadiya's marriage was annulled by the High Court of Kerala on the grounds of a report submitted by the National Investigation Agency (NIA) to the Supreme Court of India (SC), saying that Hadiya was a victim of indoctrination and psychological kidnapping and the claims that their marriage being arranged through a matrimony website, were 'bogus'. The High Court of Kerala then handed over Hadiya's custody to her father, arguing that, 'As per Indian tradition, the custody of an unmarried daughter is with the parents, until she is properly married.'

Shafin Jahan, the husband of Hadiya, appealed and moved the Supreme Court. In November 2017, the Supreme Court directed Hadiya to resume her internship and that she was free to meet whomever she wanted. In March 2018, the Supreme Court restored Hadiya's marriage, ten months after the Kerala High Court annulled it. The High Court had called the marriage a 'sham' and referred to it as 'love jihad'. The Supreme Court Bench observed that 'Freedom of faith is essential to his/her autonomy; Choosing a faith is the substratum of individuality and sans it, the right of choice becomes a shadow.' In his separate but concurring opinion, Justice Chandrachud wrote, 'Matters of belief and faith, including whether to believe, are at the core of constitutional liberty. The Constitution exists for believers as well as for agnostics.' The Constitution protects the ability of each individual to pursue a way of life or faith to which she or he seeks to adhere. 'Matters of dress and of food, of ideas and ideologies, of love and partnership are within the central aspects of identity. Society has no role to play in determining our choice of partners', Justice Chandrachud wrote.

The judgment castigated the Kerala Government for supporting 'patriarchal autocracy'. Chief Justice Misra said the High Court decision and her father's 'obstinate' attitude was an attempt to 'garrotte her desire to live with the man with whom she has entered into wedlock'. Justice Chandrachud expressed his anguish at how the High Court tried to decide 'just way of life or "correct" course of living for Hadiya'. The Supreme Court held that a person's right to choose a religion and marry is an intrinsic part of his or her meaningful existence. Neither the State nor 'patriarchal supremacy' can interfere in his or her decision.

II. Conversion by a Scheduled Caste Hindu

201. If a Scheduled Caste person professing Hindu, Sikh or Bodh religion converts to any other faith like Islam or Christianity, he loses the benefits extended to him or her and enjoyed as Scheduled Castes on such conversion. However, on reconversion to Hinduism he or she regains all benefits. This position has been affirmed in judicial decisions.[36] A Scheduled Caste on reconversion again becomes part of the caste he left. Such effects of conversion and reconversion by members of the Scheduled Castes have been affirmed in judicial decisions like *S. Swvigara doss v. Zonal Manager, Food Corporation of India (FCI)*.[37] As regards the rights of Scheduled Castes reconverting to Hinduism, the Supreme Court has observed in *CM Ammugam v. S. Rajgopal*[38] that the objects and purposes of the Constitution (Scheduled Castes) Order 1950 would be advanced rather than retarded by taking the view that on reconversion to Hinduism, a person can once again become a member of the Scheduled Caste to which he belonged prior to his conversion.

202. The implication is that once a scheduled caste always a scheduled caste as per Manu's caste classification that perpetuates the caste system. This also provides an incentive to remain Scheduled Caste and Hindu forever. Conversion by a Scheduled Castes person to Christianity or Islam would also take him out of the ambit of a law enacted by Parliament for the protection of Scheduled Castes from social atrocities of various kinds, viz., the Scheduled Castes and Scheduled Tribes (Prevention of Atrocities) Act 1989.

203. It appears that these laws as understood and interpreted and applied are aimed to keep the low-caste Hindus within the fold of Hinduism. If a Dalit Hindu who had converted to another faith or any of his descendants reconverts to Hinduism, he /she gets back to his or her original caste. So, on the one hand, allurement for conversion has been prohibited but on the other hand, when it comes to conversion to the religion of the majority, it is supported. In case of scheduled caste Hindus converting to other religions, on reconversion all benefits are restored in the form of reservations and other advantages available to schedule caste Hindus.

204. The Supreme Court has ruled that 'A person who is born to Christian parents who had converted to Christianity from Scheduled Caste Hindu can avail the benefit of caste certificate after his embracing Hinduism, subject to other qualifications. There cannot be any soundness of logic that he cannot avail the similar benefits because his grandparents were converted and he was born to parents who were Christian.' The Bench laid down a three-fold criterion for a reconverted person to get back his caste status and consequential benefits accruing to that caste for employment and education. The only caveat is that on reconversion, the Dalit community must accept him/her as a member of the community. The court stated that 'There must be absolutely clear cut proof that he belongs to the caste that has been recognized by the Constitution (Scheduled Castes) Order, 1950, there has been re-conversion to the original religion to which the parents and earlier generations had belonged and there has to be evidence establishing the acceptance by the community.' The case was related to the refusal of a Scheduled Caste certificate to one K P Manu, whose great-grandfather belonged to the Hindu Pulaya community in

36. *S. Swvigaradoss v. Zonal Manger*, FCI, AIR 1996 SC1182.
37. AIR 1996 SC 1182.
38. 1976 SC 939.

Kerala. Manu's father had embraced Christianity and took a new name, Verghese, and married Mariam, who earlier belonged to the Hindu Ezhava community and had converted to Christianity.[39]

III. Legislation on Conversion

205. The legislative history relating to the issue of conversion in India underscores the point that certain sections of society were never favourably disposed towards conversion. While British India had no anti-conversion laws, many Princely States enacted anti-conversion legislation, e.g., the Raigarh State Conversion Act 1936, the Patna Freedom of Religion Act of 1942, the Sarguja State Apostasy Act 1945 and the Udaipur State Anti-Conversion Act 1946. Similar laws were enacted in Bikaner, Jodhpur, Kalahandi and Kota and many more were specifically against conversion to Christianity. In the post-independence era, Parliament took up for consideration in 1954 the Indian Conversion (Regulation and Registration) Bill and later in 1960 the Backward Communities (Religious Protection) Bill, both of which had to be dropped for lack of support. The Freedom of Religion Bill of 1979 was opposed by the Minorities Commission due to the Bill's evident bias.

206. In 1967 Orissa and then Madhya Pradesh enacted the Orissa Freedom of Religion Act 1967 and the Madhya Pradesh Dharma Swatantrata Adhiniyam, 1968, respectively. Along similar lines, the Arunachal Pradesh Freedom of Religion Act, 1978 was enacted to provide for the prohibition of conversion from one religious faith to any other by use of force or inducement or by fraudulent means and for matters connected therewith. Subsequently, the State of Chhattisgarh passed a legislation in 2000. Each of these Acts provides definitions of 'Government', 'conversion', 'indigenous faith', 'force', 'fraud', and 'inducement' (and in the case of Arunachal, that of 'prescribed and religious faith'). These laws declared forced conversion a cognizable offence under sections 295 A and 298 of the IPC, providing that malice and deliberate intention to hurt the sentiments of others is a penal offence punishable by varying durations of imprisonment and fines.

207. 'Freedom of Religion' laws are in force in eight states in India, namely Odisha (1967), Madhya Pradesh (1968), Arunachal Pradesh (1978), Chhattisgarh (2000 and 2006), Gujarat (2003), Himachal Pradesh (2006 and 2019), Jharkhand (2017), and Uttarakhand (2018). The laws passed in Himachal Pradesh (2019) and Uttarakhand also declare a marriage to be void if it was solemnized for the sole purpose of conversion. In November 2019, the Uttar Pradesh Law Commission suggested enacting a new law to regulate religious conversions. This led the state government to promulgate the ordinance. There have been debates over the use of anti-conversion laws. Some sections of society believe that these laws are necessary to protect the cultural and social cohesion of the country, while others say that these laws are used as a tool to suppress minority religions and violate the right to freedom of religion, which is protected by international human rights laws.

39. Times of India, 28 Feb. 2015, pp. 10.

208. As early as 1967, it became evident that the concern was not just with forced conversion, but with conversion to any religion other than Hinduism and especially Christianity and Islam. In the Orissa and Madhya Pradesh Acts, the punishment was to be doubled if the offence had been committed in respect of a minor, a woman or a person belonging to the Scheduled Caste or Scheduled Tribe community. The contention of some activists was that the minority religious organizations, especially, Christian missionaries, are actively involved in the activities of mass religious conversion in the name of social service. According to them the target groups of these Christian missionaries are generally illiterate and poor Dalits and Poor tribes.

209. However, many Dalit organizations and Dalit thinkers have perceived these recurrent incidents of religious conversions as great events of Dalit emancipation from the clutches of the vicious Hindu Caste System which is and has been a constant stigma. According to them, the Hindu Caste System is founded on a rigid and stringent caste hierarchy. Due to this inhuman caste system, Dalits and Shudras (Untouchables) have been treated inhumanly, subjugated, oppressed and persecuted by the so-called upper caste Hindus or Manu Vadis in the name of caste for centuries. Dalit thinkers also allege that Hindu society was not able to make adequate reforms in the Hindu religion during the last more than three thousand years so that a lower-caste Hindu could live with human dignity in the Hindu religion. According to them, the majority of Dalits and Shudras (untouchable) are illiterate, deplorably poverty-stricken and living in sub-human conditions. They have been denied basic human rights even after independence.

210. The Chhattisgarh Religion Freedom (Amendment) Act, 2006 provide for, either three-year imprisonment and a penalty up to INR 20,000 or both for offenders. The Haryana Prevention of Unlawful Conversion of Religion Act, 2022, provides a penalty of one to five years imprisonment and a fine of INR one lakh. The Jharkhand Freedom of Religion Act, 2017 imposes imprisonment of up to three years and a fine of INR 50,000 or both. The Orissa Freedom of Religion Act, 1967 imposes one-year imprisonment and a fine of INR 5,000, or both. The Uttar Pradesh Prohibition of Unlawful Conversion of Religion Ordinance, 2020 enforces imprisonment of one to ten years in prison. According to the Karnataka Protection of Right to Freedom of Religion Act, 2022, a forced conversion is punishable by imprisonment for three to five years and a fine of INR 25,000.

211. The UN rapporteur for religious freedom, Heiner Bielefeldt, has said that 'these state laws undermine religious freedom in India. Despite lauding India as the birthplace of many religions and its heritage of pluralism', he asserts that the requirement of converts having to explain their reasons for conversion is humiliating and wrongly attributes the state with somehow having the ability to assess its genuineness. Though the UN rapporteur concedes that coercion must be prevented, he also states that 'such concepts as inducement or allurement are not only vague but that any invitation to another religion has elements of inducement or allurement'. He notes that 'these are loosely defined terms and don't meet the standards of criminal justice in which laws need to be clear'.[40]

212. The suggestions and demands from certain sections, for having a national law on conversion, have come from time to time. Bills were proposed to be introduced in the Parliament in 1954, 1960 and 1979, but fell because of lack of support. When mass conversion took place in Meenakshipuram in 1981, the Union Government advised all the States to enact law-regulating conversions. On an international level, the extreme examples come from Myanmar where a legislation has been enacted dealing with particularly Muslim minority which threatens religious freedom.[41]

213. The 1981 United Nations Declaration on the Elimination of All Forms of Intolerance and of Discrimination Based on Religion or Belief calls on States to rescind legislation where necessary to prohibit discrimination on religious grounds and to take all appropriate measures to combat intolerance on the grounds of religion.

IV. Judicial Determination of Anti-conversion Laws

214. In the 1957 case of *Ratilal Panchand Gandhi v. State of Bombay*,[42] the Supreme Court interpreted the ambit of Article 25 to include 'The right to propagate one's religion views for the edification of others'. Twenty years later, the same issues arose in the case of *Stainislaus v. State of Madhya Pradesh*.[43] While anti-conversion legislations have been challenged several times, before the judiciary, the Supreme Court judgment in the *Stainislaus* case is the main judicial pronouncement on their legal validity. The case, which adjudges the validity of the Orissa and Madhya Pradesh anti-conversion laws, arose due to divergent judgments passed by the High Courts of Orissa and Madhya Pradesh. Reverend Stainislaus of Raipur, Madhya Pradesh refused to register conversions and challenged the Madhya

40. Baijayant Jay Panda, *Losing My Religion –If Minority Communities Have the Right to Convert Others Then So Does the Majority*, Times of India, New Delhi, 25 Dec. 2014, p. 20.
41. Over eighty organizations from civil society worldwide called on Burma to scrap proposed legislation that would unlawfully restrict the right to freely choose a religion. If adopted, this law would violate fundamental human rights and could lead to further violence against Muslims and other religious minorities in the country. The draft 'Religious Conversion Law', published in state-run media on 27 May 2014, sets out a process for applying for official permission to convert from one religion to another. It confers Township-level officials from various government departments sweeping powers to determine whether an applicant has exercised free will in choosing to change religion. Those found to be applying for conversion 'with the intent of insulting or destroying a religion' could be punished by up to two years' imprisonment, raising the prospect of arbitrary arrest and detention for those wishing to convert from Theravada Buddhism – the faith of the majority in Burma/Myanmar – to a minority religion, or no religion at all. Compelling an individual to convert to another religion through 'undue influence or pressure' could carry a one-year jail penalty. The broad wording of this provision may effectively outlaw proselytizing in the country.
42. 1954 AIR SC 388.
43. 1977 AIR SC 908.

Pradesh Freedom of Religion Act, 1968 contending a violation of Article 25 of the Indian Constitution. A similar claim was brought before the Orissa High Court, challenging the constitutional validity of the Orissa Freedom of Religion Act, 1967. The Madhya Pradesh High Court upheld the Madhya Pradesh Freedom of Religion Act, on the grounds that it guaranteed religious freedom to all including those who are subject to conversion by force, fraud and allurement. The High Court of Orissa, with respect to the right to convert as a component of Article 25, held that the term 'inducement' used in the Orissa Freedom of Religion Act was too vague and capable of infringing upon the right to carry out legitimate proselytizing activities protected by Article 25 and therefore, liable to be struck down.

215. The Madhya Pradesh High Court's ruling was largely endorsed by the Supreme Court and rejected the Orissa High Court's understanding of conversion as an essential component of Article 25 and distinguished between the right to propagate and the right to convert. While the former was a fundamental right, the latter was not seen as a component of a fundamental right. It was stated that the right to religious freedom merely guaranteed the right to 'transit or spread' one's religion by an exposition of its tenets and that allowing people to 'purposely undertake' the conversion of others to their religion, as opposed to merely transmitting or spreading his religious tenets, would amount to a violation of the 'freedom of conscience' guaranteed to all the citizens. Further, the Supreme Court held that the State Government had the legislative competence to enact such legislation for the purpose of maintenance of public order as forcible conversion could result in public disorder.

216. The *Stainislaus* case overruled the Orissa High Court's judgment in the case of *Yulitha Hyde v. State of Orissa*,[44] where it was held that the definition of 'inducement' provided in the Orissa Freedom of Religion Act, 1967 impinged legitimate means of proselytizing because its ambiguous nature and wide scope. The *Stainislaus* case has been widely criticized. Mr H.M. Seervai, an authority on the Constitution, was agonized over the Supreme Court's failure to consider the legislative history behind the drafting of Article 25, as well as its failure to analyse the importance of missionary activities in the Christian religion. He argued that often, the purpose of religion propagation was not merely to spread knowledge of one's religion but also, to produce intellectual and moral conviction leading to action, namely, the adoption of that religion. And that the propagation of one's religion to another person with a view to it being accepted by the other person gives the other person an opportunity to exercise his freedom of choice of religion.

§2. Restrictions on Freedom of Religion

217. The religious liberty has been subjected to public order, morality and health. In the name of religion, no act can be done against public order and the health of the public. Section 34 of the Police Act prohibits the slaughter of cattle or indecent exposure of one's person in a public place. These acts cannot be justified

44. AIR 1973 Ori 116.

on plea of the practice of religious rites. Likewise, in the name of religion 'untouchability' or traffic in 'human beings', e.g., system of Devdasis,[45] cannot be tolerated. These rights are subjected to the reasonable restrictions under clause (2) of Article 19. For instance, a citizen's freedom of speech and expression in matters of religion is subjected to reasonable restrictions under Article 19(2).

218. The right to propagate one's religion does not give a right to anyone to 'forcibly' convert any person to one's own religion. Forcible conversion of any person to one's own religion might disturb the public order and hence could be prohibited by law. The economic, financial, political and secular activities associated with religious practices can be regulated under clause (2)(a). The freedom to practise extends only to those activities, which are the essence of religion. It would not cover secular activities, which do not form the essence of religion. It is not always easy to say which activities fall under religious practice or which are of secular, commercial or political nature associated with religious practice. Each case must be judged by its own facts, circumstances and merit.

§3. Enforcement of Religious Freedom

219. Religious freedom in India continues to be under threat and as a result, the plight of religious minorities is reaching new levels. This is despite the fact that the right to freedom of religion or belief is recognized in the Constitution and the country has acceded to the International Covenant on Civil and Political Rights (ICCPR) and so pledged to adhere to the international standards of human rights enshrined in the treaty. The latest in the Series is Citizenship (Amendment) Act, 2019 against which large-scale countrywide protests have taken place. This legislation enables granting of citizenship to members of certain religious minorities from Pakistan, Bangladesh and Afghanistan excluding Muslims. In its annual report, the United States Commission on International Religious Freedom (USCIRF) identified several limitations to the right to freedom of religion or belief and challenges faced by religious minorities in India. A number of cases of harassment, intimidation and violence being committed against Hindu Dalits (low-caste Hindus), Muslims, Buddhists, Jains, Christians and Sikhs have been reported. The level of violence is expected to increase as the perpetrators continue to enjoy impunity for their crimes. Similarly, as the government forgets the victims of such atrocities, they have little faith in ever seeing any justice done. This may lead to ever-growing mistrust between the government and religious minorities. Things can change if decisive steps are taken to address the issue by containing religiously motivated violence.

220. The discrimination of religious minorities also emanates from certain laws. For example, anti-conversion and anti-cow slaughter laws are sometimes used to discriminate against religious minorities. Anti-conversion laws have been adopted in several states like Odisha, Madhya Pradesh, Chhattisgarh, Gujrat, Arunachal Pradesh, and Himachal Pradesh, etc. These laws adversely affect the enjoyment of

45. Girls marrying the deity and remaining as virgins in the temples throughout their life.

the right to freedom of religion or belief and also violate the special protection of the rights of minorities enshrined in Article 27 of the ICCPR.

221. While conversion from Hinduism to other minority religions has been closely monitored sometimes with criminal charges like forced conversion, conversion of non-Hindus to Hinduism is alleged to be practised with relative impunity. According to USCIRF, 'These ceremonies are based on the view that all individuals born in India are Hindus by default, even if their communities have practiced other faiths for several generations.' The issues are piling up for religious minorities in India. In order for everyone to enjoy the right to freedom of religion or belief, the country needs to put in place an urgent and comprehensive legislation. Cases of religiously motivated violence or violence against religious minorities need to be fully investigated and the perpetrators brought to justice and victims of such atrocities need to be provided with assistance. The anti-conversion laws need to be repealed to give full effect to India's international law obligations (refer Ochab Evelina O, 'Religious Freedom Is on The Decrease In India' 'Forbes' of 12 January 2019).

Chapter 2. Collective Religious Freedom

222. Freedom of religion is guaranteed by the Constitution of India as a group right in the following ways:

(a) Every religious denomination or any section thereof has the right to manage its religious affairs; establish and maintain institutions for religious and charitable purposes; and own, acquire and administer properties of all kinds (Article 26).
(b) Any section of the citizens having a distinct language, script or culture of its own shall have the right to conserve the same (Article 29).
(c) Religious and linguistic minorities are free to establish and administer educational institutions of their choice, which shall not be discriminated against by the State in the matter of giving aid or compensation in the event of acquisition (Article 30).

223. Thus, freedom of religion is guaranteed by the Constitution of India as a group right as every religious denomination or any section thereof has the right to manage its religious affairs, establish and maintain institutions for religious and charitable purposes, and own, acquire and administer properties (Article 26). Any section of the citizens having a distinct language, script or culture of its own shall have the right to conserve the same (Article 29). Article 30 of the Constitution provides that religious and linguistic minorities are free to establish and administer educational institutions of their choice, which shall not be discriminated against by the state in the matter of giving aid or compensation in the event of acquisition.

224. As per Article 26, subject to public order, morality and health, every religious denomination or any section of it shall have the following rights to:

(a) establish and maintain institutions for religious and charitable purposes;
(b) manage its own affairs in matters of religion;
(c) own and acquire movable and immoveable property;
(d) administer such property in accordance with law.

225. The right guaranteed by Article 26 is the right of an 'organized body' like the religious denomination or any section thereof. Freedom from taxes for the promotion of any particular religion is provided under Article 27, which provides that no person shall be compelled to pay tax for the promotion or maintenance of any religion or religious denomination. This Article emphasizes the secular character of the State. The public money collected by way of tax cannot be spent by the State for the promotion of any particular religion.

226. The Constitution contains a number of religion-based and religion-related provisions for various communities. The special provisions of a transitory nature were included for the representation of the Anglo-Indian community in Parliament and State Assemblies (Articles 331, 333, 336–337, 366(2)). These were first reduced by the Constitution (Twenty Third Amendment) Act, 1969 and recently not continued, vide the Constitution (126th Amendment) Bill, 2019. The Constitution also includes special provisions for the Hindu, Buddhist, Jain and Sikh communities which have been retained, namely:

(a) Declaration of abolition of untouchability (mainly a Hindu religious custom) and prohibition of its practice in any form (Article 17).
(b) A Directive Principle of State Policy requiring the State to take steps to prohibit slaughter of cows and calves (reverence for whom is customary among the Hindus) (Article 48).
(c) Declaration of the validity of pre-existing and future laws made to throw open Hindu places of worship to all castes and sections of the Hindus with a supplementary provision giving the power for the Buddhist, Jain and Sikh shrines (Article 25).

Chapter 3. Organizational Religious Freedom

227. In India, there are various official establishments for religion statutory and non-statutory, set up by both the Central and the State Governments, like:

(a) Departments of Religious Affairs in some States including Jammu and Kashmir and UP.
(b) Minority Welfare Departments in most States.
(c) Union Ministry of Minority Welfare.
(d) Special bodies to manage certain religious matters of particular communities like Hindu Religious Endowment Boards, Muslims Wakf Boards, Sikh Gurdwara Prabandhak Committees, state-appointed boards, boards or committees to manage particular shrines, Central Haj Committees, etc.

228. The State is empowered to make laws for social welfare and social reform, which sometimes may limit organizational freedom. Thus, the State can eradicate social practices and dogmas, which stand in the path of the country's onward progress to modernity. Such laws do not affect the essence of any religion. Prohibition of evil practices such as Sati or the system of Devadasi (women symbolically marrying presiding deity) has thus been held to be justified. However, the State cannot regulate the manner in which the worship of the deity is performed by the authorized pujaris (persons conducting religious rituals on behalf of others) of the temple or the hours and days on which the temple is to be kept open for darshan (seeing) or puja (prayer) for devotees. The right of Sikhs to wear and carry a Kirpan (small sword) is recognized as a religious practice in Explanation 1 of Article 25. But this allows a Sikh to keep one Kirpan and he/she cannot keep a second or more Kirpans without taking a licence.

§1. Religious Holidays and Processions

229. The Government announces public holidays for Hindu, Muslim and Christian festivals (or days of mourning) including Holi, Deepavali, Dussehra, Raksha Bandhan, Eid-ul-Fitr, Eid-ul-Azha, Muharram and Good Friday. Birthdays of founders of religions are also observed as public holidays. Among these are the following festivals associated with the birth of the religious figures noted against them:

- Shivaratri (Lord Shiva).
- Ram Naumi (Ram).
- Janmashtami (Krishna).
- Buddha Jayanti (Gautam Buddha).
- Mahavir Jayanti (Mahavira).
- Gurpurb (Guru Nanak).
- Eid-e-Milad-un-Nabi (Prophet Mohammad).
- Christmas (Jesus Christ).

While these festivals are generally public holidays throughout India, in some parts of the country birthdays of some other religious figures including Ganesh, Hanuman, Guru Gobind Singh, Guru Ravidas and Rishi Valmiki are also observed as closed days.

230. There has been an old tradition in India, shared by all communities, to take out religious processions on public streets. Such processions are organized on most of the religious festivals. The law approves this right of the religious communities subject to maintaining law and order and protecting public mobility. In the case of *Muhammad Jalil v. Ram Nath,* it was held that the right to take out a procession is inherent and does not depend on custom. It is not, however, a licence for 'committing nuisance' on the highway. Protecting the right of the processionist to observe their religious practices, the court observed that worshippers in a mosque or temple which abuts a highway have no right to compel the processionist to stop their music completely while passing through a mosque or temple on the ground that there was continuous worship inside it.[46]

231. On the right to take out processions, the Allahabad High Court in the case of *Mmizur Hasan v. Muhammad Zaman*[47] held that the right is inherent but not a licence for 'committing nuisance' on the highway. With respect to the right of the processionist to observe their religious practice, the court observed:

> Worshippers in a mosque or temple which abuts on a highway have no right to compel the processionist to stop their music completely while passing through a mosque or temple on the ground that there was continuous worship inside it. Even if music, whether religious or not, offends against the religious sentiments of another community, it cannot be objected to on such grounds. The stopping of the music would offend the religion sentiments of the processionist just as much as its continuance may affect the religion sentiments of others. Therefore, there can be no right to insist on its complete stoppage.[48]

§2. Religious Trusts, Endowments and Wakfs

232. Religious Endowments and Waqfs which are variants of Trusts, are formed for some religious purposes, e.g., for providing support functions relating to the deity, charity and religion. These arise from the dedication of property for religious purposes. The corresponding action among the Muslim community led to the creation of Waqfs which is regulated and governed by Wakf Act, 1995. The Sikh Gurudwara Act, 1925, pertains to the management of Gurudwaras. For Hindu temples, the law is the Religious Endowments Act 1863, Indian Trusts Act 1882 and some state legislations like the Tamil Nadu Hindu Religious and Charitable Endowments Act 1959, The Andhra Pradesh/ Telangana Charitable And Hindu Religious

46. (1930) ILR All 484.
47. (1924) 52 IA 61: *Muhammad Siddique v. State of UP* (1955) 1 All 121.
48. *Muhammad Jalil v. Ram Nath* (1930) 53 All 484.

Institutions and Endowments Act, 1987. These put the Hindu temples and religious institutions under direct state control. Almost every State Government has enforced special codes or laws or Acts by which Hindu religious institutions viz. temples, mutts and charities (endowments) are controlled.

233. The government has recently brought the Bill for amendment of the Waqf Act 1995 introduced in the Lok Sabha on August 8, 2024. The proposed amendments seek to reform the law by enhancing the Centre's regulatory authority over waqf properties. The draft legislation, proposed to be renamed the Unified Waqf Management, Empowerment, Efficiency, and Development Act, 2024, is presented by the government as a comprehensive overhaul aimed at enhancing the efficiency of the administration and management of the waqf properties. The Bill has been referred to the Joint Parliamentary Committee of the Parliament.

Part III. Legal Status of Religious Communities

Chapter 1. Formal Status of Religious Communities

234. There are different forms of status that religious communities can acquire. Every group of people organizing for religious reasons has access to legal status as an organization under conditions that are usually very easy to meet, i.e., by forming religious or charitable trusts. A religious group can also form an association or society and get it registered and such registered body formed for non-profit purposes shall have a legal entity. Even otherwise a member of any religious community is a full-fledged citizen in India without any infirmity and as such has legal status as a legal person. Further, minority religious communities have also been provided with certain benefits so that they can develop their potential in full measure.

§1. Status of Religious Minorities

235. The religious minorities in India besides other specific rights have access to a number of national and State level commissions, set up to oversee the enforcement of their constitutional and legal rights. The first such national-level commission was established by a Union Cabinet Resolution in January 1978 and was known as the 'Minorities Commission'. To start with, this Commission had jurisdiction over both religious and linguistic minorities. But, in 1988 by another Government Resolution, the linguistic minorities were taken out of its jurisdiction and it was confined to religious minorities. Fourteen years after the establishment of the Minorities Commission, it was renamed the National Commission for Minorities (NCM) and given statutory status and quasi-judicial powers by the NCM Act, 1992.

§2. National Minority Educational Institutions Commission Act, 2004 (NCMEI)

236. A three-member NCMEI came into existence in 2004 originally under an Ordinance, which was later replaced by the NCMEIs Act, 2005. This Commission has jurisdiction over both religious and linguistic minorities and is meant to look after educational rights under Article 30 of the Constitution. Initially, the NCMEI had limited powers but its governing provisions were extensively amended in 2006 to widen the scope of its powers and functions.

§3. Ranganath Misra Commission for Minorities

237. In 2004, the government constituted a special commission for the educationally and economically backward sections among the minorities with a specific mandate. Chaired by former Chief Justice of the Supreme Court Mr Ranganath Misra, the Commission resolved that it was not bound by the description of minorities under the charters of the two Commissions formed earlier limiting it to five major religious communities. The Commission extended its work and recommendations also to Jains, Jews, Bahais, tribal faith groups and the Hindus (wherever they are a minority).

§4. Defining Minorities

238. The Constitution of India uses the expression 'minorities whether based on religion or language', but does not specify criteria or as to who are to be regarded as 'minorities'. The NCM Act, 1992 and the NCMEIs Act, 2005 define the term 'minority' as meaning the 'religious communities notified as such by the Central Government'.[49] A notification issued by the Central Government in 1993 under the NCM Act 1992 listed the Muslims, Christians, Sikhs, Buddhists and Parsi Zoroastrians to be the minorities for the purposes of the Act.[50]

239. The Notification issued by the Central Government in 1993 under the NCM Act 1992 was silent about the minority status of the Jain community. The community was pursuing it in the National Minorities Commission, which has repeatedly recommended minority status for it. As no action was taken on this recommendation, some leaders of the community went to court. The Supreme Court, in *Bal Patil v. Union of India,*[51] did not accept the claim (not on religious grounds) but in the interest of national integration. But later on, the Supreme Court upheld the validity of a UP Government Notification recognizing the Jains as a minority community in the State.[52] In several States, the Jains are recognized as a minority under notifications issued either under the local Minorities Commission Acts or otherwise. In TN religious minority status of the Jains is legally established and was noted in *AM Jain College v. Tamil Nadu Government.*[53] Now Central Government has issued notification-granting status of minority to Jains.

49. National Commission for Minorities Act 1992, s. 2(c); National Commission for Minority Educational Institutions Act 2004, s. 2(f).
50. SO No, 816(E), F 1/11/93 – MC (D) of 23 Oct. 1993.
51. (2005) 6 SCC 690.
52. *Committee of Mgt., Bal Vidya Mandir v. Basic Shiksha Parishad* 2006 (SC) 9 JX 633.
53. (1993) 1 ML 140.

§5. Religious Minorities in States

240. The State Minorities Commissions Acts either provide that 'minorities in the concerned states' would mean the religious communities notified as such by the Central Government, or empower the State Government concerned to notify the minorities. Under both these kinds of provisions in the local Minorities Commission Acts, Muslims, Christians, Sikhs, Buddhists and Parsis are recognized as religious minorities in all those states where such Acts are in force. In April 2007 a single judge of the Allahabad High Court gave a ruling that the Muslim community had 'ceased to be a minority' in the State of UP (where their population is 18.5% as per the Census Report of 2001) and directed the government to modify rules and regulation to its effect. In his judgment, the learned judge had ruled that Muslims in UP could no longer be treated as a religious minority because they comprised about 18.5% of the population in the state. The order directed the State Government to treat Muslims at par with the non-minority communities without any discrimination.

241. A Division Bench of the Allahabad High Court on 24 July 2009 quashed its April 2007 judgment delivered by the single judge bench. A Division Bench held that Muslims were declared a minority community by a notification dated 23 October 1993 and nobody can challenge either the validity of the National Minorities Commission Act, 1992 or the said notification issued under section 2(c) of the Act. The Bench, while allowing the special appeal filed by the State Government against the 2007 order of the single judge, observed that it was not open for the single judge to direct the Centre to modify the 1993 notification. 'The Minority Commission has been set up with a statutory status … it could also aid and advise the government regarding the identification of any community as minority. Though the ultimate power in this regard shall vest with the Central government under Section 2(c) of the Act, it is always open for the Commission to consider this aspect', said the Bench.

The court observed that the status of Muslims as a religious minority ought not to have been examined by the judge in the way it was done.

§6. Sikhs, Jains, Buddhists Are Hindus

I. Position of Sikhs

242. Sikh scholar Birendra Kaur questioned the constitutional and past legislative attempts to obliterate identities of separate faiths by recognizing them under the broad religious connotation of Hindus. She said this negated the constitutional guarantee to each individual to practise and propagate the religion of his/her choice. However, the Punjab and Haryana High Court dismissed the petition, with caustic observations and questioning the constitutional and past legislative attempts to obliterate identities of separate faiths by recognizing them under the broad religious connotation of Hindus. However, a Supreme Court Bench not only entertained her appeal but also framed the question for adjudication. If Sikhism, Jainism and Buddhism are separate and distinct religions, can followers of these faiths be bracketed as Hindus under the Constitution and be governed by Hindu personal law, the Supreme Court asked before issuing notice to the Centre.

243. The petitioner argued that 'This petition is seeking to express and make clear the frustration and disappointment of a large part of the Sikh community which feels its identity as Sikh is undermined by certain clauses and titles of certain statutes which club Sikhs under the definition of Hindu.' The Hon'ble Supreme Court directed issuance of notice on the question as to 'whether people professing the Sikh, Jain or Buddhist faiths could be included in the enactments relating exclusively to persons professing the Hindu religion, within the ambit of Explanation II to Article 25(2) of the Constitution'. However, the petitioners said constitutional mischief arose through Explanation II, which said, 'The reference to Hindus shall be construed as including a reference to persons professing the Sikh, Jain or Buddhist religion, and the reference to Hindu religious institutions shall be construed accordingly.'

244. The petitioner contended that making a law applicable to all religions was one thing but it would be discriminatory to refer to different religions by the name of a single religion. The petitioner added, 'The Hindu Marriage Act, 1955, the Hindu Succession Act, 1956 and the Hindu Minority and Guardianship Act, 1956, use the word Hindu to include Sikhs, Buddhists, Jains and others, even though it is clarified that these are separate religions.' Would it be acceptable if the name of the HMA was changed to Buddhist Marriage Act and made applicable to all four religions, the petitioner asked. The petition is still pending in the Supreme Court.

245. For the purpose of registration of marriage, the Anand Marriage (Amendment) Act, 2012 was passed after which Sikhs were able to register their marriages under the Anand Marriage Act, 1909 instead of the HMA. The Act paved the way for the validation of Sikh traditional marriages and provided for compulsory registration of 'Anand Karaj' marriages. According to the amendment, couples whose marriages have been registered under this Act will not be required to get their marriage registered under the Registration of Births, Marriages and Deaths Act, 1969, or any other law for the time being in force.

II. Position of Jains

246. The legal status of the Jains vis-à-vis Hindus has been a subject of dispute and controversy for long. The *Privy Council in Bhagawandas Tejmal v. Rajmal*[54] holding that the Jains come under codified 'Hindu law', dominated the case law until 1955–1956 when 'Jain law' was officially subsumed under the new statutory 'Hindu Code' (which grants the same rights to widows as the Jain texts centuries ago granted) with the dispensation that Hindu law is to be applied to Jains in the

54. (1873) 10 B.H.C.R. 241.

absence of proof of special customs. Article 25(2) b Explanation II of the Constitution of India recognizes Jains, Sikhs and Buddhists as separate religious groups, but subsumes them into 'Hindu' law, as do sections 2 of the HMA of 1955 and the Hindu Succession Act of 1956, as well as the Hindu Minority and Guardianship Act and the Hindu Adoptions and Maintenance Act of 1956.

247. Despite the fact that Jains have different religious beliefs and practices, for all practical legal purposes 'Jains' are treated as 'Hindus'. Jains were not even granted religious 'minority' status after the enforcement of the National Commission of Minorities Act of 1992. The judgment of *Bal Patil v. Union of India*[55] states, '"Hinduism" can be called a general religion and common faith of India whereas "Jainism" is a special religion formed on the basis of refinement of Hindu religion.' The process in modern Indian legal history of narrowing the range of the modern term 'Jain law' from 'Jain scriptures' down to 'Jain personal law' and finally 'Jain custom' may thus culminate in the official obliteration of Jain legal culture, which continues to thrive outside the formal legal system, in monastic law, ethics and custom.

248. The issue of whether Jains are Hindus or not is largely based on ambiguous legal definitions.

249. 'If a Hindu be defined as one born in India, or at the best one born in India and who was not a Mohamadan or Christian by birth then certainly every Jain is a Hindu. Some say Hindu is one from whom injury (Him-sa) is removed (Du-r). If this is so, only Jains are the first and best Hindus. For some, a Hindu is one who owes allegiance to the Vedas or the Brahman. In this definition Jains are not Hindus. To raise the self-awareness amongst Jains, British educated Jain reformers who campaigned from the mid nineteenth century onwards for the public self-identification of the Jains as "Jains", particularly at the time of the Census when many Jains, because of ignorance or for other reason identify themselves as Hindu.'

A. Jainism as a Separate Religion

250. On the issue of whether there is proof that Jainism is older than Hinduism, the High Court of Judicature of Bombay observed:

> It is true, the Jain reject the scriptural character of the Vedas and repudiated the Brahmanical doctrines relating to obsequial ceremonies the performance of sharadhas and the offering of ablution for the salvation of the soul of the deceased. Amongst them there is no belief that a son by birth or adoption confers spiritual benefit on the father. They also differ from the Brahminical Hindus in their conduct towards the dead; omitting all obsequies after corpse is burnt or buried. Now it is true as latter historical researches have shown that Jainism prevailed in the country long before Brahmanism came into existence

55. 2005 AIR 3172 SC.

or converted into Hinduism. It is also true that owing to their long association with the Hindus, who formed the majority in the country, the Jains have adopted many of the customs and even ceremonies strictly observed by the Hindus and pertaining to Brahminical religion.[56]

251. In the opinion of Justice Kumar-Swami Shastri[57] 'Were the matter res-integra, I would be inclined to hold that the Jains are not Hindu dissenters but that Jainism has an origin and history long and anterior to the Smritis and commentaries which are recognized authorities on Hindu law and usage. In fact, Mahavira, the last of the Jain Tirthankaras, was a contemporary of Buddha and died about 527 B.C. The Jain religion refers to a number of previous Tirthankara and there can be little doubt that Jainism as a distinct religion was flourishing in India. Jainism rejects the authority of the Vedas, which is the main source of Hinduism and denies the efficiency of the various ceremonies, which Hindus consider essential. Jain law has its own law books of which Bhadra Bahu Samhita is an important one. Vardhman Neeti by great Jain teacher Hemchandra deals with Jain law.'

252. In *Sugan Chand Bhic Chand v. Magni Bhai Gulabchanda*,[58] the Bombay High Court held that 'In view of the arguments and evidences of the eminent Scholars the following arguments of the government of Bombay to include Jains in the category of Hindus that "All legislation which is intended for the benefit or uplift of Hindu society has in the past been made applicable to Jains also without discrimination", does not stand to reason on equality and justice. True devotee of truth and non-violence should not take pride in his past mistaken notions rather he is expected to rectify this erroneous stand as early as possible.'

253. Madras High Court in Gateppa v. Eramma and Others[59] held that 'Jainism as a distinct religion was flourishing several centuries before Christ.' In *Hirachand Gangji v. Rowji Sojpal*,[60] it was observed that 'Jainism prevailed in this country long before Brahmanism came into existence and held that field, and it is wrong to think that the Jains were originally Hindus and were subsequently converted to Jainism.' A Division Bench of the Bombay High Court consisting of Chief Justice Chagla and Justice Gajendragadkar in respect of the Bombay Harijan Temple Entry Act, 1947 (C.A. 91 of 1951) held that 'Jains have an independent religious entity and are different from Hindus.'

254. In the *Commissioner Hindu Religious Endowments, Madras v. Sri Lakshmindra Thirtha Swamiar of Sri Shirur Mutt,*[61] the court observed that there are well-known religions in India like Buddhism and Jainism which do not believe in God. Jainism and Buddhism are equally two distinct religions professed in India in contrast with Vedic religion. In *Commissioner of Wealth Tax, West Bengal v. Smt.*

---

56. AJR 1039 Bomb. 377.
57. 50 Madras 228.
58. AIR 1927 Bomb. 185.
59. AIR 1927 Madras 228.
60. AIR 1939 Bom. 377.
61. AIR 1954 SC 282.

Champa Kumari Singhi and Others, a Division Bench of the Calcutta High Court observed that 'Jains rejected the authority of the Vedas which forms the bedrock of Hinduism and denied the efficacy of various ceremonies which the Hindus consider essential. It will require too much of boldness to hold that the Jains, dissenters from Hinduism, are Hindus, even though they disown the authority of the Vedas.'

B. Oath Taking by Jain

255. The question of whether the administration of an oath is lawful does not depend upon what may be the considerable intricacies of the particular religion which is adhered to by the witness. It concerns two matters, first of all, is the oath an oath which appears to the court to be binding on the conscience of the witness? And if so, second, is it an oath which the witness himself considers to be binding upon his conscience? Jains may choose either to affirm or possibly swear an oath. Since there are many different groupings, no single text can be specified, but some may choose to swear an oath on a text such as the Kalpa Sutra.

C. Minority Status of Jain Community

256. Despite different religious beliefs and practices, for all practical purposes 'Jains' are treated as 'Hindus' under the Indian law. Jains were not even granted religious 'minority' status after the introduction of the National Commission of Minorities Act of 1992. There are several cases dealing with the minority status of Jains. In *Kerala Education Bill's* case, the Supreme Court held that to claim minority rights, the community must be numerically a minority by reference to the entire population of the State or country where the law is applicable. Thus, by applying this criterion, the Jain community is eligible to claim minority status.

257. In *Arya Samaj Education Trust, Delhi & Others v. The Director of Education, Delhi Administration, Delhi and Others*,[62] it was held that 'Not only the Constitution but also the Hindu Code and the Census Reports have recognized Jains to belong to a separate religion.' The court also referred to the observations of various scholars on this behalf. The court quoted Heinrich Zimmer in 'Philosophies of India' where he has stated that 'Jainism denies the authority of the Vedas and the orthodox traditions of Hinduism. Therefore, it is reckoned as a heterodox Indian religion.' The court also quoted J. N. Farquhar in Modern Religious Movements in India wherein he stated that 'Jainism has been a rival of Hinduism from the beginning.' In the said judgment, in conclusion, the court held that 'for the purpose of Article 30(1), the Jains are a minority based on religion in the Union Territory of Delhi'.

62. AIR 1976 Delhi 207.

258. In *A.M. Jain College v. Government of Tamil Nadu*,[63] the court observed that it is also an admitted fact that the Jain community in TN is a religious and linguistic minority. In several States, including UP, the Jains are also recognized as a minority under notification issued either under the local Minorities Commission Acts or otherwise. The Supreme Court upheld the validity of a UP Government Notification recognizing the Jains as a minority in that state – committee of Management.

259. In the following states, Jains have been declared as minority:

(1) Maharashtra (which has the largest population of Jains in India).
(2) Karnataka.
(3) Madhya Pradesh.
(4) UP.
(5) Jharkhand.
(6) Delhi.
(7) Uttarakhand.
(8) West Bengal.
(9) Andhra Pradesh.
(10) Haryana.
(11) Punjab.
(12) Assam.
(13) Gujarat.
(14) TN.
(15) Rajasthan.

260. It would be worthwhile to mention that officially, the category 'Jain' was used for the first time in the Census of India of 1881. The Census still remains the only government institution, which classifies the Jains as a separate religious group. The Jain demand for minority status is almost a century old, when in British India the Viceroy and Governor General of India, Lord Minto took a decision in principle of giving representation to important minorities in the Central Legislature. Seth Manek Chand Hirachand from Mumbai, an eminent Jain leader and the then Acting President of the Bharatvarshiya Digamber Jain Subha made an appeal in 1909 to the Governor General for the inclusion of the Jain community for representation in the Council. Seth Manek Chand's petition was transferred to the Government of Bombay, and the Secretary to the Government of Bombay stated in its reply dated 15 October 1909 as follows:

> I am directed to inform you that a number of seats have been reserved for representation of minorities by nomination and that in allotting them, the claim of the important Jain Community will receive full consideration.

---

63. (1993) 1 MLJ 140.

261. In a memorandum by the Representative of the Jain Community to the Constituent Assembly in March/April 1947 a strong appeal was made for the inclusion of the Jain community as a minority religious community. In 1993, the National Minorities Commission arrived at their recommendation that the Jain community be declared as a minority religious community after considering the constitutional provisions, judicial pronouncements, the fundamental differences in philosophy and beliefs (theism versus atheism principally) vis-à-vis Hinduism, and the Jain population in the country.

It resolved to recommend to the Government of India that the Jains deserve to be recognized as a distinct religious minority, and the Government of India may consider including them in the listing of 'Minorities'.

D. Freedom of Religion Bill Controversy in Gujarat and Position of Jains

262. The Freedom of Religion Bill was a controversial legislation passed by the Gujarat State Assembly. The Bill was passed in 2003. An amendment was passed on 19 September 2006, which banned the forced conversion from one religion to another. The Anti-Conversion Act passed earlier was not clear on what forced conversion meant and to whom should it apply. Under the Amendment Bill, a person need not seek permission in case he/she is converting from one sect to another of the same religion. It clubbed Jainism and Buddhism as denominations of Hinduism like Shia and Sunnis are of Islam or Catholicism and Protestantism of Christianity. The move evoked strong protests from the state's Jain, Buddhist and Christian communities. The NCM also criticized the Gujarat Assembly's decision to club Jainism and Buddhism with Hinduism terming it to be in contravention of its 23 October 1993, notification classifying Buddhists as a 'minority community'.

263. Ultimately on 31 July 2007, finding it not in conformity with the concept of freedom of religion as embodied in Article 25(1) of the Constitution, the Governor returned back the Gujarat Freedom of Religion (Amendment) Bill, 2006. The Governor observed that Jainism and Buddhism are recognized as religions rather than denominations of Hinduism, something that the Amendment Bill sought to wrongly convey. A press release issued by Raj Bhavan said 'the proposed amendment would amount to withdrawing the protection against forceful or inappropriate religious conversions, particularly in case of Jains and Buddhists'. The release cited large-scale protests from different religious and social organizations, especially from the Jain and Christian communities, indicating the unacceptability of the proposed amendment.

264. It comes out that Jainism is to be accepted as a religion and Jains are to be treated as a separate entity in all manners. Jain legal rules may not be taken as a subset of Hindu law. It is necessary for the proper growth of the Jain community that Jain law exists like Hindu and Muslim law in the legal system. Recently the Central Government granted Jains the status of a religious minority throughout India; however, for the purpose of applicability of statutes, Jains are still Hindus except where they are governed by customs.

§7. PARSIS

265. The Parsis have migrated to India from Persia (Faris) and adhere to the Zoroastrian faith. Parsis are found in the greatest numbers in the old Bombay Presidency. They have also settled in recent times in all major cities and towns throughout India. Large immigrant communities are now found in the United States, Canada, Britain, and Pakistan. The Zoroastrian community is still found in Iran, but its members are not considered Parsis. The Parsis are those Zoroastrians who migrated first to India and were named Parsis. In 1901, the total population consisted of 93,952 Parsis throughout India. There was a very slight population increase up to the mid-century; since then, the population has declined dramatically by almost 10% each decade. The birth rate is lower than the death rate, and emigration has long taken place, so in 1976 the population was estimated at 82,000 in India and according to the 2011 Census of India, there are only 57,264 Parsis in India. Additional factors that have been cited for this decline are low fertility, late age at first marriage, and not marrying outside the Parsi community.

266. Zoroastrianism as a religion had been in existence in Persia for well over a thousand years, usually as a state cult. When Arabs overthrew the last Zoroastrian king, Yazdegerd III, in A.D. 651, numerous refugees fled, some following the Great Silk Route went to China where they established trading communities and built fire temples in various cities. All traces of these Chinese Parsis had disappeared by the tenth century AD. Others who had sought refuge in the mountainous region of Kohistan were finally driven to the port of Ormuz (Hormuz), from where they sailed to India. The story of their flight and their landing on the west coast of India at Diu has since been romanticized. In reality, they eked out a subsistence on marginal land provided by their Hindu hosts. With the coming of the Europeans, the Parsis moved into an intermediary position between the foreigners and the natives in the cities. As a result, the Parsis are the most urbanized and Westernized community in India. They were the first to avail themselves of the opportunities that came from Western-style education and the growth of industry and commerce and took government jobs under the British.

267. The first Indians to become surgeons, barristers, pilots, and members of the British Parliament were mainly Parsis. Despite their long residence in the country, Parsis have not been absorbed into the Indian caste system. Like the Europeans, they have been viewed as foreigners. The native Hindu and Muslim states accorded them positions of high authority and privilege, including prime ministerships and guardianship of the treasuries, because of their education, relative incorruptibility, and impartiality towards caste allegiances.

268. In Mumbai, the Parsi population arrived in about 1750 A.D. from the small towns and cities of Gujarat. Today some 95% live in urban areas. They are usually found in exclusively Parsi housing estates endowed by Parsi charitable funds. Parsis have not been bound to certain occupations or excluded from others by religious norms or taboos. The Parsis traditionally worked as entrepreneurs, in trade, in finance (as bankers), or in government service. The modernization of Indian manufacturing and transportation owes much to Parsis. Families such as the Tatas, the Wadias, and the Petits were the owners of the largest private enterprises. A decline in community wealth and therefore entrepreneurial capital has prompted highly educated younger Parsis to seek their fortunes overseas in every profession.

269. The relationship of Parsis to the state of India has always been one of loyalty since as a minority their survival depended on accommodation to the political authority. The British enhanced this loyalty by elevating a number of Parsi families to noble rank. Out of four hereditary barons in British India, three were Parsi. For a long time, Parsis played a dominant role in local government, particularly in the Bombay municipality. They were also instrumental in forming the Bombay Presidency Association to influence British policies in India. Later, with the movement for Indian independence, Parsis were a moving force in the Indian National Congress.

270. In independent India, Parsi political influence has waned because of the joint electorate system, although eminent Parsis are still to be found in all branches of government, especially the judiciary. The internal affairs of the community relating to questions of membership, religious practice, and use of community funds are governed by Parsi panchayats. These are local bodies (of which Bombay's is the most important), made up of priests and wealthy persons of the community. The juridical powers of the panchayats have slowly been yielded to government civil authorities, and the panchayats today are primarily involved in welfare activities and management of community trusts.

§8. Hindus as Minority

271. In 1998, the NCM recommended that the Hindus be formally recognized as minorities in the States of Jammu and Kashmir, Meghalaya, Mizoram, Nagaland and Punjab and in the Union Territory (UT) of Lakshadweep, in each of which places they are in a numerical minority. No action has yet been taken by the government on this recommendation. The Supreme Court of India in a 1971 ruling held that the minority status of a community was to be determined 'in relation to the particular legislation which in sought to be impugned'.

272. On 17 December 2019, the Supreme Court dismissed the Public Interest Litigation (PIL) seeking declaration of Hindus as minorities in eight states of India. The petition has sought for extension of benefits given to minority communities to the Hindus in these eight states being in minority in these states. It was prayed that minorities be identified based on their status in a State. It sought a direction to the Central Government to define the term 'Minority' and lay down guidelines for identification, to ensure that only those religious and linguistic groups that are socially, economically and politically non-dominant and numerically inferior may enjoy rights and protections guaranteed under Articles 29 and 30 of the Constitution. The petitioner prayed for the striking down of section 2(c) of the NCM Act, 1992 and for quashing of a notification issued by the Central Government in 1993 by which Muslims, Christians, Sikhs, Buddhists and Zoroastrians were notified as minorities.

273. During the course of the hearing, the Supreme Court allowed the petitioner to make a representation before the NCM, and in pursuance thereof, four prayers[64] were made before the Commission which included defining minorities in accordance with the United Nations General Assembly Resolution of 1992, formulation of guidelines for identifying minority communities at the state level, and declaration of Hindus as minorities in states where they are not in the majority. In July 2019, the Commission informed the Supreme Court that it does not have the jurisdiction to declare Hindus as minorities in states where they are not in the majority and further stated that the repository to declare a community as a minority lies with the Centre. The Commission also added that in a 1999 judgment in the case of *Bal Patil v. Union of India*, the Supreme Court had directed the Commission to desist from entertaining such claims from different communities and to instead work towards proposing ways to create such social conditions that would lead to doing away with the majority-minority divide.

274. The three-judge bench of the Supreme Court refused to entertain the petition and held that it has never held that religious minority status must be decided in accordance with state boundaries. CJI Bobde said, 'Religion must be construed as pan India, not on political boundaries of States.' The petitioner's request for guidelines for identification of minorities in States as units was turned down by the Supreme Court. The court said, 'Who doesn't know who is Hindu, who is Muslim … You need guidelines to tell you who is Hindu, who is Muslim, etc.?'

---

64. Word 'prayer' when used in court proceedings, means a request for judgment, relief, or damages made by the plaintiff at the end of a complaint or petition. It tells the judge what the plaintiff wants, such as money, injunctive relief, etc. As per Law.com, 'Prayer' means the specific request for judgment, relief and/or damages at the conclusion of a complaint or petition. A typical prayer would read: 'The plaintiff prays for 1) special damages in the sum of $17,500; 2) general damages according to proof [proved in trial]; 3) reasonable attorney's fees; 4) costs of suit; and 5) such other and further relief as the court shall deem proper.' A prayer gives the judge an idea of what is sought, and may become the basis of a judgment if the defendant defaults (fails to file an answer).
   https://dictionary.law.com/Default.aspx?selected=1571#:~:text=n.,of%20a%20complaint%20or%20petition.
   Can also *see* https://search.app/H5SKjw86fzg4E29Z7: Format of Writ Petition in Supreme Court of India; https://search.app/SZ4sUgYdisbJj19z6.

Chapter 2. Autonomy of Religious Communities

§1. General Principles

275. The religious communities in India have their own personal laws, freedom of religion and right to equality. They are autonomous in various respects like having religious institutions of their choice. The state shall not interfere in their working and management unless such institutions or other bodies take public funds. The religious and linguistic minorities have the right to establish and administer the educational institutions of their choice.

276. Looking from the angle of basic human rights, it is understood that the right to self-determination accrues to people. The UN Committee on the Elimination of Racial Discrimination has stated that the right to self-determination involves 'the rights of all peoples to pursue freely their economic, social and cultural development without outside interference' and that 'Governments are to represent the whole population without distinction as to race, colour, descent or national or ethnic origin.'

277. The individuals and groups should be consulted about decisions likely to impact them. This includes ensuring that they have the opportunity to participate in the making of such decisions through the processes of democratic government, and are able to exercise meaningful control over their affairs.' Self-determination is widely understood to be exercised in a manner that preserves the territorial integrity, political unity and sovereignty of a country. The international community has recognized the significance of the right to self-determination to indigenous peoples in the Declaration on the Rights of Indigenous Peoples. In India, people of all faiths have one vote per person and they are free to take part in elections and through the democratic process of election be part of the decision-making process.

§2. Limitations on Right of Self-Determination

278. Under Article 4 of the ICCPR, countries may take measures derogating from certain of their obligations under the Covenant, 'in time of public emergency which threatens the life of the nation and the existence of which is officially proclaimed'. Such measures may only be taken 'to the extent strictly required by the exigencies of the situation, provided that such measures are not inconsistent with their other obligations under international law and do not involve discrimination solely on the ground of race, colour, sex, language, religion or social origin'.

§3. Religious Communities and State Court System

279. There are parallel community and religious forums/courts in existence whose interference has sometimes been deprecated by the courts since some of such bodies are unauthorized and unwarranted and work without the authority of law and not part of the judicial system. But as a matter of fact, these forums are in the nature of alternate dispute resolution forums and with the consent of the parties resolve issues in the same manner as conciliators and/or arbitrators. Sometimes, in the matter of inter-caste or inter-religious marriages or divorces such self-styled extra-constitutional authorities take upon themselves the power of courts of law to issue community mandates to people within the community. Such religious edicts result from summary hearings often in violation of fundamental rights guaranteed by the Constitution of India.

I. Shariat Courts or Darul-Qaza

280. The Supreme Court of India on 27 March 2006 in the case of *Vishwa Lochan Madan v. Union of India and Others* issued notices to the Central Government, State Governments, All India Muslim Personal Law Board (AIMPLB) and Darul Uloom, an Islamic seminary, in the matter of the existence of parallel Islamic and Shariat Courts in the country, which were allegedly posing a challenge to the Indian judicial system. In this petition filed as a PIL petition in the Supreme Court of India, Advocate Vishwa Lochan Madan[65] sought immediate dissolution of all Islamic and Shariat Courts in India. Earlier, on, 16 August 2005 in *Vishwa Lochan Madan v. Union of India and Others*, the Supreme Court of India had also issued notices to the States of UP, Haryana, Assam, Madhya Pradesh, Rajasthan, West Bengal and Delhi, where, according to the petition, Islamic courts had been formed and were posing a challenge to the existing judicial system of the country.

281. The Petition sought an immediate dissolution of all Islamic and Shariat Courts in India, alleging that the AIMPLB claimed to have established Darul-Qaza (Muslim Courts) in some cities. The petitioner sought a ban on the establishment of such Islamic courts, along with a declaration that these Fatwas have no legal sanctity, and requested the court to direct the central and the State Governments to take effective steps to dissolve all Darul-Qazas and Shariat Courts in India. In addition, the petition further sought a direction from the court to the AIMPLB and Darul Uloom, Deoband, other seminaries and Muslim organizations, to refrain from establishing a parallel Muslim judicial system (Nizam-e-Qaza).

282. A direction from the court was also sought to restrain these organizations from interfering with the marital status of Indian Muslim citizens or passing any judgments, remarks, Fatwas or deciding matrimonial disputes among Muslims. This petition no doubt raises a crucial issue as to whether there could be two parallel legal systems in operation-one legal and the other religious, particularly when the Constitution of India prohibits discrimination on grounds of caste or religion, and whether the right to freedom of religion could be extended to the establishment of a parallel judicial system.

65. JT 2014(8) SC 176.

283. In this case, the Supreme Court pronounced the following landmark-detailed judgment:

> 'As it is well settled, the adjudication by a legal authority sanctioned by law is enforceable and binding and meant to be obeyed unless upset by an authority provided by law itself. The power to adjudicate must flow from a validly made law. Person deriving benefit from the adjudication must have the right to enforce it and the person required to make provision in terms of adjudication has to comply that, and on its failure, consequences as provided in law to ensue. These are the fundamentals of any legal judicial system. In our opinion, the decisions of Dar-ul-Qaza or the Fatwa do not satisfy any of these requirements. Dar-ul-Qaza is neither created nor sanctioned by any law made by the competent legislature. Therefore, the opinion or the Fatwa issued by Dar-ul-Qaza or for that matter anybody, is not adjudication of dispute by an authority under a judicial system sanctioned by law. A Qazi or Mufti has no authority or powers to impose his opinion and enforce his Fatwa on any one by any coercive method. In fact, whatever may be the status of Fatwa during Mogul or British Rule, it has no place in independent India under our Constitutional scheme. It has no legal sanction and cannot be enforced by any legal process either by the Dar-ul-Qaza issuing that or the person concerned or for that matter anybody. The person or the body concerned may ignore it and it will not be necessary for anybody to challenge it before any court of law. It can simply be ignored. In case any person or body tries to impose it, their act would be illegal. Therefore, the grievance of the petitioner that Dar-ul-Qazas and Nizam-e-Qaza are running a parallel judicial system is misconceived'.

284. About the issuance of fatwa, the Supreme Court observed:

> 'the Fatwa has no legal status in our Constitutional scheme. Notwithstanding that it is an admitted position that Fatwas have been issued and are being issued. All India Muslim Personal Law Board feels the "necessity of establishment of a network of judicial system throughout the country and Muslims should be made aware that they should get their disputes decided by the Quazis". According to the All India Muslim Personal Law Board "this establishment may not have the police powers but shall have the book of Allah in hand and sunnat of the Rasool and all decisions should be according to the Book and the Sunnat. This will bring the Muslims to the Muslim Courts. They will get justice." The object of establishment of such a court may be laudable but we have no doubt in our mind that it has no legal status. It is bereft of any legal pedigree and has no sanction in laws of the land. They are not part of the corpus juris of the State. A Fatwa is an opinion, only an expert is expected to give. It is not a decree, not binding on the court or the State or the individual. It is not sanctioned under our constitutional scheme. But this does not mean that existence of Dar-ul-Qaza or for that matter practice of issuing Fatwas are themselves illegal. It is informal justice delivery system with an objective of bringing about amicable settlement between the parties. It is within the discretion of the persons concerned either to accept, ignore or reject it. However, as

the Fatwa gets strength from the religion; it causes serious psychological impact on the person intending not to abide by that. As projected by respondent No. 10 "God fearing Muslims obey the Fatwas". In the words of respondent No. 10 "it is for the persons/parties who obtain Fatwa to abide by it or not". It, however, emphasizes that "the persons who are God fearing and believe that they are answerable to the Almighty and have to face the consequences of their doings/deeds, such are the persons, who submit to the Fatwa". Imrana's case is an eye-opener in this context. Though she became the victim of lust of her father-in-law, her marriage was declared unlawful and the innocent husband was restrained from keeping physical relationship with her. In this way a declaratory decree for dissolution of marriage and decree for perpetual injunction were passed. Though neither the wife nor the husband had approached for any opinion, an opinion was sought for and given at the instance of a journalist, a total stranger. In this way, victim has been punished. A country governed by rule of law cannot fathom it.'

285. On the issue of motivation behind seeking a fatwa, the Supreme Court laid down the following:

'In our opinion, one may not object to issuance of Fatwa on a religious issue or any other issue so long it does not infringe upon the rights of individuals guaranteed under law. Fatwa may be issued in respect of issues concerning the community at large at the instance of a stranger but if a Fatwa is sought by a complete stranger on an issue not concerning the community at large but individual, then the Darul-Qaza or for that matter anybody may consider the desirability of giving any response and while considering it should not be completely unmindful of the motivation behind the Fatwa. Having regard to the fact that a Fatwa has the potential of causing immense devastation, we feel impelled to add a word of caution. We would like to advise the Dar-ul-Qaza or for that matter anybody not to give any response or issue Fatwa concerning an individual, unless asked for by the person involved or the person having direct interest in the matter. However, in a case the person involved or the person directly interested or likely to be affected being incapacitated, by any person having some interest in the matter. Issuance of Fatwa on rights, status and obligation of individual Muslim, in our opinion, would not be permissible, unless asked for by the person concerned or in case of incapacity, by the person interested. Fatwas touching upon the rights of an individual at the instance of rank strangers may cause irreparable damage and therefore, would be absolutely uncalled for. It shall be in violation of basic human rights. It cannot be used to punish innocent. No religion including Islam punishes the innocent. Religion cannot be allowed to be merciless to the victim. Faith cannot be used as dehumanizing force.'

'In the light of what we have observed above, the prayer made by the petitioner in the terms sought for cannot be granted. However, we observe that no Dar-ul-Qazas or for that matter, anybody or institution by any name, shall give verdict or issue Fatwa touching upon the rights, status and obligation, of an individual unless such an individual has asked for it. In the case of incapacity of such an individual, any person interested in the welfare of such person may be permitted to represent the cause of concerned individual. In any event, the decision or the Fatwa issued by whatever body being not emanating from any judicial system recognized by law, it is not binding on anyone including the person, who had asked for it. Further, such an adjudication or Fatwa does not have a force of law and, therefore, cannot be enforced by any process using coercive method. Any person trying to enforce that by any method shall be illegal and has to be dealt with in accordance with law.'

II. Panchayats

286. The Panchayat system in the country is very old wherein elders of the society come together to resolve disputes. This system has been recognized in Gram Panchayats (Village Council) established under the Panchayati Raj System of the Government. However, there are some caste panchayats, which are not mandated by law and resort to mob justice. The khap panchayats are also there which are related to particular castes.

287. The caste panchayats (village councils) exist in many rural areas of India, e.g., in the State of Haryana and western UP. These caste panchayats make several lives miserable, often by declaring marriages invalid. Generally, their victims belong to the weakest sections of society. Traditionally, caste panchayats have played a powerful role at the village level in several other states of the country. The caste panchayats also exist in the form of khap panchayats. These are not elected bodies and their decisions are not enforceable by law. They derive support from community recognition. Khap panchayats are powerful because of their ability to mobilize a large number of people. So they appear to be democratic from the outside, but they are not as being dominated by certain powerful elements and their decisions are like the collective conscience of mob mentality. They exclude from the decision-making process women, the youth, as well as the groups who are lower down in the caste hierarchy in the village.

288. In response to a PIL filed by the Haryana unit of the People's Union for Civil Liberties (PUCL), the state's High Court directed the government to protect the life and liberty at all costs of a couple who had entered into an inter-caste wedlock. The High Court also directed the authorities to ensure that nobody coerced the couple to change the status of their marriage. A similar situation had arisen when the Punjab and Haryana High Court heard a number of writ petitions challenging the dictate issued by the self-styled caste-based khap panchayats in the State of Haryana, ordering married couples to dissolve their marriages and live separately and ordering their expulsion from the villages on their refusal to do so.

289. It is a matter of concern that government authorities have done little to check the activities of these extra-constitutional bodies, which is a blatant interference with the fundamental rights of the citizens. The responsibility of the state cannot be abdicated. If this be so, judicial Courts in India seem to be the best recourse in giving relief in individual matters involving blatant violation of fundamental rights of the citizens which are dictated by community councils enforcing their edicts by force and extrajudicial means on alleged moral grounds.

Chapter 3. Fundamental Rights and Religious Communities

290. India is one of the largest and most plural societies in the world where all the major religions like Buddhism, Christianity, Hinduism, Islam, Sikhism, and Zoroastrianism have a large number of followers. India is home to a wide variety of castes, tribes, communities, religions, languages, customs and living styles. The Anthropological Survey of India estimated that there are nearly 4,599 separate communities in India with 325 languages and dialects in 12 distinct language families and some 24 scripts. Few Indians are not immigrants, most people have come to a particular part of the country from another part, may be from a neighbouring district, or state, more occasionally from distant parts of India.

291. A society is a mixture of distinct cultures and religious communities cherishing their identities and rightly wishing to preserve them. Correspondingly one can notice the division of population into a majority and several minorities on the basis of religion and ethnicity, language and culture. Though everyone should have the right to protect, preserve and practise their beliefs, minorities often feel neglected, discriminated and looked down upon. Therefore, for the protection of minorities, their distinct religious and cultural identities are preserved. The basic object of such minority protection is to instil confidence in them, create a feeling that they will never be overrun by the majority, homogenize the pluralities in a civil society and integrate minorities fully and equally into the national life of the state characterized by the ethos and interest of majority.

292. History shows that there can be no stability in any country so long as an attempt is made to crush a minority or to force it to conform to the ways of the majority. Although in India, the Hindus constitute an overwhelming majority, there is a considerable number of Muslims, Christians, Parsees, Buddhists and Jains religions too. The diversity in India is noticed on various fronts other than religion and culture such as language. Diversity is coupled with linguistic diversity. In addition to that, there are also a number of Scheduled tribes and certain unidentified communities, which are internally heterogeneous. All these make India a country, which has not only religious but also linguistic and cultural diversity.

293. The Constitution provides certain fundamental rights, chief among them being the rule of law, equality and special provisions for certain vulnerable groups. The Constitution envisages a secular state offering justice, social economic and political to all the citizens. The freedom of speech and expression and the right to form associations and unions are guaranteed to all. The Constitution declares India a republic consisting of a representative government deriving its power from the people and exercising the same through representatives freely chosen and responsible to the people. The government is run by a majority party and political power is distributed between them. The rights guaranteed by the Constitution are available to all citizens and in some cases even to persons who may or may not be citizens, irrespective of race, religion, region, language, etc., or any other distinction. But for the protection of minorities so that they are not hampered by the majority, the Constitution went a step further and adopted a separate group of articles to infuse confidence in the minority communities of the country.

294. The National Anthem emphasizes diversity in a similar manner. The first verse is a series of names of different geographic regions, ethnicities and cultures. India is hailed as Punjab, Sindh, Gujarat, Maratha, Dravida, Utkala, Banga in the same verse. India was among the major democracies in the world to recognize and provide for the rights of the diverse religious and linguistic communities living in the country.

295. The Constitution articulates a four-fold response to define the constituent elements of secularism. First, the principle of religious freedom, which gives to every citizen the right to freedom of conscience and the right to profess, practise and propagate religion. Second, the Constitution does not recognize the special status of any religion. Third, the principle of non-discrimination on grounds of caste, place of birth, residence or religion is applicable and there is guarantee of equal citizenship with certain exceptions. Fourth, these rights are subject to public interest and public order, which requires religions to yield to regulation in the interests of social welfare and reform.

§1. Religious Freedom as a Fundamental Right

296. Article 25 provides that 'subject to public order, morality and health … all persons are equally entitled to freedom of conscience and the right to freely profess, practice and propagate religion'. Under Article 27, 'no person is compelled to pay any taxes, the proceeds of which are specifically appropriated in payment of expenses for the promotion or maintenance of any particular religion or religious denomination'. Under Article 28(3), 'no person attending any educational institution … shall be required to take part in any religious instruction or to attend any religious worship that may be conducted in such institution' Articles 14, 15(1), and 29(2) guarantee equality of citizenship. Article 29 allows minorities to conserve their language and culture. Article 15(1) states that the state shall not discriminate against any citizen on grounds only of religion, race, caste, sex, or place of birth. Article 16(1) and (2) provide equal opportunity for all citizens in matters of employment or appointment to any office under the state. Article 30(1) provides that: 'All minorities, whether based on religion, or language, shall have the right to establish and administer educational institutions of their choice.'

297. This constitutional scheme was actually necessitated by three overriding factors specific to India. The first was the magnitude of India's diversity. There are few countries in the present-day world with such cultural diversity as India. These numerous diversities had to be accommodated if India was to become a nation. The secular pluralist state is a fundamental condition of nationhood. Second, the partition of India on religious lines in 1947, especially the bloody aftermath of deteriorating Hindu-Muslim relations, made secularism a necessity. The partition meant that Pakistan might become a homeland for Muslims, but India would remain a home for Hindus, Muslims, Christians and others, and though Pakistan was declared a Muslim state, there was a very large and significant minority of Muslims in India who will remain in India and Hindus in Pakistan particularly in east – while East Pakistan (now Bangladesh) who were to remain in Pakistan. The Partition plan did not envisage any transfer of population from one dominion to another.

298. The Indian legal system is pluralistic in at least two ways. It is pluralistic in the sense that there are distinct personal laws for adherents of different religious faiths which is as a matter of fact continuing from the British period. A state-sponsored system of codified law and civil and criminal courts coexist with a family court system. The State shall not deny to any person equality before the law or the equal protection of the laws within the territory of India (Article 14). The State shall not discriminate against any citizen on grounds only of religion, race, caste, sex, place of birth or any of them (Article 15(1)). No citizen shall, on grounds only of religion, race, caste, sex, place of birth or any of them, be subject to any disability, liability, restriction or condition with regard to: (a) access to shops, public restaurants, hotels and places of public entertainment; or (b) the use of wells, tanks, bathing ghats, roads and places of public resort maintained wholly or partly out of State funds or dedicated to the use of the general public (Article 15(2)). However, the State can make special provisions for women and children (Article 15(3)). The State is also allowed to make any special provision for the advancement of any socially and educationally backward class of citizens or for the Scheduled Castes and the Scheduled Tribes (Article 15(4)) in so far as such special provisions relate to their admission to educational institutions including private educational institutions, whether aided or unaided by the State, other than the minority educational institutions referred to in clause (1) of Article 30 (Article 15(5)).

299. No person shall be deprived of his life or personal liberty except according to the procedure established by law (Article 21). Article 25 states that: (1) subject to public order, morality and health and to the other provisions of this Part I, all persons are equally entitled to freedom of conscience and the right freely to profess, practise and propagate religion. (2) nothing in this Article shall affect the operation of any existing law or prevent the State from making any law:

(a) regulating or restricting any economic, financial, political or other secular activity which may be associated with religious practice;
(b) providing for social welfare and reform or the throwing open of Hindu religious institutions of a public character to all classes and sections of Hindus.
    Explanation I. – The wearing and carrying of kirpans shall be deemed to be included in the profession of the Sikh religion.
    Explanation II. – In sub-clause (b) of clause (2), the reference to Hindus shall be construed as including a reference to persons professing the Sikh, Jaina or Buddhist religion, and the reference to Hindu religious institutions shall be construed accordingly.

§2. Religious and Linguistic Communities

300. As per the Constitution, two types of communities are considered minority communities in the country. The first one is a religious minority community and the second one is a linguistic minority community. Followers of all religions except Hinduism are considered religious minorities on national and state levels. The religious minority communities include Muslims, Christians, Sikhs, Buddhists, Jains, Parsis, etc. The contradiction is that Sikhs, Buddhists and Jains are covered in the definition of Hindu and all laws applicable to Hindus are also applicable to them. In other words, these are Hindus as well as minorities, a strange legal position. Apart from these major religious communities, there are small numbers of Jews and Bahais. Religious minorities get certain rights, especially in the field of education and educational institutions. Minority communities can establish their own educational institutions and can reserve 50% of the seats of the students for their own community members. In addition, they can recruit 100% staff from their own community. The religious minorities can also be a linguistic minority.

I. Linguistic Minorities

301. The term linguistic minority or minorities has not been defined. If the country is taken as a unit, all who speak a language other than Hindi can be treated as linguistic minorities but not so if the State is taken as the unit. Within a State, there may be linguistic minorities who speak a language or languages other than the language spoken by the majority in that State. Dialects of a language spoken in a State may proliferate the number of minorities. In *TMA Pai Foundation and Others v. State of Karnataka,*[66] it was settled that a linguistic minority is determinable with reference to the State as a unit.

Thus, linguistic minorities are those who have different first language than the first language of majority of the people in that state. For example, Gujarati-speaking people living in Maharashtra are linguistic minorities in Maharashtra and Marathi speaking people living in Gujarat are linguistic minorities in Gujarat. Such minority communities enjoy some special benefits in that state, especially in educational fields.

302. Chapter I of Part XVII of the Constitution comprising Articles 343 and 344 deal with the official language of the Union and Chapter II deals with regional languages. Article 345 of the Constitution provides that subject to the provisions of Articles 346 and 347, the legislature of a State may by law adopt any one or more of the languages in the State or Hindi as language or languages to be used for all or any of official purposes. Article 347 provides that on a demand, the President may if he is satisfied that a substantial proportion of the population of a State desire the use of any language spoken by them to be recognized by that State, direct that such

66. AIR 2003 SC 355; JT 2002(9) SC 1.

language shall also be officially recognized throughout that State or any part specified. Article 347 can, thus, be treated as a specific measure directed towards linguistic minorities inhabiting a State facilitating preservation, and even propagation, of such a language. Read in conjunction with Article 347, Article 350 also affords protection to the language spoken by linguistic minorities. It provides that every person shall be entitled to submit a representation for the redress of any grievance to any officer or authority of the Union or a State in any of the languages used in the Union or in the State.

303. Article 350 A of the Constitution contains a specific measure of protection of linguistic minorities. It provides that 'it shall be the endeavour of every State and every local authority within the State to provide adequate facilities for instruction in the mother-tongue at the primary stage of education to children belonging to linguistic minority groups; and the President may issue such direction to any State as he considers necessary or proper for securing the provision of such facility'. Article 350 A, thus, is an amplification of the cultural and educational rights guaranteed under Article 29(1) and Article 30(1). Under Article 29(1), a linguistic minority has the fundamental right to conserve its own language. Article 350 A directs every state to provide facilities for education at the primary stage in the language of a linguistic minority for the children belonging to such a community. Read with Article 45, Article 350 A provides an important policy direction to the State for preservation of the language of linguistic minorities.

304. Article 350-B provides for the appointment of a Special Officer for linguistic minorities by the President. It is the duty of the Special Officer to investigate all matters relating to the safeguards provided for linguistic minorities under the Constitution and report to the President upon those matters at such intervals as per the directions of the President. All such reports are to be laid before each House of Parliament and also sent to the Governments of States concerned.

305. India is linguistically very diverse as there are as many as 1,652 languages and dialects spoken. India has twenty-two officially recognized languages. Within a decade of India's independence in 1947, the language issue threatened to tear apart the national fabric and posed a big challenge. However, the political leadership showed exemplary political wisdom and foresight by not only recognizing all major languages as national languages but also created linguistic states. The Reorganization of States Act of 1956 set up linguistically homogeneous state units, thereby recognizing the validity of language as a basis for forming a distinct group.

A. *Welfare of Linguistic Minorities*

306. The concept of 'backwardness' is confined in its application to religious minorities, as it has no relevance for the linguistic minorities as States were reorganized on linguistic lines. Linguistic minorities may be facing some other problems like discrimination and denial of constitutional rights in practice, but no linguistic group can be regarded as backward by itself. However, linguistic minority groups keeping their education restricted to their own language may be handicapped in the matter of competing with others in respect of educational development and economic advancement.

II. Religious Minorities

307. The Constitution of India uses the word 'minority' or its plural form 'minorities' in Articles 29, 30, 350A and 350B – but does not define it anywhere. Article 29 has the word 'minorities' in its marginal heading but speaks of 'any sections of citizens .... having a distinct language, script or culture'. This may be a whole community generally seen as a minority or a group within a majority community. Article 30 speaks specifically of two categories of minorities – religious and linguistic. The remaining two Article – 350A and 350B relate to linguistic minorities only. In ordinary sense, the expression 'minority' means a group comprising less than half of the population and differing from others, especially the predominant section, in race, religion, traditions and culture, language, etc. *The Oxford Dictionary* defines 'Minority' as 'a smaller number or part; a number or part representing less than half of the whole; a relatively small group of people, differing from others in race, religion, language or political persuasion'. A special Subcommittee on the Protection of Minority Rights appointed by the United Nations Human Rights Commission in 1946 defined the 'minority' as those 'non-dominant groups in a population which possess a wish to preserve stable ethnic, religious and linguistic traditions or characteristics markedly different from those of the rest of population'.

308. As regards religious minorities at the national level, all those who profess a religion other than Hinduism are considered minorities since 79.80% population of the country professes Hindu religion. At the national level, Muslims are the largest minority. Other minorities are much smaller in size. As per 2011 census figures Muslims constitute 14.23%, Christians 2.30%, Sikhs 1.72% and Bodhs 0.70%; while all the other religious groups are still smaller. As regards linguistic minorities, there is no majority at the national level and the minority status is to be essentially decided at the State/UT level. At the State/UT level – which is quite important in a federal structure – the Muslims are the majority in the UT of Jammu and Kashmir, the UT of Ladakh and the UT of Lakshadweep. In the States of Meghalaya, Mizoram and Nagaland, Christians constitute the majority. Sikhs are the majority community in the State of Punjab. No other religious community among the minorities is a majority in any other State/UT.

The NCM Act, 1992 says that 'Minority for the purpose of the Act, means a community notified as such by the Central Government' – section 2(7). Acting under this provision on 23 October 1993, the Central Government notified the Muslim, Christian, Sikh, Buddhist and Parsi (Zoroastrian) communities as 'minorities' for the purpose of the Act.

309. In *TMA Pai Foundation & Others v. State of Karnataka and Others*,[67] the Supreme Court has held that for the purpose of Article 30 a minority, whether linguistic or religious, is determinable with reference to a State and not by taking into consideration the population of the country as a whole. Incidentally, 'Scheduled Castes' and 'Scheduled Tribes' are also to be identified at the State/UT level. In terms of Articles 341–342 of the Constitution, castes, races or tribes or parts of or groups within castes, races or tribes are to be notified as Scheduled Castes or Scheduled Tribes in relation to the State or UT, as the case may be.

310. The State Minorities Commission Acts usually empower the local governments to notify the minorities, e.g., Bihar Minorities Commission Act, 1991, section 2(c); Karnataka Minorities Commission Act 1994, section 2(d); UP Minorities Commission Act 1994, section 2(d); West Bengal Minorities Commission Act 1996, section 2(c); A.P. Minorities Commission Act 1998, section 2(d). Similar Acts of M.P. (1996) and Delhi (1999), however, say that Government's Notification issued under the NCM Act, 1992 will apply in this regard – M.P. Act 1996, section 2(c); Delhi Act 1999, section 2(g); section 2(d).

311. The Jain community approached the Supreme Court seeking a direction to the Central Government for a similar recognition at the national level and their demand was supported by the NCM. But the Supreme Court did not issue the desired direction, leaving it to the Central Government to decide the issue (*Bal Patil's* case, 2005). In a later ruling, however, another Bench of the Supreme Court upheld the UP Law recognizing Jains as a minority[68]

312. The UN Declaration against all Forms of Religious Discrimination and Intolerance 1981 outlaws all kinds of religion-based discrimination. The UN Declaration on the Rights of Minorities 1992 enjoins the States to protect the existence and identity of minorities within their respective territories and encourage conditions for promotion of that identity; ensure that persons belonging to minorities fully and effectively exercise human rights and fundamental freedoms with equality and without any discrimination; create favourable conditions to enable minorities to express their characteristics and develop their culture, language, religion, traditions and customs; plan and implement national policy and programmes with due regard to the legitimate interests of minorities. Further, the UDHR 1948 and its two International Covenants of 1966 declare that 'all human beings are equal in dignity and rights' and prohibit all kinds of discrimination – racial, religious, etc.

313. In India, Articles 15 and 16 of the Constitution prohibit the State from making any discrimination on the grounds only of religion, race, caste, sex, descent, place of birth, residence or any of them either generally, i.e., every kind of State action in relation to citizens (Article 15), or in matters relating to employment or appointment to any office under the State (Article 16). However, the provisions of these two Articles take adequate cognizance of the fact that there had been a wide

---

67. 2002 (8) SCC 481.
68. *Kanya Bal Vidyalaya v. State of UP* (2006) 11 SC 92.

disparity in the social and educational status of different sections of a largely caste-based, tradition-bound Hindu society with large-scale poverty and illiteracy. An absolute equality among all sections of the people regardless of specific handicaps may result in perpetuation of those handicaps. There can be equality only among equals. Equality means relative equality and not absolute equality. Therefore, the Constitution permits positive discrimination in favour of the weak, the disadvantaged and the backward. It admits discrimination with reasons but prohibits discrimination without reason. Discrimination with reasons entails rational classification having nexus with constitutionally permissible objects. Article 15 permits the State to make 'any special provisions' for women, children, 'any socially and educationally backward class of citizens' and Scheduled Castes and Scheduled Tribes.

314. Article 15 has been amended by the Constitution (Ninety-third Amendment) Act, 2005 to empower the State to make special provisions, by law, for admission of socially and educationally backward classes of citizens or Scheduled Castes/tribes to educational institutions including private educational institutions, whether aided or unaided by the State, other than minority educational institutions. Article 16, also permits the State to make provisions for the reservation in appointments of posts in favour of 'any backward class of citizens, which, in the opinion of the State, is not adequately represented in the services under the State'. Article 15 speaks of 'any socially and educationally backward class of citizens' and the Scheduled Castes and Scheduled Tribes without qualifying backwardness with social and educational attributes and without a special reference to Scheduled Castes/Scheduled Tribes, whereas Article 16 speaks of 'any backward class of citizens'.

315. Articles 15 and 16 empower the State to make special provisions for backward classes, but prohibit discrimination only on the ground of 'caste' or 'religion'. In other words, positive discrimination on the ground of caste or religion coupled with other grounds such as social and educational backwardness is constitutionally permissible and, therefore, under a given circumstance it may be possible to treat a caste or religious group as a 'class'. Article 15 does not mention minorities in specific terms, minorities who are socially and educationally backward are clearly within the ambit of the term 'any socially and educationally backward classes' in Article 15 and 'any backward class' in Article 16. Indeed, the Central Government and State Governments have included sections of religious minorities in the list of backward classes and have provided reservations to them.

316. The *Supreme Court in Indira Sawhney and Ors. v. Union of India*[69] held that an entire community may be treated as a 'class' based on its social and educational backwardness. The court took into consideration the fact that the Government of Karnataka based on an extensive survey conducted by them, had identified the entire Muslim community inhabiting that State as a backward class and have

69. AIR 1993 SC 477.

provided for reservations for them. The expression 'backward classes' is religion-neutral and not linked with caste and may include any caste or religious community, which as a class suffered from social and educational backwardness. Though economic backwardness is one of the most important reasons responsible for social and educational backwardness alone of a class, the Constitution does not specifically refer to it in Articles 15 and 16. In Indira Sawhney case, the Supreme Court further observed – 'It is, therefore, clear that economic criterion by itself will not identify the backward classes under Article 16(4). The economic backwardness of the backward classes under Article 16(4) has to be on account of their social and educational backwardness. Hence, no reservation of posts in services under the State, based exclusively on economic criterion, would be valid under clause (1) of Article 16 of the Constitution.'

317. Article 46 in the Directive Principles of State Policy mandates the State to 'promote with special care the educational and economic interests of the weaker sections of the people … and shall protect them from social injustice and all forms of exploitation'. This Article refers to Scheduled Castes/ Scheduled Tribes 'in particular' but does not restrict the scope of 'weaker sections of the society'. Article 340 of the Constitution empowers the President to appoint a Commission 'to investigate the conditions of socially and educationally backward classes'.

A. Mechanism for Protection of Rights of Minorities

318. Legislations such as the Protection of Civil Rights Act, 1955, formerly known as Untouchability (Offences) Act, 1955 and the Scheduled Castes and the Scheduled Tribes (Prevention of Atrocities) Act, 1989, have been enacted by the Central Government to protect persons belonging to Scheduled Castes and Scheduled Tribes from untouchability, discrimination, humiliation, etc. No legislation of similar nature exists for minorities though, unlike the latter Act Viz., the Scheduled Castes and the Scheduled Tribes (Prevention of Atrocities) Act 1989, the former Act, viz., the Protection of Civil Rights Act, 1955 is applicable to all cases of untouchability-related offences regardless of religion. Therefore, if a Scheduled Caste converts to Islam or Christianity (or any other person) is subjected to untouchability, the perpetrators of the offences may be proceeded against under the provisions of the Act. It seems that the understanding of law enforcing agencies is that the Protection of Civil Rights Act, 1955 is available only to the Scheduled Castes against enforcement of untouchability-related offences. Thus, the law enforcement authorities/agencies are required to be sensitized in this regard.

319. With a view to evaluating the progress and development of minorities, monitoring the working of safeguards provided to them under the Constitution and laws, etc., the Central Government had constituted a non-statutory Minorities Commission in 1978. In 1992, the NCM was established as a statutory Commission. The NCM was constituted under the Act in 1993. The functions of the Commission include:

(a) evaluating the progress of the development of minorities under the Union and States;
(b) monitoring the working of the safeguards provided in the Constitution and in laws enacted by Parliament and the state legislatures;
(c) making recommendations for the effective implementation of safeguards for the protection of the interests of minorities by the Central Government or the State Governments;
(d) looking into specific complaints regarding deprivation of rights and safeguards of the minorities and taking up such matters with the appropriate authorities;
(e) causing studies to be undertaken into problems arising out of any discrimination against minorities and recommend measures for their removal;
(f) conducting studies, research and analysis on the issues relating to socio-economic and educational development of minorities;
(g) suggesting appropriate measures in respect of any minority to be undertaken by the Central Government or the State Government; and
(h) making periodical or special reports to the Central Government on any matter pertaining to minorities and in particular difficulties confronted by them.

320. A Constitution Amendment Bill, viz. the Constitution (one hundred and third Amendment) Bill, 2004, was introduced so as to add a new article, viz. Article 340A to constitute a NCM with a constitutional status. A Bill to repeal the NCM Act, 1992 was also simultaneously introduced. In terms of section 13 of the Act, the Central Government shall cause the annual report together with a memorandum of action taken on the recommendations contained therein, in so far as they relate to Central Government, and the reasons for non-acceptance, if any, of any recommendation … as soon as may be after the reports are received to be laid before each House of Parliament. As there is no definite time frame for laying the annual report of the Commission, considerable delay takes place in tabling the annual reports of the Commission in the Parliament. Therefore, there is a need for amendment of the Act so as to provide for a reasonable time frame for the recommendations to be laid, along with action taken report before the Parliament/state legislature. The Bill was referred to a Select Committee which has given its report but no action was taken on it. The Standing Committee on Social Justice and Empowerment (2017–2018), in its fifty-third report, noted that the NCM is 'almost ineffective' in its current state to deal with cases of atrocities against minorities. The Committee recommended constitutional status to the body 'without any delay'. NCM has also from time to time requested to grant it constitutional status so that it can discharge its duties more responsibly and effectively.

321. As per clause (9) of Article 338 and 338A of the Constitution, the Union and every State Government is to consult the National Commission for Scheduled Castes and the National Commission for Scheduled Tribes on all major policy matters affecting the Scheduled Castes and the Scheduled Tribes, respectively. This consultation is mandatory and is an important constitutional safeguard for Scheduled Castes and Scheduled Tribes. There is no corresponding provision in the NCM Act, 1992. In the absence of such a provision the government may or may not consult the NCM on major policy matters impacting minorities. Therefore, the NCM Act,

1992 also needs to be amended with a view to incorporating in it a provision analogous to the provision contained in Article 338(9) and 338A. Further, a very important mechanism of ensuring the welfare of Scheduled Castes is constitution of a Parliamentary Committee on Scheduled Castes. This Committee is doing great work towards safeguarding the interests of Scheduled Castes. Such a mechanism of monitoring effective implementation of the constitutional and legal provisions safeguarding the interest of religious minorities and, also, implementation of general or specific schemes for the benefit of minorities by government and its agencies/ instrumentalities will be an effective step for ensuring the welfare of religious minorities.

322. The NCMEIs Act, 2004 was enacted and a Commission constituted with the responsibilities of advising the Central Government or any State Government on any matter relating to the education of minorities, looking into specific complaints regarding deprivation or violation of rights of minorities to establish and administer educational institutions of their choice, deciding on any dispute relating to affiliation to a scheduled University and reporting its findings to the Central Government for implementation. The Act was extensively amended in 2006 (Act No. 18 of 2006), *inter alia*, empowering the Commission to enquire suo-moto or on a petition presented to it by any minority educational institution (or any persons on its behalf) into complaints regarding deprivation or violation of rights of minorities to establish and administer educational institution of its choice and any dispute relating to affiliation to a university and report its finding to the appropriate government for its implementation. The Act also provides that if any dispute arises between a minority educational institution and a university relating to its affiliation to such university, the decision of the Commission thereon shall be final.

B. Other Constitutional Safeguards

323. India is a land of a large number of ethnic, religious, caste and linguistic minorities affiliated with distinct belief systems, subcultures and regions. Integration of these diverse communities, some large enough to aspire to a regional homeland and others content to remain as part of the Indian state has been a central preoccupation of India. It is important to understand the condition of the minority in the present and past scenarios. The efforts to improve the condition of the minority have failed despite constitutional guarantees and the creation of different institutions and commissions to monitor. Minorities face discrimination, violence, mob lynching and atrocities which have come to light many times. In the 2002 Gujarat riots, allegedly more than two thousand Muslims were killed and following Indira Gandhi's assassination around three thousand Sikhs were killed in Delhi. Atrocities against Dalits in different parts of the country are reported from time to time.

324. The purpose of guaranteeing rights to minorities and distinguishing them from the majority is not discrimination but to make them able to come to par and live in harmony with the majority. Minorities have the right to participate effectively in decision-making on the national level and, where appropriate, regional level concerning the minority to which they belong or the regions in which they live, in a manner not incompatible with national legislation. Article 26 states that subject to public order, morality and health, every religious denomination or any section thereof shall have the right:

(a) to establish and maintain institutions for religious and charitable purposes;
(b) to manage its own affairs in matters of religion;
(c) to own and acquire movable and immovable property; and
(d) to administer such property in accordance with the law.

325. The other measures of protection and safeguard provided by the Constitution in Part III or elsewhere having a bearing on the status and rights of minorities are: (i) Freedom of conscience and free profession, practice and propagation of religion (Article 25); (ii) Freedom to manage religious affairs (Article 26); (iii) Freedom as to payment of taxes for promotion of any particular religion (Article 27); (iv) Freedom as to attendance at religious instruction or religious worship in certain educational institutions (Article 28); (v) Special provision relating to language spoken by a section of the population of a State (Article 347); (vi) Language to be used in representations for redress of grievances (Article 350); (vii) Facilities for instruction in mother tongue at primary stage (Article 350A); (viii) Special Officer for linguistic minorities (Article 350 B).

C. Cultural and Educational Rights

326. Articles 29 and 30 deal with cultural and educational rights of minorities. Article 29 provides that: (1) any section of the citizens residing in the territory of India or any part thereof having a distinct language, script or culture of its own shall have the right to conserve the same; and (2) no citizen shall be denied admission into any educational institution maintained by the State or receiving aid out of State funds on grounds only of religion, race, caste, language or any of them. Unlike Article 30, the text of Article 29 does not specifically refer to minorities, though it is quite obvious that the article is intended to protect and preserve the cultural and linguistic identity of the minorities. However, its scope is not confined to minorities. The protection of Article 29 is available to 'any section of the citizens residing in the territory of India' and this may as well include the majority. The minorities, whether based on religion or language, are keen to preserve their cultural and linguistic identity and heritage. There may appear to be some overlapping in language and expressions employed in Articles 15(1) and 29(2). However, Article 15(1) contains a general prohibition on discrimination by the State against any citizen on grounds only of religion, race, caste, sex, place of birth or any of them; whereas Article 29(2) affords protection against a particular species of State action, viz., admission into educational institution maintained by the State or receiving aid out of State funds. Article 30 is a minority-specific provision that protects the right of minorities to establish and administer educational institutions. It provides that 'all minorities, whether based on religion or language, shall have the right to establish and administer educational institutions of their choice'.

327. Clause (1-A) of Article 30, which was inserted by the Constitution (Forty-fourth Amendment) Act, 1978 provides that 'in making any law providing for the compulsory acquisition of any property of an educational institution established and administered by a minority, referred to in clause (1), the State shall ensure that the amount fixed by or determined under such law for the acquisition of such property is such as would not restrict or abrogate the right guaranteed under that clause'. Article 30 further provides that 'the State shall not, in granting aid to educational institutions, discriminate against any educational institution on the ground that it is under the management of a minority, whether based on religion and language'.

328. The minority educational institutions referred to in clause (1) of Article 30 have been kept out of the purview of Article 15(4) of the Constitution which empowers the State to make provisions by law for the advancement of any socially and educationally backward classes of citizens or SCs/STs in regard to their admission to educational institutions (including private educational institutions), whether aided or unaided. Articles 29 and 30 have been grouped together under a common head, namely 'Cultural and Educational Rights'. Together, they confer four distinct rights on minorities, namely:

(1) any section of citizens to conserve its own language, script or culture;
(2) all religious and linguistic minorities can establish and administer educational institutions of their choice;
(3) an educational institution shall not be discriminated by State in the matter of State aid (on the grounds that it is under the management of a religious or linguistic minority); and
(4) protects the citizens against denial of admission to any State-maintained or State-aided educational institution.

329. Article 29, especially clause (1) is more generally worded, whereas Article 30 is focused on the right of minorities to: (i) establish; and (ii) administer educational institutions of their choice. Notwithstanding the fact that the right of the minority to establish and administer educational institutions is protected by Article 19(1)(g), the framers of the Constitution incorporated Article 30 in the Constitution with the intention of instilling confidence among minorities against any legislative or executive encroachment on their right to establish and administer educational institutions. In the absence of such an explicit provision, it might have been possible for the State to control or regulate educational institutions, established by religious or linguistic minorities, by law enacted under clause (6) of Article 19.

Article 29 provides that (1) any section of the citizens residing in the territory of India or any part thereof having a distinct language, script or culture of its own shall have the right to conserve the same. (2) No citizen shall be denied admission into any educational institution maintained by the State or receiving aid out of State funds on grounds only of religion, race, caste, language or any of them.

330. As per Article 30(1) All minorities, whether based on religion or language, shall have the right to establish and administer educational institutions of their choice:

(1) in making any law providing for the compulsory acquisition of any property of an educational institution established and administered by a minority, referred to in the clause;
(2) the State shall ensure that the amount fixed by or determined under such law for the acquisition of such property is such as would not restrict or abrogate the right guaranteed under that clause;
(3) the State shall not, in granting aid to educational institutions, discriminate against any educational institution on the ground that it is under the management of a minority, whether based on religion or language.

331. Article 30(2) provides that the State shall not, in granting aid to educational institutions, discriminate against any educational institution on the ground that it is under the management of a minority, whether based on religion or language. Government-aided educational institute should not be discriminated by the state on the ground that it is under the management of a minority, whether based on religion or language. Minority educational institutes are entitled to get financial assistance much the same way as the educational institutions run by the majority community.

332. These rights have been granted by the Constitution with certain underlying purpose. India being a country of diverse cultures, and as all citizens are equal, hence there must be equal opportunity to preserve it. The Supreme Court in *St. Xavier College v. State of Gujarat*[70] pointed out that the spirit behind Article 30 is that the minorities, religious as well as linguistic, are not prohibited from establishing and administering educational institutions of their choice for the purpose of giving their children the best general education to make them complete man and women of the country. The minorities have been given protection to preserve and strengthen the integrity of the country. The minority will feel isolated and separated if they are not given these rights.

333. Article 350A provides that it shall be the endeavour of every State and of every local authority within the State to provide adequate facilities for instruction in the mother tongue at the primary stage of education to children belonging to linguistic minority groups, and the President may issue such directions to any State as he considers necessary or proper for securing the provision of such facilities.

334. The constitutional protections provided to minorities depict that the promotion and protection of the rights of persons belonging to national or ethnic, religious and linguistic minorities has been given due importance as it contributes to the political and social stability of the States in which they live. The overall development of a country largely depends on the fact that all sections of citizenry develop without fear, favour and free from discrimination in all walks of life.

70. AIR 1974 SC 1389.

335. In *D.A.V School, Jullundur v. State of Punjab,*[71] it was contended that the college administered by the religious minority, i.e., Arya Samaj, and the affiliated university would be compelled to study the religious teaching of the Guru Nanak and this would amount to a violation of Article 29. Supreme Court declined the view and said that, 'there is no mandate in the provision for compelling affiliated colleges either to study religious teaching of the Guru Nanak or to adopt in any way the culture of the Sikh. If the university includes the teaching and life of the saint for the research and philosophical it cannot be said that the affiliated colleges are being required to compulsorily study his life and teaching. If anybody does it will be trespass on the rights of the sections of the citizens who have distinct language or script and which they have a right to conserve through their own educational institutions'.

336. As per Article 29(2), 'No citizen shall be denied admission into any educational institution maintained by the State or receiving aid out of State funds on grounds only of religion, race, caste, language or any of them.' This Article confers a special right not on the minority but to the majority also for admission in the state-maintained or aided educational institution. If it were only limited to the minority, it would mean that the majority has no right to admission in the state-maintained or aided educational institution. This is very clear through this provision that in any case, no one can discriminate on the grounds of language, caste or religion in the matter of admission to educational institutions. Now it is important to know the application of the above article. Dispute with respect to its application was raised in the *State of Madras v. Smt. Champakam Dorairajan.*[72] A Government Order (G.O.) of the state of Madras allotted seats in medical and engineering colleges in proportion to the communities. A Brahmin candidate who could not be admitted to the engineering college challenged the G.O. as being inconsistent with Article 29(2). Supreme Court held that the classification on the grounds of caste was inconsistent with the provision of Article 29. The petitioner has got much higher marks than those secured by non-Brahmins who were admitted. The reason was that he was a Brahmin.

337. The Bombay Government by an order banned the admission of those whose language is not English, to a school using English as a medium of instruction. The argument advanced by the State was that by doing so, it was trying to promote the national language. The court said that the view may be right but could not be upheld as it violates fundamental rights. So there should not be any discrimination on grounds of language in matters of admission, which has been clearly stated by the Hon'ble Supreme Court of India. Dividing states into two regions and then allocating seats for medical and engineering colleges in the state between these regions does not violate Article 29(2).

---

71. AIR 1971 SC 1737.
72. AIR 1951 SC 226.

D. Relationship Between Articles 29(2) and 30 with Article 15(1) and 15(4)

338. Article 15(1) prohibits discrimination on grounds of religion, race, sex, caste or place of birth. Still, there are significant differences between these two articles, Article 15(1) protects all citizens against discrimination by the state whereas Article 29(2) extends protection against the state, or anybody who denies the right conferred. Article 15(1) is much broader than 29(2) as it covers numerous conditions whereas Article 29(2) only deals with the protection against one wrong that is denial of admission in state-aided or maintained educational institutions. Further, whenever Article 29 (2) is not applicable Article 15 (1) will apply.

339. Article 15(4) was added by the first amendment of the Constitution. It was introduced for the advancement of the socially and educationally backward classes of citizens or of SC and ST. Rights guaranteed under Article 29(2) are limited by Article 15(4) as it has provision of reservation in an educational institution for certain sections of people. If the State prescribes some percentage of reservation in any educational institution under Article 15(4) but does not increase more than the prescribed limit, then reservation of the rest cannot be set aside as it would violate the fundamental right guaranteed under Article 29(2). As per Article 30, minorities, whether based on religion or language, shall have the right to establish and administer educational institutions of their choice. In making any law providing for the compulsory acquisition of any property of an educational institution established and administered by a minority, the State shall ensure that the amount fixed by or determined under such law for the acquisition of such property is such as would not restrict or abrogate the right guaranteed under that clause. The benefit of Article 30 extends only to linguistic or religious minorities and not to any other section of Indian citizens.

1. Establish and Administer

340. The words 'establish and administer' used in Article 30(1) have to be read together. This means that the religious minority will have the right to establish the educational institution and can administer it only if the institution has been established by the community. Like Aligarh Muslim University was held to be established by the statutory provision and hence cannot be designated as a minority educational institution. The Supreme Court has observed in *Azeez Basha v. Union of India*[73] that Article 30(1) postulates that the religious community will have the right to establish and administer the educational institute of their choice meaning thereby where a religious minority establishes an education institution, it will have the right to administer such institution provided that they have established the same and not otherwise. It has to be proved by producing satisfactory evidence that the institution was established by the minority claiming to administer it. The onus of the proof lies on one who asserts an institution is a minority institution. On this

73. AIR 1968 SC 662.

behalf, critics of this approach contend that for conferring degrees, it was and is necessary to have the statutory sanction and for that purpose, a statute was passed. The statute does not establish educational institutions; it only provides authority to confer degrees. Looking from this angle and in the background that for conferring degrees statutory sanction is required, no minority will be able to establish an educational institute if this interpretation of Article 30 is applied. This interpretation if carried further, will mean that minorities have the right to pass legislation which would amount to the establishment of the institution of their choice. Obviously, minorities do not have legislative power, so by this interpretation, this article of the Constitution cannot be put into operation and minorities cannot exercise this right, thereby making it inapplicable. This cannot be the intention of the framers of the Constitution. When the intention is to protect the interest of a group whose voice may not be counted in a majority-based system, i.e., democracy, such narrow and literal interpretation even otherwise is against the cannons of construction and interpretation. A right which was given after a lot of deliberations to minorities and provided in the Constitution has been taken away through interpretation. Further, it also does not take into account cases where some member or body from the majority community establishes an educational institution and gives its administration to the minority community.

341. In *Yogendra Nath Singh v. State of Uttar Pradesh,*[74] the government recognized an institution as a minority institution. This order was challenged in the High Court and the court looking into the antecedent history of the institution, right from its inception, decided that the institution was not established as a minority institution, and, therefore, it could not be granted minority status even though presently it was managed by the minority community. Under this article, both the condition 'established and managed' should be read together and the absence of even one aspect would render the institution unfit for giving it the status of minority institution.

2. Interrelationship of Articles 29(2) and 30(1)

342. The framers of the Constitution never intended that Article 29(2) act as a restraint on the content of the right available under Article 30(I). The way in which Article 29(2) came to assume its final shape in the Constituent Assembly in an interesting story. Originally the present Article 29(2) was part of the integrated scheme devised to protect the educational interests of religious and linguistic minorities. The simple object of what now constitutes Articles 29(2) was to protect minorities from being discriminated against in regard to admission into state educational institutions. The recommendation of the minorities Subcommittee made on 19 April 1947 for being incorporated as fundamental rights in the Constitution contains a

74. 1999 (2) AWC 1563.

provision which read: no minority whether based on religion, community or language shall be deprived of its right or discriminated against in regard to the admission into state education institutions. Since they have not done so, it becomes obvious that the intention of the framers was not to treat Article 29(2) as an exception to Article 30.

E. Welfare of Religious Minorities

343. As religious communities mainly Muslims have lagged behind in development, some schemes have been framed and scholarships and other help offered to minority students by Central and State Governments. Business loans with a low-interest rate are also offered to young entrepreneurs from minority communities. There is a fifteen-point development programme for minorities by the Prime Minister of India. Jains are now on the central list of minorities, and the Central Government has declared this status for the community.

344. There are Minority Commissions on national and state levels. These commissions look into various matters related to minorities. The Central Government has established the Minority Commission of India under the NCM Act, 1992. The Commission has a Chairperson, a Vice Chairperson and five members. Besides The Minority Commission of India, there are State Minority Commissions in the states of Andhra Pradesh, Assam, Bihar, Chhattisgarh, Delhi, Jharkhand, Karnataka, Maharashtra, Madhya Pradesh, Manipur, Rajasthan, TN, Uttarakhand, UP, West Bengal, etc.

345. It is ironic that recognition of personal laws does not guarantee that a community will be treated with respect or dignity. The crux of the problem is the impression created because of the apparent incompatibility of certain personal laws with the Western standards of justice and equality. The question is whether these standards are to be set by the intelligentsia of religious groups themselves or to be dictated by other religious groups or by the majority. It is to be considered what are the limits of cultural rights of communities; should these be determined by constitution makers, states or communities and further; should there be a set of individual rights which can under no circumstances be shadowed by majority community thinking and concepts. Women's rights must be enforced irrespective of the group to which women belong, but it has to be seen that it may not totally change the basic structure of religious aspects by which women of a particular religion are governed as the same may create imbalances. The Apex Court has developed a distinct jurisprudence that the solutions must come out from within the religious group and not be imposed from outside.

346. In the matter of criteria for identifying backward classes there should be absolutely no discrimination whatsoever between the majority community and the minorities; and, therefore, the criteria applied for this purpose to the majority community must be unreservedly applied also to all the minorities. Therefore, all those classes, sections and groups among the minorities should be treated as backward whose counterparts in the majority community are regarded as backward under the present scheme of things. Further, all those classes, sections and groups among the various minorities as are generally regarded as 'inferior' within the social strata and societal system of those communities should be treated as backward. To be more specific, all those social and vocational groups among the minorities who but for their religious identity would have been covered by Scheduled Castes should be unquestionably treated as socially backward, irrespective of whether the religion of those other communities recognizes the caste system or not. Whether the caste system prevalent in the majority community is part of religion and whether it should remain part of the religion, which goes against the basic spirit of the Constitution, which abolishes untouchability, the hallmark of the caste system. It may be pointed out that government policy or as a statutory recognition, caste system seems intended to be further perpetuated.

F. Minorities as Weaker Section of Society

347. As democracy is a game of numbers, the numerically weaker sections in any society may and often get marginalized by the majority. This is true of the religious minorities in India where the society remains intensively religious and religion-conscious and the religious minorities live with a predominant religious community accounting for over 79% of the national population. In such a situation legal protection from the hegemony and preponderance of the majority community becomes a pressing need of the religious minorities as a whole, and not just that of the 'backward' sections among them. To provide such necessary protection by law, the Constitution contains the Directive Principle of State Policy. Article 46 speaks about 'weaker sections of the people' without subjecting them to the condition of backwardness and requires the State to 'promote with special care' the educational and economic interests of such sections. It is well known that in India backwardness, both social and economic, is the result of educational backwardness. Hence, measures are required to be taken in a systematic and sustained manner for the educational advancement of religious minorities under the National Education Policy of 1986 and now under the draft National Education Policy of 2019.

1. Educational Welfare Measures

348. As the meaning and scope of Article 30 of the Constitution have become quite uncertain, complicated and diluted due to varied and sometimes conflicting judicial interpretations, a comprehensive law should be enacted to detail all aspects of minorities' educational rights under that provision with a view to reinforcing its original dictates in letter and spirit. The statute of the National Minority Educational Institutions Commission should also be amended to make it broad-based in its composition, powers, functions and responsibilities and to enable it to work as the watchdog for a meticulous enforcement of all aspects of minorities' educational rights under the Constitution.

349. As by the force of judicial decisions the minority intake in minority educational institutions has, in the interest of national integration, been restricted to about 50%, thus virtually earmarking the remaining 50% or so for the majority community by the same logic and for the same purpose, some seats in all non-minority educational institutions should be earmarked by law for the students of the minority communities. As regards the backward sections among all the minorities, the concessions in terms of lower eligibility criteria for admission and lower rate of fee as available to the Scheduled Castes and Scheduled Tribes should be extended to such sections among the minorities. Since women among some minorities are educationally backward, the same measure be taken for them as well.

350. In respect of the Muslims – who are the largest minority at the national level with a countrywide presence and yet educationally the most backward of the religious communities – certain exclusive measures are to be taken like: (i) Select institutions in the country like the Aligarh Muslim University and the Jamia Millia Islamia should be legally given a special responsibility to promote education at all levels to Muslim students by taking all possible steps for this purpose. At least one such institution should be selected for this purpose in each of those States and Union Territories, which has a substantial Muslim population. (ii) All schools and colleges run by the Muslims should be provided enhanced aid and other logistic facilities adequate enough to raise their standards by all possible means and maintain the same. (iii) The Madarsa Modernization Scheme of the government should be suitably revised, strengthened and provided with more funds so that it can provide finances and necessary paraphernalia either: (a) for the provision of modern education up to Standard X within those madarsas themselves which are at present imparting only religious education or, alternatively; (b) to enable the students of such madarsas to receive such education simultaneously in the general schools in their neighbourhood. The Madarsa Modernization Scheme may, for all these purposes, be operated through a central agency like the Central Wakf Council or the proposed Central Madarsa Education Board. (iv) The rules and processes of the Central Wakf Council should be revised in such a way that one of its main responsibilities should be educational development of the Muslims. For this purpose, the Council may be legally authorized: (i) to collect a special 5% educational levy from all wakfs, and (ii) to sanction utilization of wakf lands for establishing educational institutions, polytechnics, libraries and hostels. (refer Ranganath Mishra Commission recommendations).

2. Reservation to Minorities

351. The Ranganath Mishra Commission recommended reservation for Muslims on the basis as explained hereinafter. Since the minorities – especially the Muslims – are very much under-represented, and sometimes wholly unrepresented, in government employment, so they should be regarded as backward in this respect within the meaning of that term as used in Article 16(4) of the Constitution – notably without qualifying the word 'backward' with the words 'socially and educationally' – and that 15% of posts in all cadres and grades under the Central and State

Governments should be earmarked for them as follows: (a) The break-up within the recommended 15% shall be 10% for the Muslims (commensurate with their 73% share of the former in the total minority population at the national level) and the remaining 5% for the other minorities. (b) Minor adjustment inter se can be made within the 15% earmarked seats. In the case of non-availability of Muslims to fill 10% earmarked seats, the remaining vacancies may be given to other minorities if their members are available over and above their share of 5%; but in no case shall any seat within the recommended 15% go to the majority community. Yet, should there be some insurmountable difficulty in implementing this recommendation, as an alternative, since according to the Mandal Commission Report the minorities constitute 8.4% of the total OBC population, in the 27% OBC quota an 8.4% sub-quota should be earmarked for the minorities with an internal break-up of 6% for the Muslims (commensurate with their 73% share in the total minority population at the national level) and 2.4% for the other minorities – with minor adjustments inter se in accordance with the population of various minorities in various States and UTs. The reservation now extended to the Scheduled Tribes, which is a religion-neutral class, should be carefully examined to assess the extent of minority presence in it and remedial measures should be initiated to correct the imbalance, if any.

352. The situation in Meghalaya, Mizoram, Nagaland and Lakshadweep which are minority-dominated and predominantly tribal, as also such tribal areas/districts in Assam and all other States, is to be especially taken into account in this respect. The judicial reservation recently expressed in several cases about the continued inclusion of the creamy layer in various classes enjoying reservation, inclusive of the Scheduled Castes and Scheduled Tribes, should be seriously considered for acceptance as a State Policy.

353. Almost all States have one or more minority groups within their territories, characterized by their own ethnic, linguistic or religious identity differing from the majority population. Harmonious relations among minorities and between minorities and majority and respect for each group's identity is a great asset to the multi-ethnic and multicultural diversity of the country. Meeting the aspirations of national, ethnic, religious and linguistic groups and ensuring the rights of persons belonging to minorities acknowledges the dignity and equality of all individuals, furthers participatory development, and thus contributes to the lessening of tensions among the different strata of population.

354. In recent years, however, there has been a heightened interest in issues affecting minorities as ethnic, racial and religious tensions have escalated, threatening the economic, social and political fabric of the society. Discrimination, which affects minorities in a negative manner, unfortunately persists and is a major source of tension. Discrimination has been interpreted to 'imply any distinction, exclusion, restriction or preference which is based on any ground such as race, colour, … , language, religion, … , national or social origin, … , birth or other status, and which has the purpose or effect of nullifying or impairing the recognition, enjoyment or exercise by all persons, on an equal footing, of all rights and freedoms'. The prevention of discrimination has been defined as the '… prevention of any action which denies to individuals or groups of people equality of treatment which they may wish' (refer Ranganath Mishra Commission Recommendations).

355. Discrimination has been prohibited in a number of international instruments that deal with the situations in which minority groups and their individual members are denied equality of treatment. Differences in the treatment of such groups, or individuals belonging to minorities, is justified if it is exercised to promote effective equality and the welfare of the community as a whole. This form of affirmative action may have to be sustained over a prolonged period in order to enable minorities to benefit from society on an equal footing with the majority.[75]

356. India has developed an affirmative action programme for the upliftment of downtrodden, which by any standards is unprecedented in both its scope and extent. This system comprises of quotas designed to increase opportunities in employment, education and legislatures for lower castes. In India social inequality goes beyond caste-based discrimination; it revolves around three main axes, which include caste and tribal status, religion and gender, yet, religion and caste remains the crux of reservation policies. The Constitution in Article 16(4) permits the state to make 'any provision for the reservation in appointments or posts in favour of any backward class of citizens which, in the opinion of the state, is not adequately represented in the services under the state'. After independence the state sought to eliminate the effects of historical disadvantage by bringing in reservations for identified Scheduled Castes and Scheduled Tribes in governments services and representation in legislatures.

357. In Part XVI (Special Provisions Relating to Certain Classes), the Constitution provided for the reservation of seats in the legislatures as also in public employment and educational institutions funded by the state; and for the creation of a body to monitor all these safeguards. These policies reserved government jobs, college and university admissions, and legislative seats for groups officially identified as Scheduled Castes and tribes. It has given them an influential presence in national and state legislatures. Though the government's position was that only these two groups are entitled to reservations, it has been extended to the Other Backward Classes (OBCs) in education and public employment since 1994. The rationale of the Mandal Commission (1990) was to break the monopoly on government jobs and the professions, unchanged by two centuries of modern education and nearly seventy-two years of democracy.

75. The above discussion and measures are based on the Report of the National Commission for religious and linguistic minorities by Justice Ranganath Misra.

Chapter 4. Contractual Religious Freedom

358. People participate in a political and social order based on some understanding of what its terms are – what the government can expect of them, what can be expected of the government, and what we can expect the government not to do. These terms form a sort of contract. These are real terms, partly written but largely unwritten, that are perceived in law, traditions, and practices. The terms are subject to interpretation, of course, and no doubt they may change over time – occasionally through deliberately enacted law, more often through gradual and almost imperceptible cultural evolution. So long as the government honours the terms, one may feel some obligation to render support and allegiance. Conversely, if the government disregards or violates the terms of the 'contract', regarding religious freedom, loyalty is betrayed and commitment compromised. People may come to perceive the government no longer as representing them.

359. A special commitment to religious freedom has been a central part of contract. For many religious people, this term is still an essential one; but even non-religious people might acknowledge that religious freedom has been and continues to be an understood term of the contract. And violations of a central term – by the courts or Administration – will be perceived by those who care about it as a betrayal and a fundamental injustice. It is true that people who remain committed to this particular term of the contract – to constitutional respect for religious freedom – may be acting on the basis of traditional theological rationales that many other citizens no longer accept. In this way, the traditional rationales continue to influence the constitutional order.

§1. Poona Pact, 1932

360. On 16 August 1932, the British Prime Minister, Ramsay MacDonald, announced the Communal Award which provided for separate electorates for the 'Depressed Classes', the Muslims, the Europeans, the Sikhs, the Anglo-Indians and the Indian-based Christians.

Under the separate electorates system, each community was allocated a particular number of seats in the legislatures and only members from these communities would be eligible to vote to elect a representative of the same community to legislative assemblies. Mahatma Gandhi was opposed to the communal award, but Ambedkar was in favour of the award, as according to him political solutions like separate electorate would work for upliftment of depressed classes. After the series of negotiations both Gandhiji and Ambedkar agreed to a solution called Poona Pact and thereby withdrawing separate electorate for depressed classes.

I. Main Features

361. In a settlement negotiated with Mahatma Gandhi, Ambedkar agreed for depressed class candidates to be elected by a joint electorate. Also, nearly twice as many seats (147) were reserved for the depressed classes in the legislature than what had been allotted under the Communal Award. In addition, the Poona Pact assured a fair representation of the depressed classes in the public services while earmarking a portion of the educational grant for their uplift. The Poona Pact was an emphatic acceptance by upper-class Hindus that the depressed classes constituted the most discriminated sections of Indian society. It was also conceded that something concrete had to be done to give depressed classes a political voice.

The pact made the entire country morally responsible for the uplift of the depressed classes.

§2. Reorganization of States

362. After independence, the States in India were reorganized on a linguistic basis, which extended the democratic dispensation by creating many new centres of regional power with autonomous jurisdiction. The first reorganization was based on the accommodation of ethnolinguistic and cultural communities, which have since then occupied a pre-eminent place in Indian politics and in the Indian model of governance and for which demands were made from time to time. While the first reorganization affected India as a whole, the second effort at federal reorganization focused on one region, i.e., the Northeast and later on mainly based on and to accommodate geographical areas. The first was guided by the need to federalize the Union on an identifiable basis. The second was motivated by concerns over national and territorial security in the Northeast and at other places.

363. As the ethnolinguistic communities are mostly territorially rooted, territorial solutions in the form of different degrees of statehood to accommodate their demands had worked. Statehood and other such demands are predicated on collective or group of ethnic communities. The Constitution makes the conservation and cultivation of sections of society with a distinct culture, a fundamental right of every citizen of India. Article 29(1) says that any section of the citizens of India having a distinct language, script or culture of its own shall have the right to conserve the same. This means that if a cultural minority wants to preserve its own language and culture, the state cannot by law impose on it any other culture belonging to the local majority. Both religious and linguistic minorities are protected by this provision. The Constitution also defines a positive, directional role for the state in this respect. It directs every State to provide adequate facilities for instruction in the mother tongue at the primary stage of education of children belonging to linguistic minority groups, and empowers the President to issue proper direction in this regard to any state.

§3. Ethnic Peace Accords

364. State autonomy and statehood for territorially based regional/linguistic identities remains the most comprehensive method of political recognition of identity in India. The essence of the statehood demand has always been the congruence between federal political boundaries and the ethnolinguistic boundaries of the people. At the heart of such demands remains the urge for decentralization and autonomy for the protection of identity and for development. The political processes which have accompanied the legal-constitutional ones are often protracted negotiations between the governments (Union and state), and the ethnic movements, and the resultant bipartite or tripartite 'Ethnic Peace Accords' are signed, and protected by legislation, for institutionalizing peace in the shape of democratic local governing bodies. Given the complex diversity of the vast country, coupled with regional imbalances, social and economic inequalities and mass poverty, statehood or some other forum provides an institutional framework of autonomy and decentralization.

365. However, splitting up existing federal units and creating new ones is only one of the many strategies that democracies can deploy to contain ethnic conflicts. Since independence, the government has entered into various ethnic accords (as, for example, that between the Rajiv Gandhi government and Sikh and Assamese in the mid-eighties), created Regional Councils straddling several state units (as in the Northeast), and constituted district-level Autonomous Councils to address the needs of smaller ethnic regions surrounded by competing ethnic communities. Other strategies range from federal arrangement to the inclusion of nationalities based on a layered sovereignty. The special constitutional status granted under Article 370 to the State of Jammu and Kashmir is an example which has now been diluted and the State of J&K has been reorganized into two Union Territories. This is the first time that a full-fledged State with its separate State Assembly has been converted into Union Territories.

Part IV. International, Transnational, and Regional Effects on Religious Communities

Chapter 1. International Law Effects on Religious Communities

366. The struggle for religious freedom in the world has been going on for centuries and has led to a large number of tragic conflicts with great bloodshed. So, there was always a need for some safeguards, and in the twentieth century, there has been the codification of common values related to freedom of religion and belief. The UN's recognition of the importance of freedom of religion or belief is reflected in the UDHR of 1948 (Universal Declaration). Article 18 of the Universal Declaration states 'Everyone shall have the right to freedom of thought, conscience and religion. This right shall include freedom to have a religion or whatever belief of his [her] choice.' Since the Universal Declaration, attempts have been made to develop an enforceable human rights instrument[76] protecting freedom of religion and belief, which has resulted in the passage of the UN Resolution. In India, the various safeguards available under UN Resolutions and international law were embodied in the Constitution itself, which is the primary and basic law of the country, and all other laws are to be in harmony with the Constitution. Any law which is in derogation or inconsistent with the Constitution shall be stuck down. It has also been provided in the Constitution that international treaties and conventions will be respected.

367. In 1966, the UN passed the ICCPR, expanding its prior statement to address the manifestation of religion or belief. Article 18 of this Covenant includes four paragraphs related to the issue of religion, namely:

76. International legal instruments are in the form of treaty (also called an agreement, convention, covenant or protocol). There are various means by which a state expresses its consent to be bound by a treaty, with the most common being ratification or accession. A new treaty is ratified by those states that have negotiated the instrument, while a state that has not participated in the negotiations may, at a later stage, accede to the treaty. The treaty enters into force when a predetermined number of states have ratified or acceded to the treaty. While ratifying or acceding to a treaty, that state may make reservations to one or more articles of the treaty, unless the treaty prohibits this action. Reservations are exceptions that a state makes to a treaty – provisions that it does not agree to follow – and may normally be withdrawn at any time. In some countries, international treaties take precedence over national law. In others, a specific law may be required to give an international treaty the force of law.

(a) Everyone shall have the right to freedom of thought, conscience and religion. This right shall include freedom to have or to adopt a religion or belief of his [her] choice, and freedom either individually or in community with others and in public or private, to manifest his/ her religion or belief in worship, observance, practice and teaching.
(b) No one shall be subjected to coercion which would impair his/her freedom to have or to adopt a religion or belief of his [her] choice.
(c) Freedom to manifest one's religion or belief may be subject only to such limitations as are prescribed by law and are necessary to protect public safety, order, health, morals or the fundamental rights and freedoms of others.
(d) The States Parties to the present Covenant undertake to have respect for the liberty of parents and, when applicable, legal guardians, to ensure the religious and moral education of their children in conformity with their own convictions.

368. Some of the articles of the ICCPR regarding fundamental freedoms have become international conventions, which are legally binding treaties. In contrast, however, because of the complexity of the political issues involved, Article 18 of the ICCPR has not been elaborated and codified in the same way that more detailed treaties have codified prohibitions against torture, discrimination against women, and race discrimination. After twenty years, the General Assembly in 1981 adopted without a vote the Declaration on the Elimination of All Forms of Intolerance and of Discrimination Based on Religion or Belief. While the 1981 Declaration lacks any enforcement procedures, it remains the most important contemporary codification of the principle of freedom of religion and belief.

§1. UN Declaration on the Elimination of All Forms of Intolerance and of Discrimination Based on Religion or Belief, 1981

369. This Declaration contains eight articles, three of which namely Articles 1, 5, and 6 define specific rights. The remaining articles are in a supportive role and outline measures to promote tolerance or prevent discrimination. Taken together, the eight articles constitute an overall concept, advocating tolerance and preventing discrimination based on religion or belief. While human rights are individual rights, the 1981 UN Declaration also identifies certain rights related to religious institutions, parents, legal guardians, children, and groups of persons.

I. Classification of Discrimination (Article 2)

370. This article identifies categories of potential discriminators, affirming the right not to be subject to discrimination on the grounds of religion or belief by: States (national, regional, local government); Institutions (governmental, nongovernmental, religious); Groups of persons; Persons.

II. Link to Other Rights (Article 3)

371. This article links the 1981 UN Declaration to other international documents and declares that discrimination based on religion or belief constitutes an affront to human dignity and a disavowal of the principles of the Charter of the UN, and shall be condemned as a violation of the human rights and fundamental freedoms proclaimed in the UDHR, and enunciated in detail in the ICCPR and the International Covenant on Economic, Social and Cultural Rights.

III. Possible Solutions (Article 4)

372. Article 4 declares that all States, including all sectors of civil society, shall take effective measures to prevent and eliminate discrimination based on religion or belief through:

- Actions in all fields of civil, economic, political, social, and cultural life.
- Enacting or rescinding legislation where necessary to prohibit such discrimination.
- Taking all appropriate measures to combat intolerance based on religion or belief.

IV. Parents, Guardians and Children (Article 5)

373. The following rights of the parents and guardians of the child have been protected, namely the following:

(a) Right of parents or legal guardians to bring the child up in their religion or belief.
(b) Right of the child to education in religion or belief, in accordance with the wishes of parents, and the right not to be compelled to receive education against their wishes.
(c) Right of the child to protection from discrimination and to education for tolerance.
(d) Right of the child's wishes when not under the care of parents or legal guardians.
(e) Right of the State to limit practices injurious to child's development or health.

V. Manifesting Religion or Belief (Article 6)

374. At stake in the implementation of this Article are the following rights:

- Right to worship and assemble, and to establish and maintain places of worship.
- Right to establish and maintain appropriate charitable or humanitarian institutions.
- Right to make, acquire and use materials related to rites and customs.

- Right to write, issue and disseminate relevant publications in these areas.
- Right to teach a religion or belief in places suitable for these purposes.
- Right to solicit and receive voluntary financial and other contributions.
- Right to train, appoint, elect or designate appropriate leaders.
- Right to observe days of rest and celebrate holidays and ceremonies.
- Right to establish and maintain communication with individuals and communities at national and international levels.

VI. National Legislation (Article 7)

375. This article declares that all of the rights at stake in the 1981 UN Declaration need to be accorded in national legislation in such a manner that everyone shall be able to avail themselves of such rights and freedoms in practice.

VII. Existing Protections (Article 8)

376. The 1981 UN Declaration is non-binding on States so as to ensure that the Declaration does not negate existing legal protections on freedom of religion or belief. Nothing in the Declaration shall be construed as restricting or negating any right defined in the UDHR and International Covenants on Human Rights. Actually, the 1981 UN Declaration is a compromise between states after twenty years of complex discussion and debate and after final passage by the General Assembly.

VIII. Limitation on Freedom to Manifest Religion or Belief (Article 18)

377. Under Article 18 of the ICCPR, any action which falls within the four types of manifestation of belief (worship, observance, teaching and practice) can, in certain circumstances, be subject to limitation by the State. The freedom to manifest religion is qualified by the limitations set out in sub-paragraph 18(3), including those, which are 'necessary to protect ... the fundamental rights and freedoms of others'. These limitations apply whether the right is exercised by an individual or by an organization. It is clear from Article 18(3) that the recognition in human rights law of the need for a level of autonomy for religious communities does not automatically extend to protect from interference every action, which is or might be taken by a religious institution. The need to respect the autonomy of religious communities precludes the State from prohibiting internal religious practices 'merely because they do not coincide with current perceptions of human rights' as 'without respect for the differences of religious communities from general secular behaviour, pluralism would be an empty word'. However, the freedom to manifest one's religion, whether exercised by an individual or a religious organization, 'must be exercised with due regard for the rights and freedoms of others'.

378. The European Court has affirmed that when considering the actions of religious organizations, courts must conduct a balancing exercise to determine whether the rights of those affected by their actions have been violated. In a pluralistic society, it must be recognized by persons or organizations asserting their freedom of belief and expression that the same freedom attaches to others who may have contrary beliefs, and the right equally protects that other person's right to hold those different beliefs and to live in accordance with them. It follows that the manifestations of a particular belief may legitimately be limited where they threaten to destroy the autonomy of others or threaten other aspects of the social order.

379. The society has the right to defend itself against possible abuses committed on the pretext of freedom of religion. It is the special duty of government to provide this protection. Its action is to be controlled by juridical norms, which are in conformity with the objective moral order. These norms arise out of the need for the effective safeguard of the rights of all citizens and for the peaceful settlement of conflicts of rights, also out of the need for an adequate care of genuine public peace, which comes about when men live together in good order and in true justice, and finally out of the need for a proper guardianship of public morality. These matters constitute the basic component of the common welfare. When a person's or an organization's manifestation of religious beliefs affects the rights of other persons, it is legitimate for the State to try to balance the protection of these competing rights. The Indian Courts have also recognized that at the point at which a person's actions based upon religious beliefs, impact on the rights of others, in order to appropriately resolve the conflict of rights, there needs to be an assessment of what is at stake for each person involved. As the person or group whose rights are impacted has the basic right to manifest so some balance and harmony is to be brought between the conflicting aspects so that both groups can enjoy the freedom without conflict.

380. The United Nation General Assembly on 16 March 2009 in its Sixty-Third session adopted a resolution on the report of the Third Committee on Elimination of all forms of intolerance and of discrimination based on religion or belief. The General Assembly, recalling its various resolutions, expressed its serious concern at all attacks on religious places, sites and shrines in violation of international law, in particular human rights and humanitarian law, including any deliberate destruction of relics and monuments, seriously concerned also at any misuse of registration procedures and at the resort to discriminatory registration procedures as a means to limit the right to freedom of religion or belief of members of religious communities, at the limitations placed on religious materials and at the obstacles placed in the way of construction of places of worship, inconsistent with the exercise of the right to freedom of religion or belief.

381. The General Assembly was convinced of the need to address the rise in various parts of the world of religious extremism that affects the rights of individuals, the situations of violence and discrimination that also affect many women as well as other individuals on the grounds or in the name of religion or belief or in accordance with cultural and traditional practices, and the misuse of religion or belief for ends inconsistent with the Charter of the UN, as well as other relevant instruments of the UN. The General Assembly, *inter alia*:

(1) condemned all forms of intolerance and discrimination based on religion or belief, as well as violations of freedom of thought, conscience and religion or belief and stressed that the right to freedom of thought, conscience and religion applies equally to all people, regardless of their religions or beliefs, and without any discrimination as to their equal protection by the law;
(2) emphasized that restrictions on the freedom to manifest one's religion or belief are permitted only if limitations are prescribed by law, are necessary to protect public safety, order, health or morals, or the fundamental rights and freedoms of others, are non-discriminatory and are applied in a manner that does not vitiate the right to freedom of thought, conscience and religion;
(3) recognized with deep concern the overall rise in instances of intolerance and violence directed against members of many religious and other communities in the world, including cases motivated by Islamophobia, anti-Semitism and Christianophobia;
(4) recognized with concern the situation of persons in vulnerable situations, including persons deprived of their liberty, refugees, asylum seekers and internally displaced persons, children, persons belonging to national or ethnic, religious and linguistic minorities and migrants, as regards their ability to freely exercise their right to freedom of religion or belief;
(5) urged States to step up their efforts to protect and promote freedom of thought, conscience and religion or belief, and to this end to:
    (a) ensure that their constitutional and legislative systems provide adequate and effective guarantees of freedom of thought, conscience, religion and belief to all without distinction;
    (b) ensure that no one is deprived of the right to life, liberty or security of person because of religion or belief and that no one is subjected to torture or other cruel, inhuman or degrading treatment or punishment, or arbitrary arrest or detention on that account and to bring to justice all perpetrators of violations of these rights;
    (c) ensure that no one is discriminated against on the basis of his or her religion or belief when accessing, *inter alia*, education, medical care, employment, humanitarian assistance or social benefits;
    (d) ensure the right of all persons to worship or assemble in connection with a religion or belief and their right to establish and maintain places for these purposes and the right of all persons to write, issue and disseminate relevant publications in these areas;
    (e) ensure that, in accordance with appropriate national legislation and in conformity with international human rights law, the freedom of all persons and members of groups to establish and maintain religious, charitable or humanitarian institutions is fully respected and protected;
    (f) exert the utmost efforts, in accordance with their national legislation and in conformity with international human rights law, to ensure that religious places, sites, shrines and symbols are fully respected and protected and to take additional measures in cases where they are vulnerable to desecration and destruction;

(g) ensure that all public officials and civil servants, including members of law enforcement bodies, the military and educators, in the course of fulfilling their official duties, respect all religions or beliefs and do not discriminate for reasons based on religion or belief.

(6) condemns any advocacy of religious hatred that constitutes incitement to discrimination, hostility or violence, whether it involves the use of print, audio-visual or electronic media or any other means;

(7) urges States to step up their efforts to eliminate intolerance and discrimination based on religion or belief, notably by:

(a) taking all action, in conformity with international standards of human rights, to combat hatred, discrimination, intolerance and acts of violence, intimidation and coercion motivated by intolerance based on religion or belief, as well as incitement to hostility and violence, with particular regard to members of religious minorities, and devoting particular attention to practices that violate the human rights of women and discriminate against women, including in the exercise of their right to freedom of thought, conscience and religion or belief;

(b) promoting and encouraging, through education and other means, understanding, tolerance and respect in all matters relating to freedom of religion or belief and undertaking all appropriate efforts to encourage those engaged in teaching to promote mutual understanding, tolerance and respect.

(8) emphasized that no religion should be equated with terrorism, as this may have adverse consequences on the enjoyment of the right to freedom of religion or belief of all members of the religious communities concerned;

(9) invited all actors to address, in the context of inter-religious and intercultural dialogue, *inter alia*, the following issues within the framework of international human rights:

(a) the rise of religious extremism affecting religions in all parts of the world;

(b) the situations of violence and discrimination that affect many women as well as other individuals on the grounds or in the name of religion or belief or in accordance with cultural and traditional practices; and

(c) the misuse of religion or belief for ends inconsistent with the Charter of the UN, as well as other relevant instruments of the UN.

(10) welcomes and encourages the continuing efforts of all actors in society, including Non-governmental Organizations (NGOs) and bodies and groups based on religion or belief, to promote the implementation of the Declaration on the Elimination of All Forms of Intolerance and of Discrimination Based on Religion;

(11) recommends that States, the UN and other actors, including NGOs and bodies and groups based on religion or belief, in their efforts to promote freedom of religion or belief, ensure the widest possible dissemination of the text of the Declaration on the Elimination of All Forms of Intolerance and of Discrimination Based on Religion or Belief, in as many different languages as possible, and promote its implementation;

(12) urges all governments to cooperate fully with the Special Rapporteur, to respond favourably to her requests to visit their countries and to provide all necessary information for the effective fulfilment of her mandate.

382. In India, Constitution has taken care of international commitments with respect to rights of the religious communities and incorporated in a number of articles particularly from Articles 25 to 30, the very essence of religious freedom. Further, the decisions of the courts have also tried to harmonize the conflicting interests of the religious communities. Manifestation of religious belief by one religious group must be such that it may not impinge upon the right to manifest of other religious groups.

Chapter 2. Transnational Law Effects on Religious Communities

383. The rights of minority communities including religious communities consist of two elements, namely normal individual rights as applied to members of racial, ethnic, class, religious, linguistic or sexual minorities, and second, collective rights accorded to minority groups, e.g., religious groups forming minority in a particular country. The term may also apply simply to the individual rights of anyone who is not part of the majority decision. It is to be ensured that individual rights are not denied on the basis of membership in a minority group, such as global women's rights or the various racial, religious, and linguistic minority rights around the world.

§1. Congress of Vienna, 1814

384. At the international forum, the issue of minority rights was first raised in 1814, at the Congress of Vienna, which discussed the fate of German Jews and the Poles. The Congress of Paris in 1856 paid special attention to the status of Jews and Christians in the Ottoman Empire. The Congress of Berlin in 1878 dealt with the status of Jews in Romania, especially, and also Siberia, and Bulgaria. However, these congresses failed to impose significant reforms. Russia was active in protecting Orthodox Christians, and Slavic people under the control of the Ottoman Empire. The first minority rights were proclaimed and enacted by the Parliament of Hungary in July 1849. Subsequently, minority rights were recognized and codified in Austrian law in 1867.

§2. Minority Rights and the Paris Peace Conference of 1919

385. At the Versailles Peace Conference, the Supreme Council established 'The Committee on New States and for the Protection of Minorities'. All the new successor states were required to sign minority rights treaties as a precondition of diplomatic recognition as states. It was agreed that although the new states had been recognized, they had not been 'created' before the signatures of the final Peace Treaties. The issue of German and Polish rights was a point of dispute as Polish rights in Germany remained unprotected, in contrast to the rights of German minorities in Poland. However, the Minorities Treaties were ignored by the respective governments, with the system mostly collapsing in the late 1930s. Despite the political failure these treaties remained and provided the basis for the development of international law on the rights of minorities. Therefore, after World War II, the legal principles and protections evolved were incorporated into the UN Charter and reflected in the international human rights treaties.

§3. Minority Rights and International Law

386. Minority rights, as applicable to ethnic, religious or linguistic minorities and indigenous peoples, are now an integral part of international human rights law. Like children's rights, women's rights and refugee rights, minority rights ensure that a specific group which is in a vulnerable, disadvantaged or marginalized position in a particular society, is provided with the necessary support so that it is able to achieve equality and is protected from majority persecution. The first post-war international treaty to protect minorities was the UN Convention on the Prevention and Punishment of Crime and Genocide. Subsequently, the minority rights were codified in the ICCPR (Article 27), the United Nations Declaration on the Rights of Persons belonging to National or Ethnic, Religious and Linguistic Minorities, two Council of Europe treaties (the Framework Convention for the protection of National Minorities and the European Charter for Regional or Minority Languages), and the Organization for Security and Co-operation in Europe (OSCE) Copenhagen Document of 1990.

387. The rights of minorities cover protection of existence, protection from discrimination and persecution, protection and promotion of identity, and participation in political life. For the rights of Lesbian, Gay, Bisexual, and Transgender (LGBT) people, certain principles have been approved by the United Nations Human Rights Council and for the rights of persons with disabilities; the Convention on the Rights of Persons with Disabilities was adopted by the United Nations General Assembly. The UN treated indigenous people as a subcategory of minorities but there is a body of international law specifically devoted to them, in particular Convention 169 of the International Labour Organization and the UN Declaration on the Rights of Indigenous Peoples as adopted on 14 September 2007.

§4. Bilateral Pacts and Treaties

388. Besides multilateral treaties and international conventions, individual countries may enter into bilateral pacts or treaties for the protection of the rights of minorities in their respective territories. In this respect, pacts entered into India and Pakistan after attaining independence and partition of the country are relevant in the Indian context.

I. The Delhi Pact of 1950 Between India and Pakistan: The Nehru-Liaqat Pact

389. The Nehru-Liaqat Pact or Delhi Pact of 1950 was a bilateral treaty between India and Pakistan, by which refugees from both countries were allowed to return unmolested to dispose of their property, abducted women and looted property were to be returned, forced conversions were not to be recognized, and minority rights were confirmed to be protected. The treaty was signed in New Delhi by the Prime

Minister of India and Pakistan on 8 April 1950 and was the outcome of talks sought to guarantee the rights of minorities in both countries after the Partition of India.

390. By this Pact, the governments of the two countries agreed that each shall ensure, to the minorities throughout their respective territory, complete equality of citizenship, irrespective of religion, a full sense of security in respect of life, culture, property and personal honour, freedom of movement within each country and freedom of occupation, speech and worship, subject to law and morality. Members of the minorities shall have equal opportunity with members of the majority community to participate in the public life of their country, to hold political or other offices, and to serve in their country's civil and armed forces.

391. Both governments accepted these rights as fundamental and undertook to enforce them effectively. These rights are guaranteed to all minorities in India by its Constitution, and a similar provision exists in the Objectives Resolution adopted by the Constituent Assembly of Pakistan. The enjoyment of these democratic rights is assured to respective nationals without distinction and the allegiance and loyalty of the minorities is to the State of which they are citizens, and that it is to the government of their own State that they should look for the redress of their grievances.

392. Rights of ownership in or occupancy of the immoveable property of a migrant shall not be disturbed. If, during his absence, such property is occupied by another person, it shall be returned to him provided that he comes back by the 31 December 1950. Where the migrant was a cultivating owner or tenant, the land shall be restored to him provided that he returns not later than the 31 December 1950. In exceptional cases, if a government considers that a migrant's immoveable property cannot be returned to him, the matter shall be referred to the appropriate Minority Commission for advice. Where restoration of immoveable property to the migrant who returns within the specified period is found not possible, the government concerned shall take steps to rehabilitate him.

393. That in the case of a migrant who decides not to return, ownership of all his immoveable property shall continue to vest in him and he shall have unrestricted right to dispose of it by sale, by exchange with an evacuee in the other country, or otherwise. A committee consisting of three representatives of minority and presided over by a representative of government shall act as trustees of the owner. The Committee shall be empowered to recover rent for such immoveable property according to law. The Governments of East Bengal, West Bengal, Assam and Tripura shall enact the necessary legislation to set up these Committees. The Provincial or State Government, as the case may be, will instruct the district or other appropriate authority to provide assistance for the discharge of the Committee's functions. Those who are found guilty of offences against persons and property and of other criminal offences shall be punished. In view of their deterrent effect, collective fines shall be imposed, where necessary. There was also provision for appointment of special courts to ensure that wrongdoers are promptly punished and every possible effort shall be made to recover looted property.

394. The pact also provided that an agency will be set up, with which representatives of the minority shall be associated, to assist in the recovery of abducted women and derecognize forced conversions. Any conversion effected during a period of communal disturbance shall be deemed to be forced conversion. Those found guilty of converting people forcibly shall be punished. A Commission of Enquiry will be set up to enquire into and report on the causes and extent of the disturbances and to make recommendations with a view to preventing the recurrence of similar trouble in future. The personnel of the Commission, presided over by a judge of the High Court, shall be such as to inspire confidence among the minority. Prompt and effective steps shall be taken to prevent the dissemination of news and mischievous opinion calculated to rouse communal passion by press or radio or by any individual or organization. Those guilty of such activity shall be rigorously dealt with.

395. In the Cabinets of East Bengal, West Bengal and Assam, a representative of the minority community is to be included. In order to assist in the implementation of this Agreement, the two governments have decided to set up Minority Commissions, one for East Bengal, one for West Bengal and one for Assam. Each Commission will consist of one minister of the Provincial or State Government concerned, who will be Chairman, and one representative each of the majority and minority communities from East Bengal, West Bengal and Assam, chosen by and from among their respective representatives in the Provincial or State Legislatures, as the case may be. The two Ministers of the Governments of India and Pakistan may attend and participate in any meeting of any Commission. A Minority Commission or any two Minority Commissions jointly shall meet when so required by either Central Minister for the satisfactory implementation of this Agreement.

396. The Commission shall maintain contact with the minorities in districts and small administrative headquarters through Minority Boards formed in accordance with the Inter-Dominion Agreement of December, 1948 (Dominion Agreement). The Minority Commissions in East Bengal and West Bengal shall replace the Provincial Minorities Boards set up under the Dominion Agreement.

397. The functions of the Minority Commission shall be the following:

(a) To observe and report on the implementation of this Agreement and, for this purpose, to take cognizance of breaches or neglect.
(b) To advise an action to be taken on their recommendations.
(c) Each Commission shall submit reports, as and when necessary, to the Provincial and State Governments concerned. Copies of such reports will be submitted simultaneously to the two Central Ministers during the period referred to in E.
(d) The Governments of India and Pakistan and the State and Provincial Governments will normally give effect to recommendations that concern them when such recommendations are supported by both the Central Ministers. In the event of disagreement between the two Central Ministers, the matter shall be referred

to the Prime Ministers of India and Pakistan who shall either resolve it themselves or determine the agency and procedure by which it will be resolved.

Except where modified by this Agreement, The Inter-Dominion Agreement of December 1948 relating to canals in West Punjab shall remain in force except as modified by this Pact.

II. Accord Between India and Sri Lanka, 1987

398. The Prime Minister of India and the President of Sri Lanka signed an agreement on 29 July 1987 at Colombo wherein it was acknowledged that Sri Lanka is a multi-ethnic and multilingual plural society consisting, *inter alia*, of Sinhalese, Tamils, Muslims (Moors) and Burgers and that each ethnic group has a distinct cultural and linguistic identity which has to be carefully nurtured. It was also recognized that the Northern and Eastern Provinces have been areas of historical habitation of Sri Lankan Tamil-speaking peoples, who have lived together in this territory with other ethnic groups.

399. Both countries agreed that the Government of Sri Lanka proposes to permit adjoining Provinces to join to form one administrative unit and also by a referendum to separate as may be permitted to the Northern and Eastern Provinces as outlined in this Agreement. During the period, which shall be considered an interim period (i.e., from the date of the elections to the provincial council, to the date of the Referendum), the Northern and Eastern Provinces as now constituted, will form one administrative unit, having one elected provincial council. Such a unit will have one Governor, one Chief Minister and one Board of Ministers.

400. The Accord also envisaged a referendum to enable the people of the Eastern Province to decide whether:

(a) the Eastern Province should remain linked with the Northern Province as one administrative unit, and continue to be governed together with the Northern Province;
(b) the Eastern Province should constitute a separate administrative unit having its own distinct provincial council with a separate governor, Chief Minister and Board of Ministers. The President may, at his discretion, decide to postpone such a referendum.

401. All persons, who have been displaced due to ethnic violence or other reasons, will have the right to vote in such a referendum. Necessary conditions to enable them to return to areas from where they were displaced will be created. The Referendum, when held, will be monitored by a committee headed by the Chief Justice, a member appointed by the President, nominated by the Government of Sri Lanka, and a member appointed by the President, nominated by the representatives of the Tamil-speaking people of the Eastern Province. A simple majority will be sufficient to determine the result of the Referendum.

402. Elections to provincial councils were to be held. The emergency will be lifted in the Eastern and Northern provinces. A cessation of hostilities will come into effect all over the island within forty-eight hours of the signing of this Agreement. All arms presently held by militant groups will be surrendered in accordance with an agreed procedure to authorities to be designated by the Government of Sri Lanka. Consequent to the cessation of hostilities and the surrender of arms by militant groups, the army and other security personnel will be confined to barracks in camps.

403. The Government of Sri Lanka will utilize for the purpose of law enforcement and maintenance of security in the Northern and Eastern Provinces the same organizations and mechanisms of government as are used in the rest of the country. The President of Sri Lanka will grant a general amnesty to political and other prisoners now held in custody under the Prevention of Terrorism Act (POTA) and other emergency laws, and to combatants, as well as to those persons accused, charged and/or convicted under these laws. The Government of Sri Lanka will make special efforts to rehabilitate militant youth with a view to bringing them back into the mainstream of national life. India will cooperate in the process.

404. The Government of India will underwrite and guarantee the resolutions, and cooperate in the implementation of these proposals. The proposals are conditional to the Government of India cooperating directly with the Government of Sri Lanka in their implementation. These proposals are also conditional to the Government of India taking the following actions if any militant groups operating in Sri Lanka do not accept this framework of proposals for a settlement, namely:

(a) India will take all necessary steps to ensure that Indian territory is not used for activities prejudicial to the unity, integrity and security of Sri Lanka.
(b) The Indian Navy/Coast Guard will cooperate with the Sri Lankan Navy in preventing Tamil militant activities from affecting Sri Lanka.
(c) In the event that the Government of Sri Lanka requests the Government of India to afford military assistance to implement these proposals the Government of India will cooperate by giving to the Government of Sri Lanka such military assistance as and when requested.
(d) The Government of India will expedite repatriation from Sri Lanka of Indian citizens to India who are resident there concurrently with the repatriation of Sri Lankan refugees from TN.
(e) The Governments of Sri Lanka and India will cooperate in ensuring the physical security and safety of all communities inhabiting the Northern and Eastern Provinces.

405. The Government of Sri Lanka shall ensure free, full and fair participation of voters from all communities in the Northern and Eastern Provinces in electoral processes envisaged in this Agreement. The Government of India will extend full cooperation to the Government of Sri Lanka in this regard.

406. Under the Accord, the Indian Peace Keeping Force was inducted into Sri Lanka. In 1990, India withdrew its forces from Sri Lanka, and fighting between the

Liberation Tigers of Tamil Eelam (LTTE) and the government of Sri Lanka resumed. The LTTE and government forces committed serious human rights violations against one another. In January 1995, the Sri Lankan Government and the LTTE agreed to a ceasefire as a preliminary step in a government-initiated plan for peace negotiations. After three months, the LTTE unilaterally resumed hostilities.

407. The government of Sri Lanka then adopted a policy of military engagement with the Tigers, with government forces liberating Jaffna from LTTE control by mid-1996 and moving against LTTE positions in the northern part of the country. An LTTE counteroffensive, begun in October 1999, reversed most government gains and by May 2000, threatened government forces in Jaffna. Heavy fighting continued into 2001. On the eve of the signing of the Indo-Sri Lanka Accord, Rajiv Gandhi was assaulted by Leading Rate Vijitha Rohana at the Guard of Honour. Four years later, in 1991, Rajiv Gandhi was assassinated by an LTTE suicide bomber. This radically reduced support for the LTTE within India. In 2009, the Sri Lankan army mounted a major military offensive in the north and eradicated the LTTE and captured all areas, which were under LTTE.

408. The devolution of limited powers at the provincial level was to establish a power-sharing arrangement between the island's Sinhala and Tamil elites. After defeating the LTTE in 2009, the Sri Lankan Government is attempting to take back the powers granted to the provincial councils, including over police, land and the merger of adjoining councils. The Sri Lankan Government had not adhered to its commitments for a political settlement to the protracted civil war in Sri Lanka.

Chapter 3. Regional Law Effects on Religious Communities

409. There are certain laws, which vary from region to region taking care of specific conditions prevailing in a particular area and their application being restricted to certain areas. Article 371 contains these types of departures relating to the application of the Constitution to the State of Nagaland and Mizoram with respect to local community law. The State of Goa has a personal law code applicable to all the communities. Further, with respect to religious conversions, some States have enacted anti-conversion laws in the name of freedom of religion whereas other States do not have any such law.

§1. Special Provision with Respect to the State of Nagaland and Mizoram

410. Article 371 A of the Constitution contains a special provision with respect to Nagaland which provides that:

(1) Notwithstanding anything in this Constitution:
   (a) no Act of Parliament in respect of:
      – religious or social practices of the Nagas;
      – Naga customary law and procedure;
      – administration of civil and criminal justice involving decisions according to Naga customary law;
      – ownership and transfer of land and its resources, shall apply to the State of Nagaland unless the Legislative Assembly of Nagaland by a resolution so decides.

411. The Governor of Nagaland has special responsibility with respect to law and order in the State of Nagaland for so long as in his opinion internal disturbances occurring in the Naga Hills-Tuensang Area immediately before the formation of that State continue therein or in any part thereof and in the discharge of his functions in relation thereto the Governor shall, after consulting the Council of Ministers, exercise his individual judgment as to the action to be taken. In case any question arises whether any matter is or is not a matter as respects which the Governor is under this subclause required to act in the exercise of his individual judgment, the decision of the Governor in his discretion shall be final, and the validity of anything done by the Governor shall not be called in question on the ground that he ought or ought not to have acted in the exercise of his individual judgment. If the President on receipt of a report from the Governor or otherwise is satisfied that it is no longer necessary for the Governor to have special responsibility with respect to law and order in the State of Nagaland, he may by order direct that the Governor shall cease to have such responsibility with effect from such date as may be specified in the order.

412. As from such date as the Governor of Nagaland may by public notification specify, there shall be established a regional council for the Tuensang district consisting of thirty-five members and the Governor shall in his discretion make rules providing for:

(1) the composition of the regional council and the manner in which the members of the regional council shall be chosen:
  (i) provided that the Deputy Commissioner of the Tuensang district shall be the Chairman ex-officio of the regional council and the Vice-Chairman of the regional council shall be elected by the members from among themselves;
  (ii) notwithstanding anything in this Constitution, for a period of ten years from the date of the formation of the State of Nagaland or for such further period as the Governor may, on the recommendation of the regional council, by public notification specify in this behalf:
    (a) the administration of the Tuensang district shall be carried on by the Governor;
    (b). where any money is provided by the Government of India to the Government of Nagaland to meet the requirements of the State of Nagaland as a whole, the Governor shall at his discretion arrange for an equitable allocation of that money between the Tuensang district and the rest of the State;
    (c) no Act of the Legislature of Nagaland shall apply to Tuensang district unless the Governor, on the recommendation of the regional council, by public notification so directs and the Governor in giving such direction with respect to any such Act may direct that the Act shall in its application to the Tuensang district or any part thereof have effect subject to such exceptions or modifications as the Governor may specify on the recommendation of the regional council;
    (d) the Governor may make regulations for the peace, progress and good government of the Tuensang district and any regulations so made may repeal or amend with retrospective effect, if necessary, any Act of Parliament or any other law which is for the time being applicable to that district:
      – one of the members representing the Tuensang district in the Legislative Assembly of Nagaland shall be appointed Minister for Tuensang affairs by the Governor on the advice of the Chief Minister and the Chief Minister in tendering his advice shall act on the recommendation of the majority of the members as aforesaid;
      – the Minister for Tuensang affairs shall deal with, and have direct access to the Governor on, all matters relating to the Tuensang district but he shall keep the Chief Minister informed about the same.
    (e) notwithstanding anything in the foregoing provisions of this clause, the final decision on all matters relating to the Tuensang district shall be made by the Governor at his discretion.

413. It is clear from above that a wide range of exceptions from the applicability of the Constitution of India is available to certain parts of the State of Nagaland relating to religious practices, social and cultural life, and devolution of property and even with respect to the applicability of penal laws. The general practices and customs have been implemented as a carve-out from general or normal laws applicable in other parts of the country.

414. With respect to the State of Mizoram similar special provision exists in Article 371 G, which is as follows:

(1) Notwithstanding anything in this Constitution:
   (a) no Act of Parliament in respect of:
      – religious or social practices of the Mizos;
      – Mizo customary law and procedure;
      – administration of civil and criminal justice involving decisions according to Mizo customary law;
      – ownership and transfer of land and its resources, shall apply to the State of Mizoram unless the Legislative Assembly of Mizoram by a resolution so decides.

§2. UCC in Goa

415. The Goa Civil Code, collectively called family laws, was framed and enforced by the Portuguese colonial rulers through various legislations in the nineteenth and twentieth centuries. After the liberation of Goa in 1961, the government scrapped all the colonial laws and extended the central laws with the exception of retaining the family laws. The most significant provision in this law is the prenuptial Public Deed regarding the disposal of immoveable and movable property in the event of divorce or death. During matrimony, both parents have a common right over the estate, but on dissolution, the property has to be divided equally. As per this law, sons and daughters have equal rights on the property. The procedure requires compulsory registration of marriage, which effectively checks the menace of child and bigamous marriage.

416. The Family Law of Goa is cited as an example of the Uniform Civil code. However, when examined closely, it is not uniform at all in important matters of marriage and divorce. Actually, it is a misnomer to call it a Uniform Civil Code. It is a Common Civil Code where some provisions are applicable to all but others highly objectionable and discriminatory provisions exist and are applied to different communities.

§3. Law Relating to Conversion in Different States

417. To regulate conversion many states have enacted special laws on religious conversions. The Freedom of Religion Acts, known as ‘anti-conversion laws’, are brought about to curb religious conversions made by 'force', 'fraud' or 'allurement'. But rights groups allege that in reality, the laws obstruct normal conversions as well. Besides, some disgruntled elements also invoke the law with the sole purpose of harassing with spurious arrests and incarcerations. It is also alleged that these laws define 'force', 'fraud' and 'inducement' vaguely, which enables some organizations belonging to a converted individual to levy false charges against individuals and organizations involved in such conversions. They also object that these laws require that all conversions be reported to the government, failing which both the priest and convert can be imprisoned or fined like ordinary criminals.

418. To defend the various anti-conversion laws, a 1977 judgment of the Supreme Court in the *Reverend Stanislaus v. State of Madhya Pradesh*,[77] is important which upholds the Madhya Pradesh Dharma Swatantrata Adhiniyam (Freedom of Religion Act) 1969. According to the verdict, the right to propagate does not include the right to convert another person to the former's faith on the premise that the latter is equally entitled to the freedom of conscience. However, not all in the legal fraternity agree with the judgment. Besides, the 1977 judgment dealt with only one argument, i.e., what entails Christians' right to 'propagate', while there are several other arguments against the legislation that have been looked into by the courts. It is widely believed that the anti-conversion laws enacted by States are brought for political reasons being part of majoritarian vote bank politics and they make conversion not only difficult but also impossible. The object seems to not disturb the demographic composition of the population, and certain critics allege that these laws mainly serve the interest of the community, which is prone to conversion.

77. 1977 AIR 908; 1977 SCR (2) 611.

Part V. Religion and Politics

419. There are four major religious communities in India, namely Hindu, Muslim, Sikh and Christian. From a religious point of view, there are two dominant political ideologies, namely secular and other equating Hinduism with nationalism and now being termed as 'Hindutva'. Some parties project themselves as 'secular' while others call them pseudo-secular and blame that they are indulging in vote bank politics. Secularism in India as understood through judicial decisions and general understanding broadly means equal treatment of all religious groups and provision for special protection to and welfare schemes for religious minorities. However, some sections promote majoritarian nationalism, which sees India as a Hindu nation as more than 79% of the country's 1.4 billion population consists of Hindus, while Muslims and Christians account only for 14.23% and 2.3% of the population, respectively. Dalits among Hindus, who are classified in the Constitution as 'Scheduled Castes', account for 16.2% of the total population. Another cluster of communities is recognized as the 'Other Backward Classes' or OBCs communities, which are socially and educationally backward and come from all religions. According to some estimates, the OBCs account for more than 50% of the country's population.

420. India has religion-based parties registered and recognized by the Election Commission, such as the Muslim League in Kerala state, the All India Majlis-e-Ittehadul Muslimeen in Telangana and Maharashtra states, the Shiromani Akali Dal (SAD, a Sikh party) and its breakaway SAD-S (Simranjit Singh Mann) in the State of Punjab. However, barring the SAD, which remained in power in Punjab state, the other religion-based parties have a small number of representatives in the Parliament or in the State Assemblies.

421. In the Indian way of life, religion plays an important role and is the basis of day-to-day life. It was felt from the beginning that to retain unity in India, it should remain secular. That is why Gandhiji preached brotherhood among the different religious groups. Nehru was also a strong supporter of secularism. However, their efforts could not divorce religion from politics even after independence, rather in politics the vested interests started exploiting and continue to exploit caste and religion for gaining political advantage.

422. Religious places are also sometimes used for political propaganda, and the sentiments of the people are exploited to gain political mileage through winning elections and to take control of the state and its resources. The emergence of religion-based political parties and their agenda polarize the public on communal lines and is a serious threat to the delicate secular fabric of India. Mixing of religion with politics is a dangerous trend because religious attitude is opposed to democratic feelings and practices. Religion may encourage fanaticism and weaken and suspend reasoning power.

423. Democracy demands an open mind, and universal brotherhood and thinking based on reasoning. There are a large number of religions, castes and sub-castes in India, and some of them are opposed to one another as far as their religious practices are concerned. So, there are clear-cut fault lines in the social fabric of India. Religion must remain a private affair, and if it is allowed to be exploited and promoted for political purposes in public affairs, it corrupts politics. So, for the consolidation of democracy, secularism is to be firmly founded and to make its working successful, it is necessary that the people should keep religion separate from politics by changing the attitude of the people. Some voices are raised to make India a Hindu State but no national political party has in its official agenda or public declaration to make India a Hindu State.

Chapter 1. Religion's Influence on Politics

424. Religion influences and has influenced politics in India and sometimes in such a big way that entire elections are swayed by religious sentiments. Religious leaders have enormous followings and acceptability. Not only the people but also some politicians seek their blessings and get declarations and appeals to vote for a particular party. A nationalistic ideology focused on the majority evolved around the twentieth century when India's independence was foreseeable. A section of the majority population believed that freedom from the British alone would not mean real independence unless it resulted in the formation of a nation where the majority community would have dominance. Whereas as a matter of fact in a free democracy only the majority dominates and minorities unless protected are marginalized as they cannot gain political power by any means through elections. Particularly in India where followers of one religion have more than 79% population, no other community can come to power, and the dictate of the majority will always run. If the power of the majority is not regulated and protection is not provided to minorities, it may sometimes result in a tyranny of the majority through the imposing of laws and decisions without taking inputs from the concerned minority community.

§1. Historical Background

425. The roots of the use of religion in Indian politics can be linked to the country's pre-independence era. It is believed that the British, who ruled India for more than 100 years around the nineteenth century, particularly after the First War of Independence in 1857 fought jointly by all religious communities, pitched one community against the other to weaken the resistance against colonial rule. They succeeded in infusing a feeling of anxiety among sections of the minority community, mainly Muslims concerning their well-being in a country that had a majority Hindu population and emerging Hindu nationalist voices. As a result, the Muslims demanded reserved seats in the legislature and a separate electorate. The British acceded to their demands while bringing the Government of India Act, 1909.

426. In 1915, some Hindus formed the Akhil Bharatiya Hindu Mahasabha (All India Hindu Grand Party). In 1923, Vinayak Damodar Savarkar (Veer Savarkar), the Hindu Mahasabha founder, coined the word 'Hindutva' (Hindu-ness) to define who is a Hindu. A pamphlet entitled 'Hindutva: Who is a Hindu?' brought out by Veer Savarkar in 1923 gives a glimpse of Hindu nationalist aspirations. The Hindutva proponents see India as the homeland of the Hindus, who consider the country as their fatherland as well as their holy land. It sought to highlight the historical 'oppression' of Hindus by 'invading forces' like the Muslims and the Christians, calling for 'reversing' of the influence resulting from these 'intrusions'. It also called for the establishment of a 'Hindu nation' to 'protect Hindus and revive the Hindu culture', where religious conversions and cow slaughter would be banned.

427. In 1925, KB Hegdewar, the Hindu Mahasabha Vice President, founded the Rashtriya Swayam Sewak Sangh (RSS). The tensions between the Hindu and Muslim communities resulted in the Indian Muslim League demanding a separate nation for Muslims. When the British were to formally leave the country in 1947, British India was divided into the 'Hindu-majority' India and the 'Muslim-majority' Pakistan. The Partition resulted in a mass migration of 14.5 million people from India to Pakistan and vice versa, and the killing of around 1 million people – Hindu, Sikh and Muslim – in the violent clashes that followed the partition.

428. Some people translate word 'secular' in Hindi language as meaning 'panthnirpeksh', meaning neutrality to different religious sects, but it was 'publicized' as 'dharmanirpeksh', which means neutrality to religion per se. Panth or sect symbolizes devotion towards any specific belief, specific way of prayer and specific form of God, but dharma symbolizes absolute and eternal values, which can never change like laws of nature. Most importantly, the idea of separation of religion is opposed to the thinking of followers of Veer Savarkar, and according to them State must link India's past to its Hindu traditions and Hindu religiosity. In 1951, a political party, the Bharatiya Jana Sangh (BJS), was founded. In 1980, the BJS was succeeded by the Bhartiya Janta Party (BJP). The BJP, which is a national party, adopted a resolution in June 1989 to build a temple of Rama in Ayodhya (in the State of UP), which was claimed as the Ram Janmabhoomi (the birthplace of God Rama). The allegation was that Mughal ruler Babur had demolished a temple of Rama to build the Babri Mosque in Ayodhya in the sixteenth century.

429. On 6 December 1992, the Babri Mosque was demolished. This resulted in incitement of communal violence in several parts of the country, in which numerous people died and also polarized people along religious lines. The allegation is that political parties sometimes make an appeal to vote along religious lines. The media uses the word 'communalism' for this practice, which involves casting the religious minorities of Muslims and Christians in the role of enemies. However, the fact remains that even those political parties, which are perceived as fundamentalist, also emphasize development of all strata of society. This is an example of religion influencing politics. The Supreme Court by its judgment dated 8 November 2019 ruled that putting of idols in the mosque in 1949 and its destruction in 1992 was wrong. However, the whole land where Masjid stood has been given to a Hindu Party and the government was directed to constitute a trust for building the Ram Temple. The court invoked special powers available under the Constitution, to allot to the U.P. Wakf Board a plot of 5 acres of land in Ayodhya for construction of the mosque.

§2. Religion and Election Laws

430. As per the Constitution of India, use of religion is not allowed and religion should not play any role in elections to Parliament and State Assemblies and local Councils. For all elections to central and state legislatures, the electoral rolls are general and common and no person can either be excluded from, or included in, any such roll only on the basis of his or her religion as per Article 225 of the Constitution. To implement this provision of the Constitution, the Representation of the People Act 1951 (RP Act) declares that the use of religion during electioneering will be a 'corrupt practice' vitiating the election of the winning candidate and also makes such use a punishable offence.

431. Under section 8 of the RP Act 1951, a person guilty of offences relating to religion as listed below may be disqualified to contest election for a period of six years:

(a) RP Act 1951, section 125 (using religion for electoral gain).
(b) IPC, sections 153-A and 505 (offences against religion).
(c) Religious Institutions (Prevention of Misuse) Act 1988 (misusing shrines for unlawful activities).
(d) Places of Worship (Special Provisions) Act 1991 (distorting nature of particular shrines).

Promoting or attempting to promote feelings of enmity or hatred between different classes of people in connection with an election on the grounds of religion, race, caste, community or language, is declared by the Act to be an offence punishable with imprisonment up to three years, fine, or both (section 125 of RP Act). This provision applies irrespective of the civil action provided for in section 123 read with section 100.

432. The RP Act 1951 also prohibits use of religion and religion symbol with a view to promoting an aspirant's candidacy for a public election or for adversely affecting the election of another such candidate. The Act empowers the High Courts to declare the election of a winning candidate to be void if he commits, *inter alia*, a 'corrupt practice' (section 100).

433. Indulgence in any of the following acts either for the furtherance of a candidate's election or for prejudicially affecting another candidate's election is a 'corrupt practice' under the Act:

(a) An appeal to vote, or refrain from voting, for any person on the grounds of this religion, race, caste, community or language-ground of his religion, race, caste, community or language (section 129(3)).
(b) Use of or appeal to religious symbols (unless specifically allotted under the Act) (section 122(3)).
(c) Promoting or attempting to promote enmity or hatred between different classes of citizen on grounds of religion, caste, community or language (section 122(3A)).
(d) Propagating the practice or commission of sati or its glorification as defined in the Commission of Sati (Prevention) Act, 1987 (section 122(36)).

Notably, indulgence in any of the above acts will be regarded as a 'corrupt practice' if it is indulged in:

- by the candidate himself; or
- by his agent; or
- by any other person with his or his agent's consent (section 122(3), (3A), (3B)).

I. Judicial Interpretation

434. Various symbols used in elections, speeches and statements made on different occasions have come for examination of the courts to determine if they were within the meaning of 'corrupt practice' as defined by section 122 of the R.P. Act, 1951. Some important rulings are as follows:

- Projecting the duly allotted star symbol as 'Dhruv' (meaning eternal, firm, guide, determined or devoted to religion) did not amount to corrupt practice.[78]
- Depicting the allotted symbol of a rooster as a sacred bird chirping that if she was not served, 'sons of man will suffer eternal miseries' was symbolic of a religious appeal.[79]
- The symbol of 'Om' used in an election had high spiritual efficacy but was of no religious significance.[80]
- The terms 'Hindu' and 'Hindutva' have more than a mere religious connotation and did not, therefore, by themselves fall within the scope of 'corrupt practice' as envisaged by the election law of 1951; and promising to establish a 'Hindu state' in this sense could be 'at best a pious hope'.[81]
- An appeal by the (Non-resident Indian) NRI Sikhs to vote for the 'Panth' was not a 'corrupt practice', since the word seemed to be referring to a particular party, though etymologically it could mean the Sikh religion.[82]
- A statement by a Muslim candidate that his mother was a Hindu was not an appeal to religion.[83]
- A claim by a Muslim candidate that he was better than his adversary as he was opposed to any 'interference with the Shariat law' while his adversary belonged to a party which supported changes in that law, was a 'corrupt practice'.[84]
- The allegation by a Muslim candidate that a Hindu-dominated party was anti-Muslim and a Muslim party was anti-religion did not amount to an appeal in the name of religion.[85]

435. The observations made by the courts in some cases throw light on general thinking about the meaning and scope of 'appeal to religion' as a 'corrupt practice'

78. *Ramanbhai v. Dabhi*, AIR 1965 SC 669.
79. *Slnibh Nath v. Ram Narain*, AIR 1960 SC 148.
80. *Jagdeo Sidhanti v. Pratap Singh*, AIR 1965 SC 183.
81. *Manohar Joshi v. Nitin Bhaurao Patil* (1996) 1 SCC 169; *Ramesh Yeshwant Prabhoo v. Sim Prabhakar Knntc*, AIR (1996) 1 SCC 130; *Bal Thackray v. PK Kunte* (1996) 1 SCC 130.
82. *Kultar Singh v. Mukhtiar Singh*, AIR 1965 SC 141.
83. *Abdul Hussain v. Shamsul Huda*, AIR 1975 SC 1612.
84. *ZB Bukhari v. Brij Mohan Mehra*, AIR 1975 SC 1788.
85. *Ebrahim Sulaiman Sait v. MC Mohammad*, AIR 1980 SC 354.

under the election law. The Supreme Court has observed that it would not be an appeal to religion if a candidate says, vote for him because he is a good Sikh or he is a good Christian or he is a good Muslim, but it would be an appeal to religion if it is publicized that not to vote for him would be against the Sikh religion or against Christian religion or against Hindu religion, or to vote for another candidate would be against a particular religion. It is the total effect of an appeal that has to be borne in mind in deciding whether there was an appeal to religion as such or not.

436. In *Damodar Tatyaba v. Vamanroa Mahadik,*[86] Bombay High Court observed that to take a simple example, the sentence 'garva se kaho Hindu hain' (say with pride we are Hindu) by itself would be innocent. Even a sentence as innocent as above can be a corrupt practice if made at an election time with the intention of furthering the prospect of the election of a candidate or prejudicially affecting the prospect of another on the grounds of religion, caste and/or community. This would necessarily depend on the manner in which it is said and the context in which it is made.

437. An interesting observation was made in *Abdul Hussain v. Sliamsitt Huda,*[87] an election case by Mr Justice VR Krishna Iyer:

> Religion is a terrible Satan in its decadent status when people plunge into spiritual illiteracy, miss the divine essence of the lessons of the sages, prophets and seers and kiss the holy nonsense of 'my religion right or wrong' and 'my religionists alone to me belong'. In this vulgar barbarous degeneracy humanism dies and values of tolerance and compassion perish. In the perverse reversal of higher meanings, the man on earth becomes the blind ammunition of divine rivals in the skies. Be that as it may, religions cannot be wished away or wiped out but surely must be humanized and weaned from cannibalistic habits. Comity of denominations, not a zoo of savage faiths, must be the governing code of religious pluralism in the human world.

438. The fact is that it is the misuse of religion that is prevalent in politics today, and not the use of virtues found in it. What is more unfortunate is that some political parties are, in one way or the other, use religion-related issues for political gains, and even religious leaders are involved in communal politics. This is because religion is a source of identity and a bonding factor in the lives of people, mainly in developing societies like India. There was a hope given the developments after the process of economic liberalization that began in 1991, the mind set will change and public will be more interested in development than being moved by emotion aroused by appeal to religion. The middle class has expanded, the economy is growing and a cosmopolitan culture is emerging in most metropolises. As a result, the people will increasingly become more concerned about development rather than respond to identity-based issues. Unfortunately, things have not moved in this

86. AIR 1991 Bomb. 373.
87. AIR 1975 SC 1612.

desired direction as hoped and for political gains concerted efforts are continue to be made by some elements to line up communities on the basis of religion, caste and creed and even regionalism, and sometimes they succeed.

Chapter 2. Political Influence in Religion

439. Religion is influenced by politics in many ways. Some raise religious issues, particularly in cases where there is a dispute or difference with other communities, to get political benefits. The policy of reservation with respect to Dalit Hindus, the 1950 Order restricting reservation limited to Hindus and later broadening the scope to include Sikhs, Bodhs and Jains, are some of the instances of majoritarian political influence on religion particularly in light of the fact that Muslims and Christians have been left out on the basis that there is no caste system among Muslims and Christians. If this analogy is applied, then there is no caste system in Bodhs, Jains and Sikhs but these have been covered for the purpose of reservation.

440. The policy of affirmative action for the upliftment of the communities that have been discriminated against and marginalized for centuries by the Society is also based on the influence of politics on religion. This exercise of positive discrimination for the benefit of a group of majority community has been highly politicized. The issue which comes up from time to time is that the Dalits who have converted to Christianity or Islam should also enjoy the privileges at par with the Hindu Dalits. As of now, Dalits are de-listed from the Scheduled Castes category after their conversion to Christianity or Islam. There are more than 16 million 'Dalit Christians' in India who have been fighting for the restoration of their rights for decades. According to some critics this policy was initially introduced for ten years but perpetuated, is basically part of vote bank politics and example of political patronage of a particular religion which happens to be the religion of the majority population and to prevent a vulnerable section of Hindu society from conversion to other faiths. The strange development is that to press their demands, the Scheduled Caste communities threaten the government that if their demands are not met they will en masse convert to Islam.

441. On the basis of the policy of reservation and positive action, 15% of the seats in government jobs and educational institutions are reserved for Scheduled Castes and 7.5% for Scheduled Tribes. In addition to the reservation of 22.5% seats (for Dalit and tribal communities together), there is a 27% quota for another cluster of communities, recognized as 'Other Backward Classes' (OBCs). As a result, there is resentment among those belonging to the 'general category'. Many anti-quota groups have protested and continue protesting against the policy. According to an order of the Apex Court, the total quota cannot exceed 50%. The total reservation at present amounts to 49.5% (Dalit, tribal and OBC quota put together). Therefore, if Dalit Christians and Muslims are allowed to be part of the affirmative action, the Scheduled Caste communities will have to share their 15% quota with them. Such a proposition is bound to face opposition from Scheduled Caste communities, which constitute around 16% of the population. There is yet another very important aspect with respect to Dalits that even though they have adopted Christian religion but may not have declared themselves as 'Christians', just to retain their entitlement to reservations, which otherwise they lose. Therefore, once Dalit Christians have the right to affirmative action, the percentage of Christians, which as per the latest government census stands at 2.3%, may increase.

442. The sensitivity of the quota issue can be understood from the demand of the Gujjar community, which is presently classified under the OBC list. Gujjars in Rajasthan state organized shutdowns and protests to demand that they be included in the Scheduled Tribes list. Although OBCs have 27% reservation, the number of OBCs is very high. Therefore, a member of a tribal community has a better chance of being benefited than an OBC member. The government finally had to bow down to their demand and agreed for reservation as a special category but this has been stuck down by the Supreme Court.

443. Even today, many Dalits are subjected to manual scavenging, atrocities and ostracism by Hindus. To protest their place in the Hindu society, thousands of Dalits have converted en masse out of Hinduism to Buddhism and Christianity in the past. It is estimated that more than 65% of the Indian Christians are from Dalit backgrounds.

Chapter 3. Interaction Between Religion and State on a Political and Legal Level

444. The law of countries, which as a matter of policy are based on religious beliefs, is directly influenced by religion. However, in secular countries as well, religion affects certain aspects of law and the State also brings legislation regarding religious affairs. India, a theoretically secular country as per its Constitution, must not have any interference of religion in law making or vice versa except for reformation and regulation. But still, the Hindu Religious and Charitable Endowment Act (HRCE Act) of 1951 was enacted by which State Governments appointed managers to the boards of temples for better administration. This Act allowed the State Governments to take over Hindu temples and maintain control over these temples and their property. The Temple Empowerment Act brought about 34,000 temples under government control in Andhra Pradesh. Only after large public protests, the State Government gave back most of the temples, yet the most profitable ones were kept under state control. The famous sacred temple at Tirumala-Tirupati collects a large sum every year, and the State Government has not denied the charge that as much as 85% of this is transferred to the state exchequer, much of which goes to causes that are not connected with the Hindu community or Vedic temples. At the same time, priests of temples are penniless and temples are decaying due to lack of maintenance, some people allege. Hindu priests do not want to train their children in priestly activities for lack of economic benefits.

445. For the performance of the Haj pilgrimage by Muslims, Haj Committees at Centre and State levels known as Central Haj Committee and State Haj Committees have been formed under the Haj Committee Act, 2002 to manage the affairs of Haj which include the completion of visa formalities for Hajees, their air travel arrangements, stay in Saudi Arabia, the performance of rituals of Haj and return of the Hajees from Saudi Arabia, etc.

446. The Supreme Court in the case of *Syed Intesar Mehdi v. Union of India and Ano.* [(2012) 6 SCC 266] directed the government to gradually reduce the subsidy and abolish it by 2022. In 2018, the government ended the policy of giving subsidy to Muslims heading to the holy city of Mecca to perform the annual Hajj pilgrimage. The minister for Minority Affairs declared that the move was part of 'a policy to empower minorities with dignity and without appeasement'. 'Hajj subsidy funds will be used for the educational empowerment of girls and women from minority communities.' Starting in 1954, the government has for decades offered subsidies amounting to billions of rupees purportedly to poor Muslims wanting to perform Hajj. In 2016, the sum was about INR 75 million, down from about INR 100 million in 2013, according to official data. Actually, Hajj subsidy was a major earner for the national airline and in fact it was Air India that was getting the subsidy. In 2018, after removal of Haj subsidy, elimination of middlemen and 100% online and transparent system of tendering for airfare ensured that there was no unnecessary financial burden on pilgrims.

447. A recent legislation, namely Citizenship (Amendment) Act, 2019, which enables the government to confer citizenship to major communities except Muslims, coming from Pakistan, Afghanistan and Bangladesh under relaxed conditions, is based on religion and is cited as an example of religion influencing legislation. Some religious followers consider their religion and their religious texts as science and law. This belief also causes a lot of problems. In some cases, forms of contraception are illegal, only because religion places importance on procreation. Even if concerned women are extremely impoverished, and cannot feed themselves (let alone a child), and have a large chance of dying due to unsafe birth conditions, they have no choice but to have the baby. In India legislation has been used to bring reforms in various practices prevalent among Hindus, Muslims, Christians, etc. The interaction is also found in matters related to public good and in secular sphere and enjoined by Directive Principles of State Policy as enshrined in the Constitution. The major ones are issues of UCC, Protection of Cow and calves, etc. The law dealing with triple talaq making it a criminal offence is also an example of interaction of state at legal level.

§1. Personal Laws

448. In India there are separate personal laws for Hindus, Muslims and Christians and other smaller communities dealing with matters relating to marriage, divorce, and succession. Side by side, there are also special civil laws meant for the people of all communities subjection to which is optional in matters where such laws exist. However, Article 44 in Part IV of the Constitution dealing with Directive Principals of State Policy which is of not binding nature, says that endeavour shall be made to adopt a UCC throughout the country. Many rights and pressure groups are in favour of a uniform civil code, as they believe Muslim Personal Laws in particular are oppressive for women whereas Muslims contest it. Some nationalistic political parties also advocate for it, but with a different objective. However, some parties and even Apex Court is of the opinion that adoption of a uniform code must be preceded by a national consensus and demand for change must come from the community itself. Issues arising out of the UCC are: what will be the content of the common code, in what areas will it apply and whether religious customs will be exempted from the code.

449. A common Act has been brought to deal with personal laws of all communities dealing with leprosy as ground of divorce, namely the Personal Laws (Amendment) Act, 2019. The Act amends: (i) the Divorce Act, 1869; (ii) the Dissolution of Muslim Marriage Act, 1939; (iii) the Special Marriage Act, 1954; (iv) the HMA, 1955; and (v) the Hindu Adoptions and Maintenance Act, 1956. These Acts contain provisions related to marriage, divorce, and separation of Hindu and Muslim couples. Each of these Acts prescribes leprosy as a ground for seeking divorce or separation from the spouse. The Act removed leprosy as a legal ground for divorce or separation.

I. Uniform Civil Code and Implications

450. The Union Government holds the belief that personal laws rooted in religion are a challenge to the unity of the nation and asserts that the implementation of a Uniform Civil Code (UCC) will promote the integration of India by establishing a shared platform for diverse communities. This stand is not agreed by certain communities who are in the minority and even by Schedule Tribes. The background of the UCC at the time of framing of constitution shows that the issue of UCC was discussed extensively in the constitutional debates. Some members of the Constituent Assembly, including Dr BR Ambedkar believed that a UCC was necessary to promote gender equality, secularism, and national integration. But they favoured voluntary implementation. The dominant view was that the religious laws of different communities should not be tampered with, without their consent. In his address to the Constituent Assembly, Ambedkar expressed that there was no need for concern regarding the potential misuse of state power. He emphasized that the state would not hastily employ its authority in a manner that could be deemed objectionable by various religious communities, including Muslims, Christians, or any other community. The inclusion of UCC in the Constitution was on the premise that it would be implemented at a time when the country was prepared to adopt it with sufficient social acceptance.

A. Directive Principles and Fundamental Rights

451. Part IV of the Indian Constitution lays down 'Directive Principles of State Policy' which are not enforceable by court but are nevertheless fundamental in the governance of the country and the state to apply these principles while making laws. Article 44 of the Constitution (Part IV) provides that the state shall endeavour to secure for the citizens a uniform civil code (UCC) throughout the territory of India. The question is whether in the name of uniformity, religion or religious notions of majority can be imposed on religious minorities. How to harmonize freedom of religion with interference by legislation in basic religious notions or percepts by a legislature composed of majority of followers of one religion. Whether efforts to bring UCC may be like Deen-e-Ilahi as propagated by Akbar, the Mughal Emperor.

452. In the Scheme of the Constitution, the freedom of Religion is a fundamental right enforceable by law whereas UCC is only a Directive Principle, not enforceable by law. So, Directive Principle may be understood in the light of fundamental rights granted and guaranteed by the same Constitution. As a matter of fact, a Directive Principle may not be so interpreted and applied that it obliterates one of the universal fundamental freedoms, i.e., freedom of religion.

453. From the scheme of Constitution as it exists, Directive Principle for UCC is subordinate to freedom of religion and efforts to implement Directive Principles may interfere with freedom of religion and make this freedom subservient or redundant. Besides, the yardstick and rationale for any uniformity must be based on and should emanate from the system of law itself and in consultation with those on whom this will apply. Otherwise, a change may distort the whole system whether it is Hindu law, Muslim law or Christian Law. Any imposition of law on minorities may be taken as majoritarian dominance against the will of a minority groups.

B. Implementation of UCC

1. Arguments in Favour

454. Multiple pleas filed by Muslim women highlight discriminatory practices such as instant divorce (talaq-e-bain), contract marriage (Muta), and short-term marriage to another man in case of divorce (Nikah halala) allowed under Islamic law. However, some critics contrast it with a live-in relationship recognized by the courts as 'akin to marriage' and argue that when a live-in relationship is justified then why to object Muta or Nikah Halala, which confer certain rights to the woman. Sikhs' marriage laws are covered under the Anand Marriage Act of 1909, but they lack provisions for divorce, resulting in Sikh divorces being governed by the Hindu Marriage Act.

455. Adoption laws also vary across different religions, with Parsis, for example, not recognizing adoptive daughters' rights, while an adoptive son only has the right to perform the last rites of the father, but has no other rights of inheritance or maintenance under Zoroastrian practices. Proposals to change the adoption law have been met with opposition from the community.

456. The issue of guardianship of minors is governed by various personal laws, creating distinctions between the guardianship of a minor girl and a boy. The Law Commission's 133rd report titled 'Removal of Discrimination Against Women in Matters Relating to Guardianship and Custody of Minor Children and Elaboration of The Welfare Principle' in 1989, and the 257th report on 'Reforms in Guardianship and Custody Laws in India' submitted in 2015, addressed the issue of equal guardianship by both parents not only concerning roles and responsibilities but also regarding the rights and legal position of the parents. Succession laws have also been challenged in courts on grounds of discrimination, with a pending petition in the Supreme Court seeking a change in the Hindu Succession Act to remove discrimination between heirs of deceased men and deceased women.

Currently, the Hindu Succession Act recognizes the family members of the husband as primary heirs of the deceased wife, with the wife's own parents/siblings being secondary heirs.

2. Arguments Against UCC

457. There are a large number of reasons as to why a UCC should not be applied. UCC will not only infringe on religious rights but also violate Article 14 which provides treatment of different or unequal people differently which in the given situation are the different religious customs and traditions. Treatment of people under different laws leads to violation of public rights since for the same situation, punishment might be different or no punishment at all. India being a vast country with a rich and diverse cultural trait, the manner of practice of religion and worship varies from north to south and east to west. For instance, in the southern part of India, consanguineous marriage is common among Dravidian Hindus while it is not practised among the Hindus of northern India. Polygamy is a crime under Hindu law but in Shariah law, a man can have multiple wives. In Goa, a Hindu may marry a second wife in certain circumstances. Therefore, making a common civil law for a country like India is a tough task.

C. Special Constitutional Provisions for Certain States

458. The Legislature has been sensitive to the diversity of socio-cultural practices as is evident from adoption of the Sixth Schedule which provides for autonomous districts and regions. The district councils have legislative competence to deal with inheritance, succession, marriage and divorce. Article 371 of the Constitution contains special provisions for some states. Ranging from Article 371-A to Article 371-J, this Article provides special concessions for the states of Maharashtra, Gujarat, Nagaland, Assam, Manipur, Andhra Pradesh, Sikkim, Mizoram, Arunachal Pradesh, Goa and Karnataka. The objectives behind the Article 371 granting special provisions are to meet the unique needs of the backward regions of these states, protect the economic and cultural interests of these regions, combat the local challenges and protect the customary laws in these regions.

1. Special Provisions for Nagaland

459. Article 371A was inserted by the Constitution (13th Amendment) Act, 1962 which provides that no Act of Parliament in respect of religious and social practices of the Nagas, Naga customary law and procedure et al shall apply to the state of Nagaland unless the legislative assembly of Nagaland so decides by a resolution. Article 371 A contemplates differential treatment to Nagaland while Articles 371 B – 371 I offer similar exceptions to other States in the northeast because of different social conditions prevalent in these parts.

2. Special Provision for Gujarat and Maharashtra

460. Article 371 also provides special powers to the governors of Gujarat and Maharashtra to create independent development boards for Vidarbha, Marathwada and the rest of Maharashtra and Saurashtra, Kutch and the rest of Gujarat. It gives room to provide more facilities for employment opportunities, vocational and technical education in the state.

3. Special Provisions for Assam

461. Article 371-B empowers the President to include a committee of the elected tribal representatives of the Assam Legislative Assembly for the constitution.

4. Special Provisions for Manipur

462. Article 371-C provides for creating a committee for the constitution and functions of the legislative assembly with the members elected from the hilly regions of the state. The governor will have the responsibility to secure the powers of this committee and the central government can instruct the state government on the administration of the hilly areas.

5. Special Provisions for Andhra Pradesh

463. Under Article 371-D, the President can provide equal opportunities for the local populace in public education and employment. The President can ask the state to create an administrative tribunal to solve all the disputes with regard to appointments and promotions to civil posts in the state. Via Article 371-E, a Central University was established in Andhra Pradesh.

6. Special Provisions for Mizoram

464. Article 371-G says without the consent of the State Legislative Assembly, the Parliament cannot decide on the matters of the religious and social practices of the Mizos, civil and criminal law of the land, land ownership transfer, and customary law procedures.

D. Special Provisions for Arunachal Pradesh

465. Article 371-H gives special powers to the Governor of Arunachal Pradesh, on the directions from the President with regard to the law and order in the state. Though the Governor will consult the Council of Ministers, the governor's decision will be final.

E. Special Provisions for Karnataka

466. Article 371-J provides some special provisions with respect to Hyderabad-Karnataka region. The President gives special responsibilities to the Governor of Karnataka to create a separate board to develop the Hyderabad-Karnataka regions. Every year, a report regarding the working of this board is presented before the State

Legislative Assembly. Equitable funds must be allotted for development of these regions. There will be reservation of seats for the education and vocational training of the students from this region besides reservation in the jobs with the state government for persons hailing from this region.

II. Personal Law in Concurrent List

467. The authority to enact legislation pertaining to personal laws is vested in both the Parliament and state Assemblies. The personal laws find place in the Concurrent List on which both Centre and State can legislate. The inclusion of personal law in the Concurrent List (entry No. 5) seems to be motivated by the desire to maintain legal diversity. If the primary concern had been the establishment of uniformity in laws, personal laws would have been kept in the Union List, granting exclusive jurisdiction to Parliament. In January 2023, the Supreme Court upheld the constitutional jurisdiction of states to establish committees to examine the implementation of the Uniform Civil Code. The Uttarakhand government's move to set up such a committee was deemed permissible by the court. In March 2023, the Supreme Court stated that Parliament should decide issues related to the UCC, emphasizing that courts should not direct the legislature to enact laws. The Government of Uttarakhand has brought a legislation on UCC.

III. Religious Freedom

468. The UCC could infringe upon religious freedom and clash with religious practices. Since India is a diverse nation with diverse cultures so different communities should have the right to maintain their distinct culture, customs and practices. The main contention against the implementation of the UCC is its likely infringement of the constitutional right to freely exercise one's religion. This right enables religious communities to adhere to their respective personal laws. This is embodied in Article 25, which grants each religion, the entitlement to autonomously administer its internal matters. Article 29 safeguards their prerogative to preserve their unique cultural heritage. Applying the principle of 'one nation, one law' to personal laws of communities would not be a good idea, as even codified civil laws and criminal laws, such as the Code of Criminal Procedure (CrPC) and the Indian Penal Code (IPC), do not adhere to this principle. The variation in the law of anticipatory bail across different states is an example.

IV. Tribal Customs and Practices

469. In 2016, the Rashtriya Adivasi Ekta Parishad, an organization purporting to advocate the interests of the Adivasi community and representing a population of approximately 110 million tribals, initiated legal proceedings in the Supreme Court with the objective of safeguarding their cultural traditions and religious practices. This included the preservation of their rights to engage in polygamy and polyandry.

According to the Parishad, the Adivasis possess distinct personal laws and are not classified as Hindus due to their practice of nature worship instead of idol worship and their observance of burial rituals for the deceased. The marriage and death rituals observed by tribal communities differ from Hindu customs, and there is concern that these practices may also face prohibition if a uniform civil code is imposed.

470. In the 2018 paper, the Law Commission noted that certain tribes in Meghalaya are 'matriarchate, that is, they follow a female line of descent and property is inherited by the youngest daughter. Among the Garos, the son-in-law comes to live with his wife's parents'. Among certain Naga tribes, women are not allowed to inherit property or marry outside of the tribe. These differences in cultural practices would also have to be considered when it comes to drawing up a Uniform Civil Code. Polygamy and polyandry are also permitted in certain tribal practices protected under the Constitution.

V. Judicial Verdicts and UCC

471. At present, matters including marriage, divorce and succession, are governed by religion-based personal laws. It is argued that the Uniform Civil Code (UCC) will provide for a uniform legal framework for all citizens, irrespective of their religion, race, caste or community. In the *Kesavananda Bharati* case (1973) Chief Justice SM Sikri conceded that 'no Court can compel the Government to lay down a uniform civil code'. However, pointed out that a UCC 'is essentially desirable in the interest of the integrity, and unity of the country'. In *Mohd. Ahmed Khan v. Shah Bano Begum* (AIR 1985 SC 945) the Hon'ble Supreme Court observed that a universal civil code would support the cause of national integration by doing away with different loyalties to legislation that have contradictory philosophies.

472. In *Maharshi Avadhesh v. Union of India* (1994 SCC Supl. (1) 713) the Supreme Court dismissed the petition by the petitioner to introduce a uniform civil code on the grounds that matters relating to drafting a new law are matters of the legislature. In *Sarla Mudgal v. Union of India* (1995 AIR 1531), the court in its judgment held invalid, the practice of converting to another religion to have a second marriage but did not dissolve the second marriage. In *Pannalal Bansilal v. State of Andhra Pradesh* (1996 AIR 1023), the court held that 'a uniform law, though is highly desirable, enactment thereof in one go perhaps may be counter-productive to unity and integrity of the nation'. In another case of *John Vallamattom v. Union of India* (Writ Petition (Civil) 242 of 1997), the court held that Articles 25 and 26 protect only those practices which are integral parts of a religion.

473. Thus, the Supreme Court has time and again expressed unhappiness with the fact that there is not a single set of personal laws for everyone in the country. It has been pointed out by the Courts that UCC is important for national integration and equality of genders and religions. The personal laws based on religion can sometimes lead to discriminatory practices, especially against women. Another argument is that a common civil code would reinforce the principles of secularism.

The implementation of the UCC will make legislation in terms of succession and divorce easier and will oust a lot of outdated religious personal laws.

474. In 2020, a PIL was filed in the Supreme Court seeking gender-neutral and religion-neutral uniform grounds of succession and inheritance for all Indian citizens. The PIL quoted a judgment of the Supreme Court in *Jose Paulo Coutinho v. Maria Luiza Valentina Pereira* where the court referred to Goa as a 'shining example' as it has the Uniform Civil Code applicable to all, irrespective of religion (*Ashwani Kumar Upadhyay v. Union of India, 2023 Live Law (SC)143)*

However, in this case, the Union Government asked the Supreme Court to dismiss all the PILs seeking Uniform Civil Code. The government argued that Courts cannot direct the legislature to enact a bill or law.

VI. Common Civil Code in Goa

475. A Common Civil Code is in place in Goa which is referred to as a shining example time and again. The Goa Daman and Diu Administration Act of 1962, was passed after Goa joined India as a territory in 1961. It gave Goa permission to apply the Portuguese Civil Code of 1867, subject to amendment and repeal by the appropriate legislative body. Goa is the only state where a Common Code has been in operation for many years. However, when it is closely examined, it is flawed and not uniform at all in important matters of marriage and divorce. Actually, it is a misnomer to call it a Uniform Civil Code. It is a Common Civil Code where some provisions are uniformly applicable to different religious communities but others are highly objectionable and provide different treatment for different communities.

A. Uniformity

476. The Code permits equitable distribution of wealth and income between husband and wife as well as between offspring (regardless of gender). Every birth, marriage, and death must be registered voluntarily. Muslims who register their marriages in Goa are prohibited from engaging in polygamy and triple talaq. Consent of men and women is required before marriage. All assets and wealth owned or obtained by each spouse throughout a marriage are kept jointly by the pair. In case of a divorce, each spouse is entitled to one-half of the property, and in case of death, the surviving spouse receives one-half of the property. Wife and husband jointly own the asset in property proceedings, but the husband has the authority to administer the asset. However, he cannot sell the house without the approval of his wife. Property is equally split between the couple, but this works only for those whose marital families have property of their own. This means that if a woman's husband does not have ownership rights in the property, the division of such property at the time of divorce would mean that the woman gets half of nothing.

477. Children cannot be completely disinherited by their parents. The children must inherit at least half of their possessions. The children must divide this inherited property evenly. As per the Goa Succession, Special Notaries and Inventory Proceeding Act, 2012, the distribution of property among the heirs is equal. The male and female heirs both have the right to inherit the property and no distinction is made. However, the Goa code allows for a prenuptial agreement which can alter the ratio of the distribution of assets.

B. Discriminatory Provisions for Different Religious Groups

478. There are some highly objectionable and unequal provisions for different communities. The following examples and discussion explain the objectionable and unequal nature of the Civil Code of Goa. Under this Code Catholics enjoy certain privileges, such as exemption from marriage registration and the Catholic priests have authority to dissolve marriages. Catholics can solemnize their marriages in church after obtaining a No Objection Certificate (NOC) from the Civil Registrar. For others, only a civil registration of the marriage is accepted as proof of marriage. If marriage is not consummated, a church tribunal may declare it null and void. A divorce granted by the ecclesiastical (Church) authorities is treated as a valid divorce for civil purposes. Catholics marrying in the church are excluded from divorce provisions under the civil law. However, non-Christians must obtain a divorce through the courts, and they cannot do so on the grounds that the marriage has not been consummated.

479. One of the objectionable provisions of the Code is which enables a particular type of polygamy for Hindus linked to the birth of a child that too of a particular sex. The law grants an exception to a Hindu man to marry once again if his wife doesn't conceive a child by the age of 25 or a male child by the age of 30. Code does not extend the Shariat Act to Muslims living in Goa, who are instead subject to both Portuguese law and Shastric Hindu law. A non-Hindu man must divorce his wife in order to remarry, which has led males to engage in clandestine relationships and abandon their dependent wives. If a woman believes that her own law is the only source for marriage and divorce, the law isolates her since it will not recognize her divorce and will thus prevent her from being married again.

480. In terms of gender, a man is entitled to a divorce if his wife has an affair. However, a woman can only obtain a separation on grounds of her husband's infidelity if it has resulted in a public scandal and a divorce if he brings his mistress into their marital residence. Followers of any religion can divorce someone for any reason, with the exception of Hindus, who can only get a divorce if their wife has committed adultery. The law has inequalities in case of adopted and illegitimate children.

481. The Special Marriage Act governs marriages between persons from different religions. This law is applicable throughout India and governs the divorce of such marriages and succession as well. However, in Goa, this Act applies differently. The property owned by each spouse is equally divided among the spouses during the course of the marriage. In case of divorce, each spouse is entitled to half of the property and in the case of death of both spouses, the property is equally divided among the surviving members.

C. Goa Has a Common Civil Code and Not a Uniform Civil Code

482. So, it seems a misconception that Goa has a Uniform Civil Code. In fact, Goa has adopted a common civil code and not a uniform civil code. 'Uniform' means uniformity for all despite being of any religion, race, caste, sex and age. Goa Civil Code prohibits bigamy for all other religions except for Hindus. The Hindu men have the right to bigamy under specific circumstances mentioned in Codes of Usages and Customs of Gentile Hindus of Goa (if the wife fails to deliver a child by the age of 25, or if she fails to deliver a male child by the age of 30). Such privilege particularly given to men of Hindu religion and prohibition for men of other religions clearly may not go well as part of a uniform civil code.

Roman Catholics can solemnize their marriages in church after obtaining a No Objection Certificate from the Civil Registrar. Whereas for others, only a civil registration of the marriage is accepted as proof of marriage. The Catholics marrying in the church are excluded from divorce provisions under the civil law. For any other religion, divorce can be taken on any of the valid grounds but there is an exception for Hindus, divorce is permitted only on the grounds of adultery by the wife. One more point that draws a line of differentiation is that the law has inequalities in case of adopted and illegitimate children.

In view of the fact that Goa is a very small state with 1.59 million population, it should not be a model or even a starting point for making a Uniform Civil Code for a population of 1.4 billion with people of different religions, beliefs, tribals, etc.

1. UCC and Hindu Undivided Family (HUF)

483. Under the Income Tax Act, an HUF is treated as a 'person' and is assigned a separate entity for tax purposes. Under Hindu Law, an HUF is a family which consists of all persons lineally descended from a common ancestor including their wives and unmarried daughters. An HUF cannot be created under a contract, it is created automatically in a Hindu Family. Jain and Sikh families even though are not governed by the Hindu Law, are treated as HUF under the Act. An HUF has its own PAN and files tax returns independently of its members. Muslims and Christians are not covered under this scheme and cannot claim any benefit of taxation.

484. Implementation of UCC may affect taxpayers who use HUF for tax planning. After its implementation, the concept of HUF may cease to exist which has implications for individuals and corporates in terms of tax benefits. HUF can claim tax deductions, exemptions, and other benefits available to individuals and businesses. HUF income is taxed separately from the individual income of its members. Once UCC is implemented, tax benefits associated with the HUF would no longer be applicable, which would force many taxpayers to rework their income tax planning. It will increase the tax outgo of the people who have been hitherto using HUF for tax planning.

485. The number of HUFs availing tax benefits under the Income Tax Act stood at almost 8.76 lakh in 2022–2023. While there were more than 9.25 lakh HUFs who availed tax benefits in 2020–2021, this number dropped to around 8.77 lakh in 2021–2022 and further to a little under 8.76 lakh families last year. The impact on the tax treatment under UCC has not yet been examined. Responding to a query on whether the Government has assessed the impact of UCC on tax benefits to HUFs in the country, the Minister of State for Finance said there has been no such assessment 'as there is no such Code at present'. (The Hindu, 26 May 2023)

a. Impact of Withdrawal of HUF Benefits

486. Apart from tax implications, it could also impact succession planning and the division of ancestral property within Hindu families. Currently, the HUF being a separate tax unit enjoys a separate tax exemption limit and various tax breaks under sections 80C, 80D, 80DDB, and 112A of the Income Tax Act. The income tax slab for HUF is the same as that for individuals. HUFs also qualify for tax benefits on capital gains and enjoy exemptions in this regard. Amendments to the Income Tax Act would likely be required if no specific provisions similar to the 'Kerala Joint Hindu Family System (Abolition) Act, 1975' are made in the UCC. This would mean that Hindus would no longer be entitled to claim any interest in ancestral property by birthright.

487. The HUF as a tax unit is not of recent origin. This was already there in the Income Tax Act, of 1922, the predecessor of the present Income Tax Act of 1961, under which also it has been continued. Finance Act 2023 provided that from FY 2023–2024, the HUF can avail the benefit of enhanced basic exemption of up to INR 3 lakh under the new tax regime u/s 115BAC of the Income Tax Act, 1961. The threshold limit of INR 1.5 lakh under section 80C of the IT Act pertaining to various investment-linked deductions such as tax-saving FDs, and equity-linked savings schemes applicable in the case of HUF would be in addition to the threshold limit enjoyed by the members. HUF provides a structured manner for the purpose of transferring wealth to the next generation by ensuring the interest and basic requirements of the family members are provided for and also as a structure to achieve tax optimization at the family level. Removal of tax benefits will result in increase of tax outgo of people using HUF for tax planning.

488. One alternative can be introduction of a HUF-like framework for each religion. Removing the present HUF tax benefits could substantially increase revenue for the state and end the preferential tax structure. But the removal of the HUF structure and its benefits needs to be assessed in the larger context of its impact on financial planning, tax efficiency and the social cohesion of Indian households. First, the HUF enables Hindu family members to pool their financial resources in their common family property, which provides a safety net during financial hardships. It also facilitates effective risk mitigation and promises investment options. HUF is an invaluable instrument to plan for inheritance and a support system for family members with any bereaved male member. It is also a boon to small businesses because ownership remains with the family and the corpus can be utilized for business expansion.

489. HUF tax benefits encourage and support the joint family system and foster familial harmony and unity. With the supplemented tax advantages, it recognizes the significance of 'collective economic activities' in the family. Phasing out the HUF tax structure or the available benefits will be a disincentive to the joint family system. Without tax benefits, families may be more inclined to opt for individual taxation, resulting in the fragmentation of family assets and weakened family bonds. The government must not strike out the HUF concept or its supplemental tax benefits and create a structure similar to the HUF so as to benefit all religions. In order to extend the benefits of a HUF structure to every religion, the government may change the term 'Hindu Undivided Family' to 'Undivided Family'. Treating HUF as a non-religious-centric beneficial family structure, UCC may ensure social welfare and economic stability to all regardless of religion. Simultaneously, it will also dispel the arguments of the Right to Equality embodied under Articles 14–16 against the preferential treatment of only Hindus by guaranteeing equality before the law to all within the territory of India.

§2. The Uniform Civil Code of Uttarakhand Act, 2024

490. The Uttarakhand government has passed Uttarakhand UCC Act 2024 (Act) on 7 February 2024. The Act applies not only to the whole of Uttarakhand but also to residents of the State who are living outside its territories. The Act encompasses provisions as to the registration of marriages and live-in relationships, polygamy, and certain extrajudicial divorce practices. Additionally, the bill addresses issues related to guardianship, adoption, and the legitimacy of children born out of wedlock or live-in relationships. The UCC prohibits practices such as polygamy, halal, iddat, triple talaq, and child marriage across all religious communities. The new law also makes compulsory the registration of not just marriage but also divorce. Further, Iddat which is observed by Muslim women after divorce to determine the paternity of the child in the womb, if any, has been dispensed with. It is a clear interference in religion. It is strange that the Act excludes Scheduled Tribes as some tribes in Uttarakhand practice polyandry.

§3. Conversion and Role of State

491. Swami Dayananda Saraswati, an eminent Hindu philosopher and the founder of the Arsha Vidya Hindu study centres in the U.S., has said that every conversion is an 'act of violence'. In an open letter to Pope John Paul II in 1899, Saraswati said conversion would ultimately lead to the destruction of the entire Indian culture. 'Religion and culture are not often separable', he wrote. 'This is especially true of the Hindu religious tradition. [For instance,] the greeting word, namaste, is an expression of culture as well as religion.' He also referred to the bindi, a mark worn by women on their foreheads. 'Even though a … mark on the forehead is purely religious, it is looked upon as an integral part of Hindu culture.' He said culture often disintegrated after conversion, 'leaving only dead monuments'. In other words, some converts still followed cultural traditions but abandoned the religious meaning behind these traditions.

In India, several States have limited the scope of conversion, particularly mass conversions through various enactments, regulations and a vetting process so as to protect and maintain public order. These laws were made assuming and looking into the vulnerability of group converts, especially women, lower castes, and tribal. States took the view that conversions are being done through allurement and coercion, not through personal choice.

§4. Politics and Religious Personalities

492. In the southern state of Kerala, the State Government has launched a massive crackdown against 'fake' spiritual gurus. The Government of Kerala, which has been alleged to be at loggerheads with Christians over the issue of autonomy of educational institutions run by Christian groups, is also investigating the head of the Believers Church in India and the leader of US-based evangelical organization Gospel for Asia. Religious groups allege that the atheist government is also targeting genuine religious and spiritual leaders under the pretext of the fake Godman controversy. Recently a number of religious gurus have been apprehended for various offences. These offences are committed in Ashrams, madrasas and other religious places. Actually, these gurus, Imams and others related to religion have sometimes vast followings and political parties try to get their blessing so that their followers may vote *en bloc* for their candidates.

§5. Failure of Enforcement Machinery

493. The connection between Islam and Christianity in India goes back centuries. Islam initially came and was introduced in India by Arab traders in the western coastal area and thereafter by attackers from the north. Christianity came to India with the arrival of Apostle Thomas in the port of Cranganore near Cochin in Kerala a long time ago in AD 52. It is believed that Thomas established at least seven churches in Kerala before he moved on to neighbouring TN state, where he was killed for preaching Christianity. Despite this old connection and existence, there has been violence against both Christians and Muslims and law enforcement failed to prevent it. At least 200 incidents of anti-Christian attacks, including four murders, had been recorded before an unprecedented spate of violence erupted in Orissa state's Kandhamal district during Christmas week in 2007. The Orissa attacks show the extent of suffering, which can be caused by communal violence in the country. Similarly in Hindu-Muslim communal violence hundreds of people have been killed and property worth millions has been destroyed. There has been mob violence in the form of lynching of Muslims and scheduled caste people in the name of cow protection or even otherwise.

§6. Misuse of Law Against Certain Minorities

494. India has the world's third-largest Muslim population and the community has made commendable contributions in nation-building as well as in defending the country against foreign aggression. In 1992 the Babri Masjid was destroyed leading to widespread rioting. There have also been attacks on Christians with the allegation that they promote conversion by dubious means. In 1984, there was widespread rioting against Sikhs after the killing of Mrs Indira Gandhi.

495. A terrorist group, Harkat ul-Jihad-e-Islami, allegedly launched eight bomb attacks killing dozens of people and injuring hundreds in Rajasthan's capital Jaipur on 13 May 2008. Reacting to the attacks, at that time demand was made for an anti-terror law such as the POTA of 2002, which was revoked as a draconian law by the United Progressive Alliance (UPA) in 2004. When in force, the law was grossly misused to target Muslims. The Gujarat Government registered 287 cases, mostly against Muslims, under the POTA in 2003 – a year after more than two thousand Muslims were killed in an incident of large-scale communal violence in the state.

496. On 20 December 2019, there were widespread protests after Friday prayers against Citizenship Amendment Act, 2019 throughout India and particularly in the state of UP. The Chief Minister of UP declared that the property of those found guilty of indulging in violence would be seized to compensate for damage to public property. The UP government issued notices to alleged vandals, even before guilt had been proven, to pay damages or face the seizure of their properties. According to some legal experts, it lacks any backing of the law. The UP administration has also warned that defaulting on the payment would result in the attachment of the properties. Senior Supreme Court advocate Sanjay Hegde said 'confiscation of property is normally after a criminal trial. So, this kind of action seems to be legally suspect and would be subject to further legal challenges. He added that it appeared that, 'the (UP) administration is going ahead nevertheless just as a measure to curb dissent'. Hegde further said that 'normally provisions for forfeiture of property are only after the end of a criminal trial. So, there cannot be any ipso facto confiscation'.

497. Another senior advocate termed the action blatantly illegal. 'This is grossly unconstitutional and illegal because it is not supported by any law and it results in pre-judging people without even the benefit of a fair trial.' He viewed that the action was being taken merely on the basis of an allegation. 'It is particularly pernicious in this case because there is a serious allegation that a lot of the violence was instigated by third parties. In fact, it was also alleged that it was perpetrated by the police themselves.' The senior advocate insisted that 'there are also Youtube videos which show the police destroying public and private property – so to impose demands on people to pay so-called reparations is grossly unconstitutional, completely immature and illegal'. Questioning the action when 'they have not even investigated anything' he said, the UP Government was acting like the 'judge, jury and hangman'. 'It has already decided that somebody is guilty and on that basis has issued demands, at least that is what one has read.'[88]

498. International Religious Freedom Report, 2023 (by US Commission International Religious Freedoms (USCIRF) highlights concern regarding certain laws and policies in the country that have been criticized for their potential to discriminate on the basis of religion. These include laws related to conversion, interfaith relationships, hijab, and cow slaughter, as well as the Citizenship (Amendment) Act, 2019 and the National Register of Citizens (NRC) All of these, it alleges, have not impacted minorities in a favourable way. It also raises concerns about alleged measures that may have impacted critical voices, particularly those belonging to religious minorities. These include surveillance, harassment, property demolition, and detention under the Unlawful Activities Prevention Act (UAPA), 1967. Some Non-Governmental organizations (NGOs) have also been subject to scrutiny under the Foreign Contribution Regulation Act (FCRA), 2010. USCIRF has been recommending India's designation as a country of particular concern since 2020 but it hasn't been accepted by the US government so far.

499. USCIRF is an independent, bipartisan US federal government commission, dedicated to defending the universal right to freedom of religion or belief abroad. It is an advisory body to the US Congress, headquartered in Washington DC. Established by the US government after the inaction of the International Religious Freedom Act (IRFA), 1998 the recommendations of USCIRF are non-binding on the state department. IRFA provides that US policy includes condemning violations of religious freedom and assisting other governments in the promotion of this right.

India does not recognize the view of USCIRF and has rejected the recommendations of the US Commission on International Religious Freedom's (USCIRF) 2023 report, calling it biased and motivated.

88. Gaurav Vivek Bhatnagar, No Legal Backing for UP Govt's Action Against Property of Rioters: Lawyers, 27 December 2019, The Wire https://thewire.in/law/uttar-pradesh-protest-property, accessed on 7 Jan. 2020.

Part VI. Labour Law Within Religious Communities

500. Temples, mosques and churches individually and institutions like hospitals, religious societies and charitable institutions, all of them taken together form a big chunk of employers after the state. The Hindus, Muslims, Christians and other religious communities see themselves as a community under God or presiding deity. Religious places and religious persons are considered to reflect and actively live common ideals and convictions identifying right from wrong. The work in temples, mosques and churches is regarded not just as individual work or employment but as duty for a common and religiously defined good and for carrying on the goal of the community. These religious places therefore usually do not speak of employers and employees in respect of the work in their institutions but use other terms such as service-giver and service-taker, pastor, pujari (priest) Imam (one who leads the prayer in the mosque) and muezzin's (one who gives call for prayer), Granthi (keeper of Guru Granth Sahib), Sevadars (Sikhs doing service in Gurdwara), etc.

501. In a religious body, acceptance and non-acceptance by the people of the views, teachings, and ways of life, and conduct and behaviour of each of the members and staff of the religious community is of core relevance to other members and staff within the community and for the religious body. Further, the success of religious activity by those working for religious bodies depends at its very core on the credibility of the religious community in their words and in their deeds. Any compromise of the teaching, required by the religious community by any of its employees falls back on the community itself and the religious body has to answer that. This is, even more, the case when an employee compromising these teachings holds an important and publicly visible position within the religious community and among its employees, but it also applies to any other staff member of the religious community. Therefore, labour law no doubt plays a role but the same is limited as the employed themselves do their duty to get spiritual satisfaction rather than considering it an opportunity solely for winning their bread and butter.

Chapter 1. Scope of Application of Labour Law

502. The religious places and institutions have a variety of rules of their own dealing with the terms of employment of personnel kept by them for secular and religious services. For the large majority of employees in the service of a religious community, normal state labour laws in principle should apply. It is, however, modified in many circumstances, on the basis of the religious community's right to self-determination of their religious regulations applied to their religious institution. Since in every religion there is a provision for service such employees may not insist on strict compliance with the labour laws and the State may also avoid scrutiny of labour law applications. In India, the employees of religious places are not organized so even otherwise they are not in a position to insist on compliance. Freedom of religion demands that the special conditions and circumstances that result from the religious duties of religious institutions and places must be taken into consideration when examining the status of labour.

503. Religious self-regulation is enjoyed by all religious places and institutions and is guaranteed within the constitutional and legal limits of general application. In interpreting the scope of self-determination the religious community's conception of itself is of special importance, particularly when deciding on loyalty obligations of employees. However, no one may be discriminated against because of reasons of race, ethnicity, gender, religion or belief, etc., in the field of profession and employment, social security or education, or access to social benefits, health services or goods and services open to the public including housing facilities. However, in India in religious places, male employees are generally employed with a certain exception. A different treatment because of religion or belief is prevalent in view of the employment by a religious place, body or institution.

504. A religious body, employee or their organizations owe a particular obligation of loyalty to their employer. It is the religious community itself that, within the framework of the notion of public order, good faith, and prohibition of arbitrary action, determines the contents of these obligations and enters into labour agreements. The religious communities' right to self-regulation allows them, within the limits of the law to regulate internal working conditions according to their own terms and to make obligatory specific duties of their employees. As to which basic duties of the religious community are important as part of the terms of employment is decided according to the organized religious community's own standards. In cases of dispute, the labour courts have to respect the standards of the religious community in assessing the contractual obligation of loyalty, insofar as the law recognizes the right of the religious community to determine the matter internally. It is left to the organized religious community to decide what is required for the credibility of the religious community and its teaching, what the specific duties are, what constitutes essential principles of faith and morality, and what is to be considered contrary to these norms which may be applicable to the employee.

Chapter 2. Religious Ministers, Priests, Imams, Etc., and Labour Law

505. The religious ministers, priests, imams, granthis, etc., lead the performance of religious rituals and services in religious places. It is left to the religious communities and their autonomous decision in which form and institutional linkage within the framework of law, they intend to establish and operate their institutions with respect to the employment of persons for carrying on the religious and other functions. The religious communities act in the secular sphere, as in the case of employment, for religious reasons. Termination of a contract by the religious employer because of gross misconduct in view of the religious teaching of the employing community is regarded as an act based on the freedom of religion of the religious employer. Therefore, the right of religious entities to self-regulation and non-interference and the right of the religious communities to organize their activities including the developing and keeping of an internal organizational structure is considered the internal matter of such communities.

506. The religious body can give notice to an employee when the employee in his or her public way of life publicly expresses opinions, contrary to the teachings of the specific religious community. These basic principles are implemented in applying the general secular labour law by the state, and while interpreting and applying the secular general labour law, the courts have to take into account the self-understanding of the religious communities in balancing the rights and obligations of the employees and the employers.

507. Upon being employed, the employee in his or her individual labour contract with the religious employer, may sign in addition to other general terms and conditions, a promise of loyalty to the teaching and moral standards of his or her employer. This is the individual basis on which the labour relationship rests and from which individual rights and duties result. If problems arise in this relationship, this may result finally in the termination of the labour contract by the employer, which is a religious body. In cases where there is a legislation regulating the activities, the relevant provisions of legislation shall apply as can be seen from the application of Wakf's Act.

§1. Employment Rights of Imams and Muazzins in Mosques

508. The issue of employment rights of Imams in mosques has arisen in a case related to mosques covered under the Wakfs Act. There are a large number of other mosques, which are managed by local mosque committees but not covered under the Wakfs Act. These committees appoint Imams on an oral agreement to carry on the duties of Imam. It is incumbent on mosque committees to ensure that any such agreement reflects the status of the Imam. Employing Imams enables the management committee to control activities within the mosques, such as the content of the khutbah (sermon), which may be desirable in the political climate of a given time and ensuring that anything against the law is not preached or done in the mosque.

An Imam performs the duty of offering prayer for the congregation in mosques where Muslims perform prayer like the rites performed in the church that are important and integral to the function of many churches. However, confession, penitence and confirmation do not exist and are not practised in mosques.

509. The Supreme Court of India in the case of *All India Imam Organizations and Others v. Union of India and Others*[89] observed that the objective and purpose of every mosque being community worship and it being the obligation of the Wakf Board under the Wakf Act to ensure that the objectives of the wakf are carried on. It is not correct to say that the Board has no control over the mosque or Imam. 'In the absence of any provision in the Act or the rules providing for the appointment of Imam or laying down condition of their service is probable because they are not considered as employees. At the same time, it cannot be disputed that due to changes in social and economic set-up, they too need sustenance. The nature of their job is such that they may be required to be present in the mosque nearly for the whole day. There may be some who may perform the duty as part of their religious observance or may be ordained by the community to do so. But there are a large number of such persons who have no other occupation or profession or service for their livelihood except doing duty as Imam. Should they be paid any remuneration and if so how much and by whom?

510. 'According to the Board, they are appointed by the mutawallis (caretakers) and, therefore, any payment by the Board was out of question. Prima facie it is not correct as the letter of appointments issued in some States are from the Board. But assuming that they are appointed by the Mutawallis as the Mutawallis too u/s 36 of the Act are under the supervision and control of the Board. The right to life enshrined in Article 21 means right to live with human dignity. It is too late in the day, therefore, to claim or urge that since Imams perform religious duties they are not entitled to any emoluments. Whatever may have been the ancient concept but it has undergone change and even in the Muslim countries mosques are subsidized and the Imams are paid remuneration. Therefore, it cannot be said that in our set up or in absence of any statutory provision in the Wakf Act the Imams who look after the religious activities of mosques are not entitled to any remuneration. Financial difficulties of the institution cannot be above fundamental rights of a citizen. If the Boards have been entrusted with the responsibility of supervising and administering the Wakf then it is their duty to harness resources to pay those persons who perform the most important duty namely of leading community prayer in a mosque the very purpose for which it is created.'

'Imams perform the duty of offering prayer (Namaz) for congregation in mosques. Essentially the mosque is a centre of community worship where Muslims perform ritual prayer and where historically they also gathered for political, social and cultural functions. The function of the mosque is summarized by the thirteenth Century Jurist Ibn Taymiyah as a place of gathering where prayer was celebrated and where public affairs were conducted. All mosques are where Muslims men on an equalitarian basis rich or poor, noble or humble, stand in rows to perform their

89. AIR 1993 SC 2086.

prayers behind the Imam. Imams are expected to look after the cleanliness of mosque, call Azans from the balcony of the minarets to the whole religious meetings and propagate the Islamic faith. They are expected to be well versed in the Shariat, the holy Quran, the Hadiths, ethics, philosophy, social, economic and religious aspects. Imam or prayer leader is the most important appointee. In the early days the ruler himself filled this role; he was leader (Imam) of the government of war, and of the common Salat ("ritual prayer"). Under the Abbasids, when the caliph no longer conducted prayer on a regular basis, a paid Imam was appointed. While any prominent or learned Muslim can have the honour of leading payers, each mosque specifically appoints a man well versed in the logical matters to act as its Imam. He is in charge of the religious activities of the mosque, and it is his duty to conduct prayers five times a day in front of Mihrab' (refer the Encyclopedia of Religion Vol. 10. 121–122):

> 'On nature of the duties performed by the Imams there is no dispute. But both the Union of India and various State Wakf boards of different States which have put in appearance in response to the notice issued by this Court have seriously disputed the manner of their appointment, right to receive any payment and absence of any relationship of master and servant. It is stated that the Imams or Muazzins are appointed by the Mutwallis. According to them the Wakf Board have nothing to do either with their appointment or working. It is claimed that under Islam, emoluments cannot claimed as a matter of right as the Islamic law ordains the Imams to offer voluntary service. They are said to be paid some money out of the donations received in mosques or by the Mutwallis of the Boards. Their job is stated to be honorary and not paid. Nature of duty under Islamic Shariat is stated to lead prayers, which is performed voluntarily by any suitable Muslim without any monetary benefit. Some of the affidavits claim that they are appointed by people of the locality. The Union Government has specifically stated that Islam does not recognize the concept of priesthood as in other religions and the selection of Imams is the sole prerogative of the members of the local community or the managing committee, if any, of the mosque. According to Karnataka Wakf Board Imamat in the mosque is not considered to be employment. The allegation of the petitioners that due to low payment they are humiliated or insulted in the society, is denied and it is claimed that they are respectable persons who carry on the duty of Imamat as a part of religious activity and not for earning bread and butter. The Delhi Wakf Board pointed out that the honorarium is paid to an Imam as a consideration for his five time presence in the mosque regularly and punctually. The Board has denied any right to exercise an authority over the mosque where Imams and Muazzins are appointed by the Mutawallis or by the managing committees. It is stated that holding of a certificate from a registered institution to enable a person to lead the prayer is not necessary as the only requirement for being an Imam under the Shariat is to have a thorough knowledge of the holy Quran and the rites, rules and obligation required for offering prayers according to the principles laid down by the Quran and Sunnah.

The Wakf Board has pointed out that mosque can be categorized in five categories. One, which are under direct control or management of the Government such as Mecca Masjid or the mosque situated in public garden which are not governed or regulated by the Muslim Wakf Board. Second, mosques, which are under the direct management of Wakf Board. Third, mosques, which are under the control of mutawallis under various Wakf Boards. Fourth, mosque which are not registered with the Wakf Board and are managed by local inhabitants and are under the management of the public who offer prayers; and Fifth, mosques which are not managed by mutwallis or the Muslims of the locality. It is claimed that Imams of fourth and fifth category are not regular and any Muslim can lead the prayers, whereas under the third category mosques are having regular Imams. Financial difficulty of the Wakf Board to meet the demand has also been pointed out. The Pondicherry Wakf Board has pointed that there is not even one employee except a peon working there and, therefore, it is not possible to meet the demand of the Imam. It is also claimed that the Board has no control over the pesh-Imams as they are considered to be well dignified personality of the society and they are given due respect by the Muslim community as a whole.'

'The Punjab Wakf Board has stated that Imams of mosques in Punjab were being paid on the basis of their qualification. Imams Nazara (Mubtaii grade) are in the scale of Rs. 380-20-580-25-830-30-980, whereas Imams Hafiz (Wasti grade) are paid Rs. 445-20-720-25-970-30-1120. They are also paid Rs. 30/- per month medical allowance and Muazzins are paid Rs. 310/- per month. These scales were revised in 1992. According to them Imams of all the mosques in Punjab, Haryana and Himachal Pradesh which come under the Punjab Wakf Board are being paid regularly and they are treated as regular employees. The sunni, Central Wakf Board of Uttar Pradesh stated that all the sunni mosques were managed by mutwallis of the concerned managing committees and not by the Wakf Boards.'

The mosque differs from a church or a temple in many respects. 'Ceremonies and service connected with marriages and birth are never performed in mosques. The rites that are important and integral functions of many churches such as confession, penitence and confirmations do not exist in the mosques. Nor any offerings are made as is common in Hindu temples. Ministry of Wakf (Endowments) appoints the servant, preachers and readers of the Quran. Mosques in non-Muslim countries are subsidized by individuals. They are administered by their founder or by their special fund. The Muezzin calls to prayer five times a day from the minaret.

511. In 1954, the Wakf Act was passed by the Parliament for better administration and supervision of Wakfs. To achieve the objective of the Act, section 9 provides for the establishment of a Wakf Board. The functions of which are detailed in section 15. Sub-section (1) reads as under:

(1) Subject to any rules that may be made under this Act, the general superintendence of all wakfs in a State in relation of all matters except those which are expressly required by this Act to be dealt with by the Wakf Commissioner,

shall vest in the board established for the State; and it shall be the duty of the Board so to exercise its powers under this Act as to ensure that the Wakfs under its superintendence are properly maintained, controlled and administered and the income thereof is duly applied to the object and for the purposes for which such wakfs were created or intended.

Provided that in exercising its power under this Act in respect of any wakf, the Board shall act in conformity with the directions of the wakf, the purposes of the wakf and any usage or custom of the wakf sanctioned by the Muslim law.

512. The Board is vested with supervisory, administrative and financial powers over the wakfs. One of its primary duties is to ensure that the income from the wakf is spent on carrying out the purposes for which wakf was created. Mosques are wakf and are required to be registered under the Act over which the Board exercises control. Purposes of their creation are community worship. Namaz or Salat is the mandatory practice observed in every mosque '(Among the Five Pillars (arkan; eg; rukn) of Islam, it holds the second-most important position, immediately after the declaration of faith (shahadah))' (the Encyclopedia of Britannica Vol. 18 p. 883).

513. The principal functionary to undertake it is the Imam. The objective and purpose of every mosque being community worship and it being the obligation of the Board under the Act to ensure that the objective of the wakf is carried on and the Board cannot escape from its responsibility for proper maintenance of religious service in a mosque. To say, therefore, that the Board has no control over the mosque or Imam is not correct. The absence of any provision in the Act or the rules providing for the appointment of Imam or laying down the condition of their service is probably because they are not considered employees. At the same time, it cannot be disputed that due to changes in social and economic set-up they too need sustenance. The nature of their job is such that they may be required to be present in the mosque nearly for the whole day. There may be some who may perform the duty as part of their religious observance. Still others may be ordained by the community to do so. But there are a large number of such persons who have no other occupation or profession or service for their livelihood except doing duty as Imam. What should be their fate? Should they be paid any remuneration and if so how much and by whom? According to the Board, they are appointed by the Mutawallis and, therefore, any payment by the Board was out of question. Prima facie it is not correct as the letters of appointment issued in some states are from the Board. But assuming that they are appointed by the Mutawallis the Board cannot escape from its responsibility as the Mutawallis under Section of the Act are under the supervision and control of the Board. In a series of decisions rendered by this Court, it has been held that the right to life enshrined in Article 21 means the right to live with human dignity. It is too late in the day, therefore, to claim or urge that since Imams perform religious duties they are not entitled to any emoluments Whatever may have been the ancient concept it has undergone change and even in Muslim countries mosques are subsidized and Imams are paid their remuneration. So it cannot be accepted that in the absence of any statutory provision in the Wakf Act the Imams who look after the religious activities of mosques are not entitled to any remuneration. It was argued on behalf of Union and the Wakf Boards that their financial position was not such that they could meet the obligations of paying the Imams as they are being paid in the State of Punjab. It was also argued that the number of mosques is so large that it would entail heavy expenditure, which the boards of different States would not be able to bear. We do not find any correlation between the two. Financial difficulties of the institution cannot be above the fundamental right of a citizen. If the boards have been entrusted with the responsibility of supervising and administering the wakf, then it is their duty to harness resources to pay those persons who perform the most important duty namely of leading community prayer in a mosque the very purpose for which it is created (The Encyclopedia of Religion Vol. 13. 20-21).

514. The Apex Court issued the following directions:

- The Union of India and the Central Wakf Board will prepare a scheme within a period of six months in respect of different types of mosques, some details of which have been furnished in the counter affidavit filed by the Delhi Wakf Board.
- Mosques, which are under the control of the government, shall not be governed by this order. But if their Imams are not paid any remuneration and they have no independent income, the government may fix their emoluments on the basis as the Central Wakf Board may do for other mosques in pursuance of our order.
- For other mosques, except those which are not registered with the Board of their respective States or which are not manned by members of the Islamic faith the scheme shall provide for payment of remuneration of such Imams taking guidance from the scale of pay prevalent in the State of Punjab and Haryana.
- The State Boards shall ascertain the income of each mosque and the number and nature of Imams required by it, namely full-time or part-time.
- For the full-time Punjab Wakf Board may be treated as a guideline. That shall also furnish guidelines for payment to part-time Imam.
- In all those mosques where full-time Imams are working they shall be paid the remuneration determined in pursuance of this order.
- Part-time and honorary Imam shall be paid such remuneration and allowance as is determined under the scheme.
- The scheme shall also take into account those mosques, which are small or are in the rural area or are such as mentioned in the affidavit of Pondicherry Board and have no source of income and find out ways and means to raise its income.
- The exercise should be completed and the scheme be enforced within six months.
- Our order for payment to Imams shall come into operation from 1 December 1993. In case the scheme is not prepared within the time allowed then it shall operate retrospectively from 1 December 1993.
- The scheme framed by the Central Wakf Board shall be implemented by every State Board.

515. On the direction of the Supreme Court, a Scheme was formulated and approved by the Central Wakf Council at its meeting held on 12 December 1995 providing as follows:

(1) The Scheme shall be called the scheme for remuneration to Imams and Muazzins 1995.
(2) The Scheme shall come into force on 1 December 1993.
(3) The Scheme shall apply to the following categories of Mosques:
  (a) Mosques which are under the direct management of a board of Wakfs established under the Wakf law for the time being in force.
  (b) Mosques which are registered with a Board of Wakfs established under the wakf law for the time being in force and are under the control/management of Mutawallis of various wakfs.

Provided that the Scheme shall not apply to the following categories of Mosques:

- Mosques under the control or management of the Government except as provided in paragraph 7.
- Mosques which are not registered with the Wakf Board and are managed by local inhabitants.
- Mosques which are not managed by either Mutawallis or the Muslims of the locality.
- Mosques not managed by members of the Islamic faith.

516. According to nature of duty performed by them, Imams can be either full-time/part-time or honorary:

(a) Full-time Imams.

In case of full-time Imams, the qualification and the remuneration shall be on the lines of those adopted by the Punjab and Haryana Wakf Board. The Punjab and Haryana scheme is in Annexure.

(b) Part-time and Honorary Imams.

The payment of remuneration to part-time Imams with comparable qualifications could be up to a maximum of 50% payable to the full-time Imams. The State Wakf Board shall consider payment of remuneration and allowances to Honorary Imams as follows:

- Imams who lead only Friday prayers that are once in a weak, may be paid honorarium @ INR 50 per prayer.
- Such Honorary Imams who lead all five prayers on a regular basis and are willing to accept may be paid honorarium @ INR 400, INR 500. INR 600 per month, depending on whether they are Nazara, Hafiz or Alim.
- Such Honorary Imams who do not lead all five prayers regularly may be paid an honorarium @ INR 20 per day irrespective of the number of prayers they lead.

Provided that the appropriate Board of Wakf may, in respect of mosque which are small or are in the rural areas or have no source of income, fix such rates of remuneration for Imams and Muazzins of such a mosque until that mosque is able to find out ways and means to raise its income as may be sufficient to pay remuneration at the rate mentioned in: (a) or as the case may be, (b) above. Acceptance of remuneration under the scheme in all the above-mentioned categories paras 5(a) and (b), the acceptance of the above remuneration will be on voluntary basis.

- The remuneration suggested in para 5 above shall be followed for Imams of Mosques under the control of the Government in cases where they have no independent income.
- The appropriate Board of Wakfs may determine the quantum of remuneration to various categories, of Imams taking into account, among others, the following factors:
  - (a) Whether the mosque is located in urban or rural areas.
  - (b) Existing mode of payment as also the quantum, if the payment is in kind, whether the same can be quantified.
  - (c) Qualification of Imams.
  - (d) Income of the Wakf in which the mosque is comprised.
  - (e) Income of the Wakf in which the mosque is comprised.
  - (f) Collection/donation made for the Imam.
  - (g) Grants received from any source for the purpose.
  - (h) Whether the Wakf deed provides for specified sources of payment to the Imams.
  - (i) Whether Imam is full-time, part-time or honorary.
  - (j) Whether Imam has any known source of income.
  - (k) Any other factor relevant to the local situation.
- The responsibility for implementation of this Scheme shall be on the appropriate Board of Wakfs.
- The appropriate Board of Wakfs shall harness necessary resources in accordance with powers and responsibilities vested with it under the provisions of the Wakf Law for the time being in force.

§2. Minimum Wages to Persons Working in Temples and Other Religious Places

517. In *Shree Satya Narain Tulsi Manas v. Workman Compensation* (26 May 2006) judgment was delivered by Justice S. Srivastava. The facts of the case are that the proceedings under the Minimum Wages Act, 1948 were initiated against the petitioner. Notice to the writ petition makes it clear that all twenty-nine workers in Shree Satya Narain Tulsi Manas Mandir Durga Kund Varanasi were getting a fixed amount of INR 450 to INR 650 per month and some were being paid a fixed amount of INR 1,050 per month. After receiving the notice the petitioner filed an objection/ written statement raising the question of jurisdiction and the applicability of the provisions for the Minimum Wages Act.

518. The petitioner stated that Shree Satya Naram Tulsi Manas Mandir is a temple of Sanatan Dharm Sect and is a holy place where devotees come for darshan and puja for their Adhyatmik Santushthi by Murti Puja. No Prasad is sold in the temple and it is purely a religious shrine of Hindus and not a commercial establishment. It was further stated that the temple is neither an industry within the meaning of the UP Industrial Disputes Act nor a shop or commercial establishment within the meaning of the UP Shop and Commercial Establishment Act and it is a religious and spiritual place which has no room for any sort of business, trade or manufacturing.

519. The question for consideration as framed by the court was whether the employees of religious/charitable institution/establishment are the employees protected under the Minimum Wages Act or any other statutory enactment in the matter of wages and if not, whether a citizen of India employed in any religious or charitable institution/establishment is entitled to protection in the matter of wages under Article 21 of the Constitution.

520. It is on record that the petitioner earns huge money during a certain period of the year and that money is used and appropriated by the management and the office bearers of the petitioner to their use. Each and every person working in a religious and charitable institution, whether he is an ordinary worker or an office bearer, is the custodian to protect the property of the establishment. The Mahants, Secretaries and heads of such religious and charitable institutions are like other workers who have also been engaged to achieve the same goal. The wealth collected or received by the religious and charitable institutions is to be distributed in a rational manner to protect the life and livelihood of the workers and their family members:

- In the circumstances, the court directed the State to make a certain scheme for such religious and charitable institutions and frame regulation in the scheme to provide protection to such workers. The State has every duty to enforce the constitutional rights of the workers of such institutions as applicable to other establishments, i.e., commercial establishment. The work ‘otherwise’ mentioned in Article 43 of the Constitution, contained in Directive Principles, read with Article 21 of the Constitution fully covers the case of such workers.

521. The question for consideration is as to what are the rights of employees or Sevadars, or Imams, etc., who are charged with the duty to upkeep the establishment or to perform Pooja of deity in a temple, managed either by the trustees, Committee, Manager or Savaits as the case may be, and whether in the matter of offerings to the deity or the income flowing from such trust, temple, they can lay claim to surplus income or offerings to a use other than betterment and maintenance/ upkeep of the Trust, etc., and employees/workers are entitled to get wages. The court took the view that the offerings or income from such temple/Charitable Trust, etc., is an offering/income meant for deity and Almighty and in this connection, such trustee, Savaits, etc., have no personal claim to appropriate such offering and income according to their own choice and they are also in the service of deity or Almighty at par with the other employees or Sevadars and by this reckoning, merely because, they are Savait or Mahants, etc., or at the helm of the affairs in the management of such establishments, they have no overriding claim or personal rights to the offerings/gifts/Daan received by the temple or charitable or religious establishment or its use except for the upkeep and maintenance.

522. Article 21 of the Constitution is applicable equally to all such persons working in religious places. The right to get livelihood, wages to maintain themselves and their families and to get fair wages cannot be denied merely on the ground that the establishment or institution is a religious or charitable institution or that persons who are engaged are Sevadars or employees at the pleasure of management. Employees or Sevadars are the persons who have dedicated themselves to the service of deity and Almighty and merely on that ground cannot be denied their right of living wages to maintain themselves or their families and to live a life with human dignity.

Though the service conditions of the employees of religious and charitable establishments are not governed by any statutory rules, looking to the fact that these people are committed to their works in religious and charitable establishment and service to the entire society selflessly and have been devoting their time to the service of the mankind, a humanistic approach towards their plight and predicament is required. It is settled that under Article 21 of the Constitution, the rights to live take within its sweep the right to livelihood and therefore they are also entitled to such emoluments so as to keep the pot boiling for himself and his family members.

523. The above viewpoint gets support from various decisions, namely Workmen represented by *Secretary v. the Management of Reptakos Brett & Co and Anr.*, in which five norms of fixation of minimum wages were delineated, i.e., food requirement, clothing requirement, other misc. expenses, including fuel, lighting, etc. Besides the above, the right to get education and maintain health of the children has also been recognized. It cannot be disputed that every citizen whether an employee of a religious or charitable establishment or otherwise is entitled to get living wages. It is now well settled by several pronouncements that religious activities, which are an integral part of religion, cannot be interfered with but the matters, which are not an integral part of religious activities, can be regulated by legislation or by any scheme.

524. In a decision rendered in *Raja Vir Kishore Deo v. State of Orissa*, the Constitution Bench of Apex Court held Orissa Act No. 11 of 1995 valid. In the judgment, the rights of management of the temple, which were vested in Raja of Puri and his ancestors, were taken away. The Supreme Court held that the Act so enacted has not taken away the right of Raja of Puri as Sewaks and it also does not affect religious rights of Raja. This judgment also pronounces that all persons in the management are Savaits like its employees and anyone engaged in the service and performance and upkeep of the temple/trust, etc., has no right to use the offerings of devotees personally except in the interest of all the persons and the interest of temple or religious institutions. Another Constitutional Bench decision is *Commissioner Hindu Religious Endowments (Madras) v. Sri Lakshmandra Thirtha Swamiar* (1954 S.C. 282), in which the court observed that freedom of religion in our Constitution is not confined to religious beliefs only; it extends to religious practices as well subject to the restrictions which the Constitution itself has laid down under Article 26(b). Therefore, a religious denomination or organization enjoys complete autonomy in the matter of deciding as to what rites and ceremonies are essential according to the tenets of the religion they hold and no outside authority has any jurisdiction to interfere with their decision in such matters. However, the Apex Court held that the scale of expenses to be incurred in connection with these religious observances would be a matter of administration of property belonging to the religious denomination and can be controlled by secular authorities in accordance with any law laid down by a competent legislature, for it could not be the injunction of any religion to destroy the institution and its endowments by incurring wasteful expenditure on rites and ceremonies.

525. Another Constitution Bench decision of the Apex Court in *Durgah Committee, Ajmer and Anr. v. Syed Hussain Ali and Ors.* supports the view that the matters of religion include even practices which are regarded by the community as part of its religion provided that these are regarded by the said religion as its essential and integral part; otherwise even purely secular practices which are not an essential or an integral part of religion are apt to be clothed with a religious form and may make a claim for being treated as religious practices. The State cannot interfere with the integral part of the religious functions, but such matters like payment of minimum wages or other welfare schemes for the Sevaks/workers in the employment of temple or other religious and charitable establishments can be regulated.

526. With respect to gratuity, in the case of *Administrator, Shree Jagannath Temple v. Jagannath Padhi* (1992 LAB IC 1621) a Division Bench consisting of Hon. B.L. Hansana, then C.J. and Sri A. Pasayat, observed as follows:

> It does not have foundation on any legal liability, but upon a bounty streaming from appreciation and graciousness. Long service carries with it expectation of an appreciation from the employer and a gracious financial assistance to tide over post retrial difficulties. Judged in that background, we feel that it would be unconscionable to keep temple out of the purview of the Act, more particularly when opposite party No. 1, a low paid employee has served the temple for a very long span of time.

527. Therefore, every citizen whether employees of any religious and charitable establishment/institution which includes, Math, Monastery, etc., are entitled to get living/minimum wages; it is held that employees working in the establishment of the petitioner are entitled to get minimum wages from the date the dispute was raised. The petitioners are liable to pay the same forthwith along with arrears. Besides, the State is also liable to make suitable legislation for securing to all workers, a living wage conditions of work ensuring a decent standard of life in the tenor and spirit of Article 43 of the Constitution of India.

528. A similar matter came up for consideration before the Apex Court in *All India Imam Organization v. Union of India* (1993 SC 2089). The Apex Court in paragraph 5 of the said decision laid down as below:

> Absence of any provision in the Act or the rules providing for appointment of Imam or laying down condition of their service is probably because they are not considered as employees. At the same, it cannot be disputed that due to change in social and economic set up they too need sustenance. Nature of their job is such that they may be required to be present in the mosque nearly for the whole day. There may be some who may perform the duty as part of their religious observance. – But there are large number of such persons who have no other occupation or profession or service for their livelihood except doing duty as Imam. What should be their fate? Should they be paid any remuneration and if so how much and by whom? – In series of decisions rendered by this Court it has been held that right to life enshrined in Article 21 means right to live with human dignity. It is too late in the day, therefore, to claim or urge that since Imams perform religious duties they are not entitled to any emoluments. Whatever may have been the ancient concept but it has undergone change and even in Muslim countries mosques are subsidized and the Imams are paid their remuneration.

529. The difference between the case referred to above and this case is that in case of Imams, there was a statutory body like Wakf Board covered by Central as well as State Wakf Act but there was also no provision regulating the services of Imams. Here, in the present case, there is no statutory body, which may be directed to prepare a scheme for payment of minimum/living wages to the employees-workers of the temple.

530. Therefore, to make fundamental right of such workers enforceable, the court directed that the Union of India and the State of UP prepare a scheme for constitution of an autonomous Board on the lines of the U.P. Muslim Wakf Act, 1960 with suitable amendments commensurate to the requirements of Hindu religion representing all sects falling within the fold of Hinduism. This Board shall register all such religious and charitable establishments/ endowments according to the norms represented by Maths, monasteries, temples and Religious and Charitable Trust or Societies as the case may be, through their heads or the representatives of all sects. The Central as well as the State Government may also frame a welfare scheme for providing minimum wages to such workers as well as other welfare measures relating to such workers/ employees. The scheme will be prepared on the lines of the U.P. Muslim Wakf Act, 1960 or any other legislation in this regard with suitable amendments/changes.

Chapter 3. Other Employees of the Religious Places and Labour Law

531. The religious communities may not be denied the right to set conditions of employment because it will affect the ability of these communities to carry out their missions in accordance with their beliefs and doctrines. This can also be taken as amounting to interference in the affairs of the religious community. The religious communities would suffer a violation of their right to freedom of religion or belief and may face difficulties in carrying out their affairs in ways that are consistent with their teachings. The religious communities' ability to preach their message and carry out their missions with authenticity and without compromise would be subjected to the nature of the beliefs and practices of individual employees. While any individual who does not share these religious convictions can continue to do so, and thus conserve his or her religious identity, but while acting on behalf of religious body, such an employee has to follow the belief kept and propagated by such body. Employees who do not conform to the religious teaching or the ethos of their employer can leave and find other employment. Religious communities make use of private autonomy in establishing and regulating a labour relationship. State labour law applies to such labour relations. However, religious communities' right to self-regulation remains essential. This enables religious communities to organize the personnel structure service of the religious institution according to its self-understanding and to attribute binding force to the specific obligations of their employees. The basic commitments of the religious community that can be of importance as a matter of the employment relationship are to be determined according to the standards acknowledged by the religious community. The opinion of an individual religious institution that may be affected, the forming of which may be influenced by a variety of motives, is of no relevance to the state authorities in establishing these basic commitments.

532. The labour courts have to apply the standards provided by the religious community as far as the law acknowledges the right of the religious communities to decide on these standards by themselves. It is left to the official, formally organized religious communities to decide with binding force on what the credibility of the religious community and of its teaching requires, what the specific assignments of the religious community are, what proximity to those means, what the 'essential principles of the belief and moral teaching' are and what has to be regarded as violation of those principles. Also, the decision about whether and how a gradation of loyalty obligations should take place among the staff that is active within the community service remains a matter that in principle falls under the right to self-determination of the religious community. In case there is a violation of loyalty obligations, the additional question of whether this violation justifies a termination of the employment contract is to be decided according to the employment protection provisions. The employment relationship may be terminated by either party to the contract for a compelling reason without complying with a notice period if facts are present on the basis of which the party giving notice cannot reasonably be expected to continue the employment relationship to the end of the notice period or to the agreed end of the employment relationship. Such action takes all circumstances of the individual case into account and weighing the interests of both the parties to the contract.

Part VII. Religious Communities and Protections of the Individual

533. The institutions of religious communities which do not fall in the definition of State under the Constitution are not in general bound to apply fundamental rights in their actions. Only those religious bodies which get public funds are bound to observe fundamental rights in their actions and dealings. In view of individuals who are not members of the specific religious community, these communities relate to them as do private associations with any other individual. No doubt there can be a right to manifest the belief in such a way based on freedom of religion or belief, but at the same time individuals have the right not to be disturbed and both these rights will be balanced appropriately as to give as much space as possible for expression of both of them. General rules for this balancing process are specified in the relevant laws such as emission laws on the production and avoidance of noise or in the general environmental laws. The right to take out processions and play music on roads in front of the mosque is an example of balancing of conflicting rights (right to play music and right to not be disturbed in the mosque) resorted to by the courts.

Chapter 1. Protection of Privacy

534. Religious communities can direct and oblige their members to behave in their private lives in specific ways. They can make compliance with their moral and spiritual principles a condition of membership and community relationships. The state may not interfere with merely religious sanctions that may be imposed by a religious community as a reaction to specific behaviour such as exclusion from sacraments. However, religious communities may not impose sanctions that would contradict criminal or any other state law or against the constitutional protections available to an individual. No religious community may use bodily or any other force or deprivation of personal freedom of movement against any member of such community to enforce their internal rules.

§1. Right to Privacy: A Human Right

535. Right to privacy is a human right recognized under Article 12 of the *Universal Declaration of Human Rights* of the UN issued on 10 December 1948, of which India is a signatory. Many of these rights including the right to privacy received the status of fundamental rights either explicitly or through judicial interpretation under the Constitution of India. The rules and norms prescribed by religion may be rigid or flexible. A person will not face obstacles if he or she chooses to do something that is in line with the teachings of a respective religion. The opposite might occur if a person goes against religious teachings. In such situations, religious authorities may intrude into a person's life through religious edits. *Fatwas* issued by Islamic clerics against an individual for doing something perceivably un-Islamic could have a serious effect on a person's standing within the community.

§2. Bringing Religious Privacy Through Legal Reforms

536. The law may help people in addressing privacy issues. There was no concept of divorce in Hindu marital norms, and couples had to remain in marriage against their will. However, the HMA, 1955, gave an option of divorce for Hindu couples. In case of Muslim women, in August 2017, the SC struck down the practice of instant triple *talaq* (divorce) as unconstitutional in *Shayara Bano v. Union of India and Ors.*[90] Instant triple *talaq* is a practice in Islam where the husband divorces his wife by saying '*talaq, talaq, talaq*' instantly in one sitting without due procedure. Though prohibited among Catholics, abortion is legal in India, giving women an option of pre-choice, which comes under the Right to Privacy.

90. (2017) 9 SCC 1.

§3. RESPECT FOR PERSONAL PRIVACY

537. The cost of doing something in a multireligious society against respective religious teachings may be very harsh, brutal and inhumane. A number of honour killings are reported which could be attributed to inter-caste marriages, inter-religious marriages, and intra-*gotra* (roughly translated to the clan) marriages, among others. Even dietary habits could lead to killing. Even if someone does something illegal, it is the state's prerogative to look after the matter. No one has the right to enter anybody's private space without the respective person's permission or legal warrant. Despite the presence of several strict laws, law enforcement is slack and there is a breach of the norm of privacy by lynching mobs.

538. No doubt, the practice of religion is a completely personal and private matter. In *Justice K S Puttaswamy (Retd.) and Anr. Versus Union of India and Ors* (Writ Petition (Civil) No. 494 of 2012) Justice Chelameswar's judgment said, '… the freedom of the belief or faith in any religion is a matter of conscience falling within the zone of purely private thought process and is an aspect of liberty'. This privacy should not only give freedom to practise a certain religion but also do it in a manner the individual feels comfortable, even if it is not in line with the traditions and norms. Another important aspect of privacy is religious conversion. 'Subject to public order, morality and health and to the other provisions of this Part, all persons are equally entitled to freedom of conscience and the right freely to profess, practice and propagate religion … ', as per Article 25(1) of the Constitution.

Chapter 2. Freedom to Marry

539. In India, the state does not interfere in a marriage under any religion or of any community. The right or freedom to marry is a component of the right to life under Article 21 of the Constitution which says, 'No person shall be deprived of his life and personal liberty except according to procedure established by law.' In the context of the right to marry, a mention may be made of a few Indian cases. A person who is suffering from venereal disease even prior to the marriage cannot be said to have any right to marry so long as he is not fully cured of the disease.

540. In *Mr X v. Hospital Z* (AIR 1999 SC 495) the court said that it was open to the hospital or the doctor concerned to reveal such information to persons related to the girl whom he intended to marry and she had a right to know about the Human Immunodeficiency Virus (HIV) positive status of the appellant. If that was so, there was no need for the court to go further and declare in general what rights and obligations arise in such context as to right to privacy or confidentiality or whether such persons are entitled to be married or not or in the event such persons marry, they would commit an offence under law or whether such right is suspended during the period of illness. In that view of the matter, the court held that the observations made by this Court, except to the extent of holding as stated earlier that the appellant's right was not affected in any manner in revealing his HIV-positive status to the relatives of his fiancée, are uncalled for.

541. Further, in *Lata Singh v. State of Uttar Pradesh*,[91] the Supreme Court viewed the right to marry as a component of the right to life under Article 21 of the Indian Constitution and observed that:

> This is a free and democratic country, and once a person becomes a major he or she can marry whosoever he/she likes. If the parents of the boy or girl do not approve of such inter-caste marriage, the maximum they can do is that they can cut off social relations with the son or daughter, but they cannot give threats or commit or instigate acts of violence and cannot harass the person who undergoes such inter-caste marriage.

Both the parties in the case were adults and so free to marry of their choice. There is no bar to an inter-caste marriage under the Hindu Marriage Act or any other law. Inter-caste marriages are in fact in the national interest as they will result in destroying the caste system.

542. The registration of marriage is not compulsory except for marriages solemnized under the Special Marriage Act and in the State of Goa. However, Article 44 of the Constitution requires the state to secure for the citizens a UCC throughout the territory of India. India has a unique blend of codified personal laws of Hindus, Christians, Parsis and to some extent of the laws of Muslims. However, there is no

91. AIR 2006 SC 2522.

uniform family-related law in a single statute or legislation for all Indians which is acceptable and applicable to all religious communities. The Supreme Court of India for the first time directed the Indian Parliament to frame a UCC in 1985 in the case of *Mohammad Ahmed Khan v. Shah Bano Begum*[92] but later on, in subsequent cases changed its position. In this case, a Muslim woman claimed maintenance from her husband under section 125 of the Code of Criminal Procedure after her husband pronounced triple talaq (divorce by announcing the word 'Talaq' thrice). The Apex Court held that the Muslim woman had a right to get maintenance under section 125 of the Code and also held that Article 44 of the Constitution had remained a dead letter. To undo this decision, the Muslim Women (Right to Protection on Divorce) Act, 1986 was enacted by the Parliament. This Act provided alternative ways and remedies so that a Muslim woman after divorce could get financial support but curtailed her right to claim maintenance from her ex-husband under section 125 of the Cr. PC.

543. Thereafter, in the case of *Sarla Mudgal v. Union of India*,[93] the question raised was, whether a Hindu husband married under Hindu law can, by embracing Islam, solemnize a second marriage. The Supreme Court held that a Hindu marriage solemnized under Hindu law can only be dissolved under the HMA and conversion to Islam and marrying again would not by itself dissolve the earlier Hindu marriage. Further, a second marriage solemnized after converting to Islam would be an offence of bigamy under section 494 of the IPC. The Supreme Court reiterated the need for Parliament to frame a common civil code which will help the cause of national integration by removing contradictions based on ideologies.

544. The debate still remains on the issue of whether freedom of religion granted as a fundamental right will be subservient to a Directive Principle of State Policy. Even the Directive Principle does not embody absolute uniformity in civil matters, and if it is attempted then it will impinge upon and obliterate the very spirit of constitutional guarantee of religious freedom. The majority will decide what should fall within the ambit of UCC leaving the minority religious communities at the mercy of the majority. This aspect was considered in later decisions and position was clarified that demand should emanate from within the concerned community.

545. Articles 25 and 26 of the Constitution of India guarantee freedom of religion and freedom to manage religious affairs. At the same time, Article 44 which is not enforceable in a court of law states that the State shall endeavour to secure a UCC in India. How are they to be reconciled? What will be the ingredients of a UCC? Since the personal laws of each religion contain separate ingredients, the UCC will need to strike a balance between the protection of fundamental rights and the basic principles of different religious communities. Marriage, divorce, Succession, inheritance and maintenance can be matters of a secular nature and law can

92. 1985 SCR (3) 894.
93. AIR 1995 SC 1531.

regulate them but the question as to how marriage will be performed and, how separation be effected will remain thorny issues to be resolved. Whether the provision of dower which is in favour of women will be applied to all which otherwise is an attribute of Muslim law?

546. The Directive Principle of enacting a UCC was initially urged by the Apex Court repeatedly in a number of decisions. But subsequently Apex Court itself realized the dangers of imposition of views of majority on minority in matters of civil code, so in a subsequent decision, namely *Lily Thomas v. Union of India*,[94] dealing with the validity of a second marriage contracted by a Hindu husband after his conversion to Islam, clarified that the court had not issued any directions for the codification of a common civil code and that the judges constituting the different benches had only expressed their views in the facts and the circumstances of those cases.

547. A petition challenging the practices of polygamy and nikah halala allowed in the Muslim community is pending before the Supreme Court. While the practice of polygamy is outlawed in India, an exemption has been made for the Muslim community under the Muslim Personal Law (Shariat) Application Act, 1937. The Act provides for the application of Muslim Personal Law in matters relating to marriage, succession, etc., among Muslim parties. Similarly, the practice of nikah halala is also permitted. As per this practice, once a Muslim woman has been divorced, her husband is not permitted to take her back even if he had pronounced talaq under the influence of any intoxicant unless his wife undergoes nikah halala, which involves her marriage with another man, who subsequently divorces her so that her previous husband can remarry her.

548. The petitioner argued that these practices treat women as property violating their fundamental rights enshrined in Articles 14, 15 and 21 of the Constitution. The failure to secure the same equal rights and life of dignity for Muslim women violates their most basic human and fundamental right to life of dignity unmarred by gender discrimination, which in turn has a critical impact on their social and economic rights, to say the least. The petitioner submitted that polygamy violates section 494 of IPC which prohibits bigamy and nikah halala amounts to rape under section 375 of IPC.

§1. Marriage among Hindus

549. As per the Hindu philosophy,[95] marriage is not just a process of coming together of the individuals but it is also a holy bond and a commitment which lasts a lifetime. Even the holy scriptures of the Vedas, the sacred Hindu texts, suggest that

94. 6 SCC 224.
95. Jeannine Auboyer, *Daily Life in Ancient India: from 200 BC to 700 AD* (Phoenix Press 2002). Google Books.

an individual should enter the phase of Grihastha 'household' after his or her student life. Thus, it can be said that marriage is almost a mandatory custom in the life of all Hindus. Marriage is a body for the performance of religious duties. It is deemed as a holy union in Hindu law. It is also considered to be union of flesh and flesh and blood and blood. It is a religious sacrament and not a civil contract.

550. Manu Smirti states[96] that the father or the brother, who has not married his daughter or the sister who has attained puberty, will go to hell. A Hindu marriage is to be performed according to religious rites, the performance of homa and saptapadi is essential and where they are not proved to have been performed it cannot be called a solemnized marriage. The word 'solemnize' means in connection with a marriage, 'to celebrate the marriage with proper ceremonies and in due form', according to shorter *Oxford Dictionary*. Unless the marriage is celebrated or performed with proper ceremonies and due form, it cannot be said to have been solemnized.

551. When the HMA, 1955 brought out some revolutionary changes then it was argued that 'Personal law is essentially secular in character, and cannot be treated as a part of Hindu religion properly so called. Reformers also urged that Hindu law was never "Sanatana" or static and had undergone changes from time to time.'[97]

552. Regarding the 'age of consent' the IPC 1860 has recognized the minimum marriageable age for a girl to be 15 years.[98] However, at the same time, marriageable age as prescribed under the Child Marriage Restraint Act 1929 is 18 years. Here it is clear that there is an ambiguity and contradiction as regards 'the age of consent' in the HMA, 1955 and the IPC 1860.

553. The HMA, 1955 was enacted by the Indian Parliament with the intention of regulating the personal life among the Hindus, especially their institution of marriage, its legitimacy, conditions for divorce and applicability, etc. There are many significant features in the provisions of the Act that lay down the very foundation of marriage. The basic essence of the act is that it appropriately recognizes the religious ethics and morals of the Hindus. Therefore, the HMA is applicable to all Hindus, taking within its ambit various offshoots like followers of Prarthana, Arya and Brahmo Samajas and Sikhs, Buddhists and Jains.

I. Void and Voidable Marriage under the HMA

554. A Void Marriage[99] is one that will be regarded by every court in any case in which the existence of marriage is in issue as having not been taken place and

96. A. Barua, H. Apte & P. Kumar, C*are and Support of Unmarried Adolescent Girls in Rajasthan*, XLII Econ. & Political Weekly (2007) 3-9, p. 54.
97. The 59th Law Commission Report; February 2008.
98. Proviso to s. 375 of IPC states that 'sexual intercourse by a man with his own wife, the wife not being under 15 years of age, is not rape'.
99. P. Diwan: *The Hindu Law*, 2nd edn., 695 (Orient Publishing Company 2005).

can be so treated by both the parties to it without any necessity of any decree annulling it. A decree is nonetheless advisable. It can be obtained by either party to marriage or by a person having sufficient interest in it. A Void Marriage is no marriage. It is called a marriage because two persons have undergone the ceremonies of marriage but as they absolutely lack the capacity to marry, they cannot, by just undergoing ceremonies, become husband and wife in the eyes of law.[100] So in case of void marriage, parties have no status of husband and wife. Thus, if one of them or both of them take another spouse, the offence of bigamy will not be committed. A void marriage confers no status of legitimacy and therefore children of a void marriage are illegitimate.[101] In respect of a void marriage, no decree of court is necessary. Even when the court passes a decree, it merely declares that marriage is null and void. It is an existing fact that marriage is void and the court merely makes a judicial declaration of the fact.[102] Moreover, a void marriage cannot be approbated. It cannot be ratified later.

555. A Voidable Marriage is one that will be regarded as a valid, subsisting marriage until a decree annulling it has been pronounced by a court of competent jurisdiction.[103] However, in English law, the form of the decree was the same as in the case of void marriage: pronouncing the marriage to have been and to be absolutely null and void for all intents and purposes. This led to a great deal of confusion and conflict. This confusion has been now avoided by the Nullity of Marriage Act, 1971. Section 5 lays down the decree of nullity granted after the commencement of this Act on the ground that a marriage is voidable shall operate to annul the marriage only as respects any time after the decree has been made absolute, and the marriage shall, notwithstanding the decree, be treated as if it had existed up to that time.

556. A Void Marriage is a perfectly valid marriage so long as it is not avoided. A Voidable marriage[104] can be avoided only on the petition of one of the parties to the marriage. If one of the parties does not petition for annulment, the marriage will remain valid. If one of the parties dies before the annulment of the marriage there cannot be any challenge to the marriage. The marriage will remain valid forever. So long it is not avoided all the legal consequences of a valid marriage flow from it, such as: it confers the status of husband and wife on the parties, the children are legitimate and all mutual rights and obligations arising from such a relationship are to be honoured.

II. Age for Marriage under Hindu Law

557. Almost all systems of Hindu law have permitted marriages at an early age, and the age of marriage and the age of majority have been different. The Hindu

100. *Supra* n. 35.
101. Section 16 of Hindu Marriage Act, 1955.
102. P. Diwan: *The Hindu law*, 2nd edn. p. 696.
103. *Laxhamma v. Thyamma,* AIR 1974 Andhra Pradesh, 255.
104. *Supra* n. 37.

Sages have enjoined that a girl should be married before she attained puberty though they laid down the age of 25 for the boys – the age when a child returned from Guru's ashram after completion of his education. Under ancient Hindu law, the age of majority was much less, under the Dayabhaga School it was the completion of fifteenth year, while under the Mitakshara school, it was the completion of 16 years.[105] The Hindu sages like Manu and Gautama enjoined that it was the religious duty of the father to give the daughter in marriage before the signs of puberty made an appearance. Some sages even declared that if a girl was married after she attained marriage age, she was at liberty to choose a husband for herself.[106] The HMA, 1955 originally laid down the age of 15 for girls and the age of 18 for boys. These ages were raised to 18 and 21 respectively by the Child Marriage Restraint (Amendment) Act, 1978. Section 5 (iii) of the HMA, 1955 lays down that a marriage may be solemnized between any two Hindus if the 'bridegroom has completed the age of 21 years and the bride the age of 18 years at the time of marriage',[107] However, the marriage remains even if bride and bridegroom are underage. The fifty-ninth Report of the Law Commission felt that 'the general understanding that the breach of that conditions does not effect the validity of marriage' should remain undisturbed.[108] The rationale behind this policy is that minor marriages in our country are still so rampant that if we would lay down that non-age rendered a marriage void, probably 80% of marriages would be rendered null and void.

A. Child Marriage and Freedom to Marry

558. The lines quoted below from a song sung during marriages in Rajasthan best illustrate the agony of a child's heart that is undergoing a marriage ceremony. These lines symbolize the mixed pain of leaving the father's house and at the same time the anguish as to why was she being married off at such a tender age. Such a situation is unprecedented and the inner pain unimaginable:

> '*Choti si umariya main parnanaya o babosa, kain main tharoo kario kusoor.*'
> 'Oh father why had you given me off in the marriage at such a tender age, for what sin did I commit.'

559. Prevention of child marriages is imperative not merely from the child and human rights perspective but also in the interest of meeting goals relating to health. The word 'Child Marriage' is contradictory in itself, as one would wonder how marriage and child could go together. But it is a sad reality that even to this day child marriages are being solemnized much to the chagrin of laws restraining such marriages[109]

105. P. Diwan, *The Hindu Law*, 2nd edn., p. 606.
106. *Supra* n. 40.
107. Section 5 of the Hindu Marriage Act, 195.
108. The 59th Law Commission Report February 2008.
109. Child Marriage Restraint Act 1928.

560. There is a belief that child marriage is a protection for girls against unwanted masculine attention or promiscuity. In a society, which puts a high premium on the patriarchal values of virginity and chastity of girls, they are married off as soon as possible. Furthermore, securing the girl's economic future has been put forth as a reason for early marriage.[110] The institution of marriage in communities or societies can be used to serve or strengthen economic and social ties between different families and even communities. Also, a young girl may be offered to a family in order to improve the financial and social standing of the girl's family.[111] Other reasons that have been listed for the high prevalence of child marriages in India are lack of education and knowledge, shortcomings in the law, and the lack of will and action on the part of the administration.[112]

561. Child marriage is one of the worst forms of denials of child rights. Still, in many parts of India such as Rajasthan, Madhya Pradesh, UP, Bihar and West Bengal children are forced every day into a relationship, of which they have only the faintest knowledge and for which they are not at all prepared.[113] The tragedy is that the legal system also has failed to prevent this practice and the enforcement machinery has been inadequate and ineffective.

562. Child marriage is also considered to be a violation of human rights; according to the United Nations International Children's Education Fund (UNICEF), it represents the most prevalent form of sexual abuse and exploitation of girls.[114] In many parts of the world especially underdeveloped countries parents give consent to child marriages hoping that it would benefit the girl both economically and socially. This practice is especially common in rural areas and among economically weak families and the daughter is married off at a young age to relieve the family from her economic responsibilities.

563. Many factors are responsible for this practice; the most common ones are poverty, protection of girls, family honour and the provision of stability during unstable social periods, lack of opportunities for girls, and lack of awareness about adverse health consequences. Another big problem is the lack of awareness of the law and also inadequate implementation of the existing laws. The child marriages are mainly due to the tyranny of poverty and due to lack of education. Statistics show that the majority of girls in Asia, Africa and Latin America are married by the age of 14.[115] It has been seen that child marriage is practised more in countries which have high poverty rates, birth rates and death rates, higher levels of underdevelopment and lack of education.

110. Chatterji, Jyotsna, *Child Marriage,* paper presented at India Social Forum, November 2006, New Delhi.
111. *Supra* n. 16.
112. *Supra* n. 15.
113. 'Child Marriage in India', http://www.unicef.in/Itstartswithme/childmarriage.pdf.
114. 'Child Marriage', http://www.unicef.org/protection/files/Child_Marriage.pdf.
115. 'Child Marriages Must Stop', www.unicef.org/newsline/01pr21.htm.

564. Unfortunately, marriage before attaining adulthood is a reality for a large number of women; according to UNICEF over 64 million women aged 20–24 years were married or in union before the age of 18.[116] Child marriage has many harmful consequences which include lack of freedom, decreased opportunities for education and can result in enslavement, sexual exploitation and violence against the victims. Not only that, but also a child bride who is not physically or psychologically prepared for conjugal life is also exposed to serious health risks such as early unwanted pregnancy which puts a young girl at great risk, increased risks of maternal and infant mortality, increased vulnerability to HIV and other sexually transmitted diseases.

565. Apart from affecting the health of a girl, child marriage has other consequences too. It takes away the educational opportunities limiting opportunities for employment and income generation. In terms of development, child marriage prevents women from participating fully in the life of the family, the community and society and thus results in social isolation. Child marriage prevents women as well as society from realizing their full potential. It has a negative impact on the position of women in the society and also affects the potential contribution of women to the society. The society bears a phenomenal cost by allowing the continuation of the practice of child marriage.

566. Child Marriage is a common practice in India, especially among the uneducated sections of the society, which actually forms a large chunk of the population. In fact, 40% of the world's child marriages occur in India. According to UNICEF's 'State of the World's Children-2009 Report',[117] 47% of India's women aged 20–24 were married before the legal age of 18, with 56% in rural areas. The government has taken several steps to eradicate this practice. There are flaws in the legislations on child marriage, namely the Prohibition of Child Marriage Act, 2006.

567. Birth, marriage and death are the standard trio of key events in most people's lives. Out of them, only marriage is a matter of choice. The right to exercise that choice was recognized as a principle of law even in Roman times and has long been established in international human rights instruments. Yet many girls, and a smaller number of boys, enter marriage without any chance of exercising their right to choose. Some are forced into marriage at a very early age. Others are simply too young to make an informed decision about their marriage partner or about the implications of marriage itself. They may have given what passes for 'consent' in the eyes of custom or the law, but in reality, consent to their binding union has been made by others on their behalf.[118] The assumption is that once a girl is married, she has become a woman even if she is only 12. Child marriage refers to any marriage

116. 'The Challenge', http://www.childinfo.org/marriage.html.
117. http://www.unicef.org/sowc09/report/report.php.
118. International Center for Research on Women (ICRW) *Policy Advisory on Child Marriage,* www.icrw.org/docs/childmarriage0803.pdf (accessed 29 Nov. 2011).

of a child younger than 18 years old, in accordance with Article 1 of the Convention on the Right of the Child. While child marriage affects both sexes, girls are disproportionately affected as they are the majority of the victims. Their overall development is compromised, leaving them socially isolated with little education and opportunities for employment and self-realization. This leaves child brides more vulnerable to poverty, a consequence of child marriage as well as a cause.[119]

568. While child marriage takes many different forms and has various causes, one issue is paramount, i.e., violation of human rights. The right to free and full consent to a marriage is recognized in the 1948 UDHR and in many subsequent human rights instruments and consent that cannot be 'free and full' when at least one partner is very immature. For both girls and boys, early marriage has profound physical, intellectual, psychological and emotional impacts, cutting off educational opportunity and chances for personal growth. For girls, in addition, it will almost certainly mean premature pregnancy and childbearing and is likely to lead to a lifetime of domestic and sexual subservience over which they have no control.[120]

569. According to the philosophy of the Vedas, there is a restriction on child marriage. The age of marriage for a boy is 25 years or more and that of a girl is 18 years or more. Since the Middle Ages to the present day, the custom of child marriage against Vedas has persisted in India. However, as states and governments developed, the political system modified Indian society gradually. The girl child is considered and is subject to family discipline and the honour of their clan. Since young women were considered irresponsible and irrational in love, their parents married them early before they got caught in any scandal.

570. The age at which the girl was to be married differed and it was rare for girls younger than 12 to be married in antiquity. Nevertheless, girl brides became younger towards the medieval period, and it became increasingly common for girls as young as 6 or 8 to be married. The prime concern of negotiating the marriage was to find out the compatibility between the two families. It was believed during those times that if two persons know each other right from childhood it enhanced understanding and affection. Hence parents decided on the marriages of their children at a very early age although the daughter stayed with her parents until she attained the age of puberty.

571. Child Marriages continue to be a fairly widespread social evil in India. As per Census data of 2011, 41.3% of all girls aged 19 are married and of over 10 million girls of this age at the time of Census more than 4.1 million were married or already divorced, separated or widowed. The data confirms that the age of marriage is getting pushed back. During the 2001 Census, about 25% of girls aged 15 to 19 were married. After ten years that proportion has shrunk to 20%. In the 20–24 age group, while 77% were married in 2001, it came down to 70% in 2011. In rural

119. 'Child Marriage', http://www.unicef.org/protection/files/Child_Marriage.pdf (accessed 29 Nov. 2011).
120. *UNICEF Innocenti Research Centre* www.unicef-irc.org/publications/pdf/digest7e.

India, 47.3% of 19-year-old girls have been married whereas in urban areas the corresponding figure is 29.2%.[121] The 2001 Census of India had revealed that 300,000 girls under 15 had given birth to at least one child.

572. Child marriage in India has been practised for centuries, with children married off before their physical and mental maturity. The problem of child marriage in India remains rooted in a complex matrix of religious traditions, social practices, economic factors and deep-rooted prejudices. Sexual activity starts soon after marriage, and pregnancy and childbirth at an early age can lead to maternal as well as infant mortality. Moreover, women who marry younger are more likely to experience domestic violence within the home.[122]

573. The phenomenon of child marriage can be attributed to a variety of reasons.[123] The chief among these reasons are poverty and culture, tradition and values based on patriarchal norms. Child marriage is a violation of human rights, compromising the development of girls and often resulting in early pregnancy and social isolation, with little education and poor vocational training reinforcing the gendered nature of poverty. The girls are required to perform heavy amounts of domestic work, under pressure to demonstrate fertility, and responsible for raising children while still children themselves, married girls and child mothers face constrained decision-making and reduced life choices. Boys are also affected by child marriage but the issue impacts girls in far larger numbers and with more intensity.

574. Where a girl lives with a man and takes on the role of caregiver for him, the assumption is often that she has become an adult woman, even if she has not yet reached the age of 18.[124] Dowry becomes an additional reason, which weighs even more heavily on poorer families. The general demand for younger brides also creates an incentive for these families to marry the girl child as early as possible to avoid high dowry payments for older girls. The girl in the patriarchal set-up is believed to be somebody's property and a burden. These beliefs lead parents to marry the girl child and they relieve themselves of the 'burden' of looking after the child.

575. Complications and mortality are common during childbirth for young pregnant girls. Girls who come from poor backgrounds and who are often married at an early age have little or no access to health care services. Risks associated with young pregnancy and childbearing include 'an increased risk of premature labour, complications during delivery, low birth-weight, and a higher chance that the newborn will not survive'.[125] Young mothers under age 15 are more likely to die than

121. Times of India, 3 May 2015.
122. http://middleeast.about.com/od/humanrightsdemocracy/a/child-brides.htm.
123. Black, Maggie, *Early Marriage, Child Spouses,* UNICEF, Innocenti Research Centre, Digest no. 7 (2001), p. 10.
124. Taken from UNICEF based website, www.childinfo.org/areas/childmarriage/ (accessed November 2007).
125. Black, Maggie, *Early Marriage, Child Spouses,* UNICEF, Innocenti Research Centre, Digest no. 7 (2001), p. 10.

women in their twenties due to complications.[126] Maternal mortality among adolescent girls is estimated to be two to five times higher than adult women.[127] Maternal mortality among girls aged 15–19 years is about three times higher.[128] Young women also suffer from a high risk of maternal morbidity.

576. It has been found that for 'every woman who dies in childbirth, thirty more suffer injuries, infections and disabilities, which usually go untreated and some of which are lifelong'.[129] 'Infants of mothers aged younger than 18 years have a 60% greater chance of dying in the first year of life than those of mothers aged 19 years or older [UNICEF 2007].' Babies are born premature or underweight or young mothers simply lack parenting skills and decision-making powers.[130] Young brides who run away from early marriages may end up as sex workers or eventually resort to using sex work as a way of earning additional income. Young brides also run the risk of catching diseases from their respective spouses, as older husbands often engage in sexual relations with other women outside the marriage.

577. An analysis of the HIV epidemic shows[131] that 'the prevalence of HIV infection is highest in women aged 15–24 and peaks in men between five to ten years later'. Women also undergo sexual violence in marriage and young girls are particularly vulnerable. In a study carried out in Calcutta in 1997 where half the women interviewed were married at or below the age of 15, with the youngest being married at 7 years old, findings revealed that this age group had 'one of the highest rates of vulnerability to sexual violence in marriage, second only to those whose dowry had not been paid'. The women interviewed said that sex was early and very painful, and 'many still continued to be forced into sexual activity by their husbands.

578. 'Additionally, the young girls had made their husbands aware of their unwillingness to have sex or of pain during sex, but in 80% of these cases the rapes continued.' As husbands are often much older than their brides, girl brides are likely to be widowed at an early age.

579. A child bride who is widowed can suffer discrimination including loss of status and is often denied property rights and other rights. At a 1994 Conference in Bangalore, India, participants told of being married at 5 and 6 years old, widowed a few years later and rejected by their in-laws and their own families. These widows are, quite simply, left with no resources and nowhere to go.[132] Giving education to a girl in poor families is considered, by both the girl's and boy's families

126. The 59th Law Commission Report February 2008.
127. *Supra* n. 20.
128. *Supra* n. 20.
129. *Supra* n. 19.
130. *Supra* n. 20.
131. C. Somerset, *Carron, Early Marriage: Whose Right to Choose? Forum on Marriage and the Rights of Women and Children* 21 (UNICEF 2000).
132. The 59th Law Commission Report February 2008.

unnecessary for becoming a good wife or a mother. Those who have a choice are eventually forced to drop out of school because they are forced to assume the responsibility of doing domestic chores, starting a family, etc. Researchers on child marriage in Rajasthan and Madhya Pradesh state that young married girls suffer more than boys due to the consequences of child marriage.[133]

580. To prevent and bring reform, the Prohibition of Child Marriage Act, 2006 was enacted replacing the Child Marriage Restraint Act 1929. It becomes necessary to revisit the various laws passed by the legislature in the past and contextualize them with respect to the new Act intended to prohibit the practice of child marriage. The HMA, 1955 laid down a minimum age of 10 for the bride and 21 for the bridegroom as a condition for marriage; however, this has not been given as a ground for void or voidable marriage, if violated. Hence after perusal of the Child Marriage Restraint Act, 1929 and HMA, 1955 it is clear that the validity of the marriage is not affected in any way even if the marriage was in contravention of the prescribed minimum age.

III. Valid Marriage under HMA, 1955

581. A marriage may be solemnized between any two Hindus, if the following conditions[134] are fulfilled, namely:

(1) neither party has a spouse living at the time of the marriage;
(2) at the time of the marriage, neither party:
    (a) is incapable of giving a valid consent to it in consequence of unsoundness of mind;
    (b) though capable of giving valid consent has been suffering from mental disorder of such kind and to such extent as incapable of procreation of children and unfit for marriage;
    (c) has been subject to recurrent attacks of insanity or epilepsy.
(3) the bridegroom has completed the age of 21 years and the bride the age of 18 years at the time of the marriage;
(4) the parties are not within the degrees of prohibited relationship unless the custom or usage governing each of them permits a marriage between the two;
(5) the parties are not sapindas of each other unless the custom or usage governing each of them permits a marriage between the two. (A sapinda is someone who is: within or has a common ancestor relative within three generations above one on one's mother's side of the family; within or has a common ancestor relative within five generations above one on one's father's side of the family.)

133. *Supra* n. 26.
134. Section 5 of the Hindu Marriage Act, 1955.

IV. Bigamous Marriage

582. With the commencement of HMA, 1955, one of the conditions provided for a valid marriage was that neither party should have a spouse living at the time of the marriage. Thus, there is freedom to marry but it is restricted to one marriage. Under the old law, there was a bar against a woman marrying a second husband while her first husband was alive unless custom permitted her. There was no such bar against men, till some States passed laws for the prevention of bigamous marriages, and introduced the principle of monogamy among Hindus. After 1955 second marriages came to be declared null and void *ab initio*. Under the HMA for a bigamous marriage, it is necessary that a marriage is solemnized according to the customs and rites, and second, that the spouse of the first marriage was a legally wedded spouse and the first marriage was subsisting on the date of the second marriage. In case of a spouse unheard of for more than seven years, a presumption can be drawn under section 108 of the Indian Evidence Act, 1872 (Evidence Act) that the spouse is dead. In such an event, the other spouse can marry a second time on the ground that the former marriage is dissolved due to the death of his/her spouse.

V. Judicial Pronouncement

583. Under section 13 (1) of the Hindu Marriage Act, 1955, a court can by decree dissolve a marriage on nine grounds, including certain fault- and religious-based grounds, such as adultery, desertion, cruelty, religious conversion, and insanity. There are no 'no-fault' grounds included in the law, including 'irreconcilable differences' or an 'irretrievable breakdown of the marriage'. Section 13B also provides for divorce through mutual consent, which requires the couple to wait one year after separating and a minimum of six months after filing a petition to dissolve the marriage by a decree of divorce.

584. On 1 May 2023, a five-judge constitutional bench of the Supreme Court acting under discretionary powers granted to the court under Article 142(1) of the Constitution of India, held in the case of Shilpa Shailesh (2023 SCC online SC 544) that marriages under Hindu law can be dissolved on the ground of irretrievable breakdown. The court's main holding was that the court also has the power to issue a decree to dissolve a marriage through mutual consent without the mandatory waiting period of six months, subject to certain conditions.

585. Article 142(1) of the Constitution grants the Supreme Court equitable powers to 'pass such decree or make such order as is necessary for doing complete justice in any cause or matter pending before it'. The court held that its inherent powers under Article 142(1) can be exercised to issue a decree to dissolve a marriage through mutual consent by waiving or reducing the mandatory waiting period of six months and that this discretion on the part of the court 'should be exercised with care and caution' and in 'exceptional situations'. These include circumstances where there is 'no chance of reconciliation' between the parties, 'the parties have genuinely settled their differences including alimony, custody of child or any other pending issues between the parties,' and 'the waiting period will only prolong their agony'. The court further stated that 'the courts only have to enquire and ensure that the settlement between the parties is achieved without pressure, force, coercion, fraud, misrepresentation, or undue influence, and that the consent is indeed sought by free will and choice, and the autonomy of the parties is not compromised'.

586. provisions for divorce under section 13 of HMA also provide for the remedy available to the second wife. Section 13(2)(i) of HMA says that in cases of marriages before the commencement of this Act, a second wife can seek divorce on the ground that her husband's first wife was alive at the time of the solemnization of the second marriage. Even though the law for the interim maintenance under section 24, HMA does not categorically provide for maintenance for second wife, the section has been given a wide interpretation by the courts to bring the cases of second wives within its ambit. The second wife can also claim interim maintenance under the interpretation given to section 24 of HMA. The terms 'wife' and 'husband' used in section 24, HMA are not to be given strict literal meaning as to convey only legally married wife and husband. The expression wife and husband in the context of the section and scheme of the Act should mean a person claiming to be a wife or a husband.

587. Similarly, under section 25, HMA the provisions for permanent alimony has also been interpreted widely by the courts to protect the rights of the second wife. After the declaration of the nullity of the marriage, the second wife could claim maintenance under section 25 of HMA. A woman whose marriage is void because of the existence of another wife is entitled to maintenance under this section. The second wife can claim interim maintenance under section 20 of the HAMA. No sane lady would surrender herself unless she treats her male companion as her husband – whether the marriage is proved or not that is the point to be determined by the trial Court itself – but keeping in view the fact that the petitioner cohabited with the respondent, interim maintenance under section 20, HAMA is allowed to her.

In *Ishwar Singh v. Smt Hukum Kaur,*[135] Smt. Hukum Kaur filed an application under section 488 of Criminal Procedure Code (Cr. PC) alleging that her husband was neglecting her and that she was entitled to get her monthly allowance from him for maintenance. The applicant denied to have married Smt. Hukum Kaur. It was admitted that Smt. Hukum Kaur's previous husband was alive; therefore, there could be no legal marriage between the opposite party and the applicant entitling the opposite party to receive maintenance. So long as a divorce has not been obtained, the previous marriage subsists and, therefore, the second marriage cannot be contracted by a Hindu if his spouse is living. Section 5 of the HMA provides that the marriage may be solemnized between any two Hindus, if neither party has the spouse living at the time of the marriage.

135. AIR 1965 All. 465.

In *Trailokya Mohan v. State of Assam*,[136] the petitioner already having a wife living married a second time and thus committed the offence of bigamy punishable under the IPC read with the provisions of the HMA, 1955. The court observed that under the provision of section 5(1) of HMA, one of the conditions of a valid Hindu marriage is that it should be solemnized between two Hindus, neither party having a spouse living at that time. Where the accused himself in his statement under section 342 Cr. PC had admitted that he did marry A during the lifetime of B, whom he married first. And that admission was corroborated by oral evidence of witnesses who in their cross-examination did not take a stand that the second marriage was invalid, there is a presumption of a valid marriage and when a strong satisfactory and conclusive evidence to rebut the presumption was totally lacking in the case, it must be held that a valid second marriage was solemnized and that was the basis of the admission made by the accused and it could be relied upon.

In *Banshidhar v. Chhabi Chatterjee*,[137] A Hindu woman claimed to have married in 1962 to the petitioner. Petitioner alleged that she was not his wife and that he was already married in 1952. It was held that if petitioner on the date of marriage with the claimant – woman – had already a legally wedded wife, his marriage with the claimant – woman – will be void under section 11 of the HMA. A claim under section 488 by a woman can be made only if she is the legally wedded wife of the person from whom she claims maintenance.

588. The social stigma attached with being a second wife, the absence of any legal status, and the pain of being cheated into the marriage are extremely depressing for a woman. Though monogamy is the rule from Vedic times, polygamy has, as an exception, existed side by side. But, the first wife was alone the wife in the fullest sense. One text of Manu seems to indicate that there was a time when a second marriage was allowed to a man after the death of his former wife. As a norm, the first wife had precedence over the others and her first-born son over his half-brothers. It was a settled law that a Hindu male could marry again while his previous marriage subsisted without his wife's consent and justification. Custom, however, did prevent the second marriage without the consent of the first wife and without making provision for her.

VI. Customary Divorce

589. Section 29 of the HMA, 1955 gives statutory recognition to customary divorces. This in effect means that parties relying on a custom need not go to court and obtain a decree for divorce. However, the onus on the party who relies on a custom is indeed weighty and the custom should be ancient, certain, reasonable and not opposed to public policy. Even though courts take judicial notice of customs, the validity of a deed of dissolution of marriage under a customary practice has to be established by substantial cogent evidence by the person about the existence of such custom.

136. AIR 1968, Assam 22.
137. AIR 1967 Patna 277.

§2. Muslim Law on Marriage

590. As per the Quran 'every person must marry'. Quran asserts that marriage is the only way to satisfy one's desire. Marriage (nikah) is defined to be a contract which has for its object the procreation and the legalizing of children. Thus, in Islam marriage is the norm and celibacy is not encouraged rather frowned upon. Marriage ('nikah') according to Muslim law is a contract underlying a permanent relationship based on mutual consent. A Muslim marriage requires proposal (Ijab) from one party and acceptance (Qubul) from the other as is required for a contract. Moreover, there can be no marriage without free consent and such consent should not be obtained by means of coercion, fraud or undue influence. In case a contract of marriage is entered by a guardian on behalf of a minor, the minor on attaining the age of puberty can set aside such contract. The parties to a Muslim marriage may enter into any antenuptial or postnuptial agreement which is enforceable by law provided it is reasonable and not opposed to the policy of Islam. Same is the case with a contract. The terms of a marriage contract may also be altered within legal limits to suit individual cases. The solemnization of marriage requires adherence to certain forms and formulas. They are called the essentials of a valid marriage. If any of these requirements is not fulfilled the marriage becomes either void or irregular, as the case may be. These essentials are as follows:

(a) Proposal and acceptance.
(b) Competent parties.
(c) No legal disability.

Marriage like any other contract is constituted by ijab-o-qabool, that is by declaration and acceptance. One party to the marriage must make an offer (Ijab which is done by the bride) to the other party (groom). The marriage becomes complete only when the other party has accepted the offer. According to Muslim law it is necessary that a man or someone on his behalf and the woman or someone on her behalf should agree to the marriage at one meeting and the agreement should be witnessed by two adult witnesses. The words conveying proposal and acceptance must be uttered in each other's presence or in the presence of their agents, who are called Vakils. The other condition is that the transaction must be completed at one meeting. A proposal made at one meeting and an acceptance at another meeting will not constitute a valid marriage. There must be reciprocity between offer and acceptance. The acceptance must not be conditional. Under the Sunni Law, the proposal and acceptance must be made in the presence of two males or one male and two female witnesses present to testify that the contract was properly entered into between the parties. The witnesses must be of sound mind, adult and Muslim. Under Shia Law, witnesses are not necessary at the time of marriage. In Shia Law, a marriage contracted by the spouses themselves or their guardians in private is a valid marriage and the witnesses are required at the time of dissolution of marriage. The parties to the marriage must be acting under their free will and consent and must have the capacity of entering into a contract, i.e., competent to marry. A Muslim who is of sound mind and who has attained puberty may enter into a contract of marriage. The parties to a marriage must be able to understand the nature of their act.

591. There are certain situations under which marriage is not allowed and such situations are termed as disability. Disability to marry means the existence of certain circumstances under which marriage is not permitted. These prohibitions have been classified into four categories:

(1) absolute incapacity or prohibition;
(2) relative incapacity or prohibition;
(3) prohibitive incapacity;
(4) directory incapacity.

Absolute incapacity or prohibition arises from consanguinity, affinity, and fosterage and consanguinity means blood relationship and bars a man from marrying:

- his mother or grand-mother how highsoever;
- his daughter or grand-daughter how lowsoever;
- his sister whether full, consanguine or uterine;
- his niece or great niece how lowsoever;
- his aunt (father's sister, mother's sister) or great aunt, how highsoever, whether paternal or maternal.

592. A marriage with a woman prohibited by reason of consanguinity is void. Issues from such marriage are illegitimate. Affinity prohibits a man from marrying: his wife's mother or grand-mother how highsoever; his wife's daughter or grand-daughter how lowsoever; wife of his father or paternal grand-father how highsoever; wife of his son or son's son or daughter's son how lowsoever. A marriage with a woman prohibited by reason of affinity is void.

Fosterage means when a woman other than its own mother has suckled a child under the age of two years, the woman becomes the foster-mother of the child. A man may not, for instance, marry his foster-mother or her daughter, or his foster sister.

593. The Shia jurists place fosterage and consanguinity on the same footing and refuse to recognize the exception permitted by the Sunnis. The above-mentioned prohibitions on account of 'consanguinity', 'affinity' or 'Fosterage' are absolute and the marriages contracted in contravention of these rules are void. Relative incapacity or prohibition springs from cases which render the marriage invalid only so long as the cause which creates the ban exist. The moment it is removed, the incapacity ends and the marriage becomes valid and binding. These cases are unlawful conjunction, polygamy, or marrying a fifth wife or absence of proper witnesses, differences of religion, woman undergoing Iddat (a period of seclusion after talaq or death of husband). Unlawful conjunction means contemporaneously marrying two women so related to each other by consanguinity, affinity or fosterage, which they could not have lawfully intermarried with each other if they had been of different sexes. Thus a Muslim cannot marry two sisters, or an aunt and her niece. Under the Shia Law, a Muslim may marry his wife's aunt, but he cannot marry his wife's niece without her permission. Marriage prohibited by reason of unlawful conjunction is void under Shia Law.

594. It is unlawful for a Muslim to have more wives than four at a time. A Muslim woman cannot marry more than one husband. If a woman marries a second husband, she is liable for bigamy under section 494, IPC and the issues of such a marriage are illegitimate. A Muslim marrying under or getting his marriage registered under the Special Marriage Act, 1954, cannot marry a second wife during the lifetime of his spouse.

595. A Sunni male can marry a Muslim female (of any sect) or a Kitabia. Marriage with the Kitabia, i.e., a woman who believes in a revealed religion possessing a Divine Book like Christianity and Judaism is valid under the Sunni Law. But marriage with an idolatress or a fire-worshipper is not permitted. A marriage with an idolatress or a fire-worshiper is merely irregular in Sunni Law, but void in Shia Law. A Muslim woman cannot marry any man who is not a Muslim, whether he is Kitabia (i.e., man believing in a revealed religion possessing a Divine Book) or not. Under Shia Law, no Muslim, whether male or female can marry a non-Muslim in the nikah form. A marriage between a Muslim and a non-Muslim can only take place under the Special Marriage Act, 1954. Iddat is a period during which it is incumbent upon a woman, whose marriage has been dissolved by divorce or death of her husband to remain in seclusion and to abstain from marrying another husband during such period. Under Sunni Law, marriage with a woman undergoing Iddat is irregular and not void. But under Shia Law marriage with a woman who is undergoing Iddat is void. Polygamy, i.e., to marry up to four women, is still allowed to Muslim men under the law. Since it is one of the religious practices it is claimed to be immune from any legislative enactment.

§3. Christian Law on Marriage

596. The Christian Law considers marriage to be a permanent union of one man and one woman to the execution of others. Marriage, as is seen in Christian tradition, is not merely a civil contract nor is it purely a religious contract. Roman Catholic Church considered marriage as one of the sacraments. The Christian marriages are governed by the Indian Christian Marriage Act of 1872. The matrimonial relieves among Christians in the whole of India including the former Travancore Cochin area governed by the Indian Divorce Act of 1869. Under the Christian Marriage Act, marriages can be solemnized by a minister/priest in a church. After the marriage, the priest registers the marriage and issues a marriage certificate.

597. The Supreme Court has ordered the compulsory registration of all marriages in India, irrespective of the religion. A marriage, which has already been solemnized by a priest in the church can be registered by a registrar of marriages. The parties to the registration of marriage have to apply to the concerned authority in whose Jurisdiction either party has been residing. Along with the application form they have to attach two photographs of the marriage ceremonies, invitation card of marriage, age and address proof of both parties, affidavit with regard to these as well marital status, fit mental condition and the marriage certificate issued by the priest. So the freedom to marry is regulated by their own marriage law among the Christians.

§4. Live-In Relationship

598. The new generations are considering relationships between a man and a woman from a different perspective and more liberally. One such concept is live-in relationships which are being adopted by numerous couples. A variant is maître qarar meaning friendship agreement. The relationships where two people cohabit without any legal obligations towards each other are known as live-in relationships. In this relationship, both partners enjoy individual freedom and live in a shared household without being married to each other and either of the partners can walk out of the relationship. Indian law does not provide any rights or obligations to the parties in a live-in relationship. However, the courts have evolved some principles to deal with live-in relationships through various judgments. The Supreme Court has ruled that any couple living together for a long term will be presumed as legally married unless proved otherwise. The aggrieved live-in partner can take shelter under the Domestic Violence Act 2005, which provides protection and maintenance and thereby grants the right of alimony. A man and woman cohabiting for a long term will be presumed as legally married under the law unless proved contrary. The right to maintenance in a live-in relationship is decided by the court in accordance with the Domestic Violence Act, 2005 and the individual facts of the case.

599. In *Badri Prasad v. Dy. Director of Consolidation* (AIR 1978 SC 1557), the Supreme Court of India recognized live-in relationship and interpreted it as a valid marriage. The court gave legal validity to a 50-year live-in relationship of a couple. It was held by Justice Krishna Iyer that a strong presumption arises in favour of wedlock where the partners have lived together for a long time as husband and wife.

600. In *Tulsa & Ors v. Durghatiya & Ors* [(2008) 4 SCC 520], the Supreme Court held that one of the preconditions for a child born from live-in relationship to be treated as legitimate is that the parents must have lived under one roof and cohabited for a considerably long time for society to recognize them as husband and wife. The relationship must not be a 'walk in and walk out'. The court granted the right to property to a child born out of a live-in relationship.

601. In the case of *D.Velusamy v. D.Patchaiammal* (Cr. Appeal Nos 2028–2029 OF 2010) the court pointed out certain prerequisites for a live-in relationship to be considered valid. For example, the couple must hold themselves out to society as being akin to spouses and must be of legal age to marry or qualified to enter into a legal marriage, including being unmarried. The couple must have voluntarily cohabited and held themselves out to the world as being akin to spouses for a significant period of time. However, if a man keeps women as a servant and maintains her financially and uses for sexual purposes, such relationship would not be considered marriage in the court of law. Therefore to get such benefit the conditions mentioned by the court must be satisfied, and has to be proved by evidence.

602. In *S. Khushboo v. Kanniammal & Anr,*[138] the petitioner was charged under section 499 of the IPC and it was also claimed that the petitioner endorsed premarital sex and live-in relationships. The court held that living together being right to life and hence not illegal in the eyes of law even if it is considered immoral in the eyes of the Indian society.

603. In *Indra Sarma v. V.K.V.Sarma* (2013 (14) SCALE 448), the Supreme Court pointed out five categories where the concept of live-in relationships can be considered and proved in the court of law, namely:

(i) Domestic relationship between an adult male and an adult female, both unmarried.
(ii) Domestic relationship between a married man and an adult unmarried woman, entered knowingly.
(iii) Domestic relationship between an adult unmarried man and a married woman, entered knowingly.
(iv) Domestic relationship between an unmarried adult female and a married male, entered unknowingly.
(v) Domestic relationship between same-sex partners (gay or lesbian).

The Supreme Court in this case held that such relationship will fall within the expression 'relationship in the nature of marriage' under section 2(f) of the Protection of Women Against Domestic Violence Act, 2005. Also, all facets of the interpersonal relationship need to be taken into account, including the individual factors. The Parliament has to ponder over these issues, bring in proper legislation or make a proper amendment of the Act, so that women and the children, born out of such relationships, are protected, though such relationship might not be a relationship in the nature of a marriage.

§5. Lacunas in the Existing Divorce Laws in India

604. The existing three-tier divorce structure in India, largely applicable to all communities, i.e., fault grounds, breakdown theory and the mutual consent principle provide the codified and statutory grounds for divorce in Indian Courts. There is a clear indication through judicial pronouncement that the ground of irretrievable breakdown of marriage should be rarely used. However, the Apex Court has recommended that 'irretrievable break down of marriage' should be added as a ground for divorce in the statute book.

138. (2010) 5 SCC 600.

605. There are certain technicalities which obstruct the court or the parties in giving or obtaining a decree of divorce. Like, for example, the following:

- Under consent theory the consent of both the parties is necessary for the decree of divorce. However, it may so happen that one of the parties just to harass the other party out of anger, jealousy, ill will, etc., may withhold consent, which will be a major hindrance in obtaining divorce by parties or in giving divorce by courts.
- Under fault theory, the requisite condition is that one of the parties must be at fault for any of the matrimonial offences, while the other party must be completely innocent. If it is found that the other party is also at fault for any of the matrimonial misconduct, the divorce will not be granted.
- Again under fault theory there are certain technicalities, due to which the courts are not able to give a decree of divorce, which causes such a great hardship to the innocent party, leading to a great miscarriage of justice.
- Therefore there is a demand for an irretrievable breakdown of marriage, as a separate ground for divorce, which notwithstanding these technicalities will empower the court to dissolve the marriage between the parties.

I. Law Commission Recommendations and Its Impact

606. Law Commission in Chapter 6 'Requirement of Living Apart' of 71st of its Report has described the situations from which it can be presumed de facto by the courts that marriage has irretrievably broken down. The situations are as follows:

- Agreement of separation between two married couples.
- 'Not cohabiting' should be sufficient proof for the irretrievable breakdown of marriage.
- Separate living of spouses for more than five years should be sufficient proof.
- Continuous separate living of spouses in the prime period of youth, and desire of not coming together in mind of one is sufficient proof.
- After a continuous separation arising out of the rift and no petition for conjugal rights from either side is filed during the period of one year, 'separation' should be a conducive ground for the irretrievable breakdown of marriage.
- Continuous separation for more than one year, coupled with suspicion of misconduct from either side, mental or physical cruelty arising out of admission. Discovering either of the spouses engaging in adultery covering premarital illicit relations, rendering their living together impossible.
- If a case for judicial separation or divorce or restitution for conjugal rights is pending for three years, and no attempt to settle the dispute or to compromise is made by either party.
- In some cases, it is even enough to take into account a simple submission of the spouse that he or she cannot live together.

607. In view of the above-noted position of law, a civilized parting of spouses where a marriage has irretrievably broken down should be incorporated in the statute book as an additional ground for divorce, but only in cases where both the parties to the marriage jointly petition the court for such relief. This will have an immediate twofold benefit. First, where parties have irreconcilable differences and want to part amicably, an option will be available to them to part legally and logically without resorting to a protracted, time-consuming legal battle on trumped-up grounds. Second, recourse to ex parte divorce in foreign jurisdictions by NRI against spouses on Indian soil may decline, once a proper legal option of irretrievable breakdown is available to spouses on Indian soil. However, to prevent hasty divorces or misuse, sufficient statutory safeguards can be incorporated to arm the judiciary to prevent any abuse of the process of law.

Chapter 3. Freedom of Expression

608. Religious communities are free to have and to demand special respect from their employees for their spiritual and moral teaching like priest in temples, Imam in mosques and pastor in churches. Further, in case members of a religious community make statements against the teaching of the religion, they can be excluded from the community and debarred from social functions but as per law no force can be used and they cannot be called to appear before the community forum or bodies.

609. People who have written against their community are to be given protection so as to protect right of free speech. Threats against such persons are not allowed under the law. But if an individual voluntarily agrees to undergo the punishment, law will not prevent that an example is of Giani Zail Singh, an ex-President of India who was declared a Tankhayya by Sikh body had to perform kar seva (community service) in Golden Temple at Amritsar. Communities generally try to punish themselves against any statement or act of person of their religion who criticize the religion or its practices. In some cases, if something has been written which in the estimation of the community is offensive, then pressure is mounted on the government to ban such writings, e.g., ban in India on Satanic Verses written by Salman Rushdie. However, freedom of speech and expression is not absolute under the Constitution and it can be regulated by the government. Freedom of expression is not a license to hurt the sentiments of others.

Chapter 4. Due Process Norms and Religious Groups

610. The state actions may interfere with free exercise of religion and infringe upon liberty if carried out without the due process of law. The specific legal principles and applications that are relevant for due process protections and freedom of religious practice rights remain dynamic. In case of restrictions on any religious practice, there must be a balance between the compelling nature of the state's interest in restricting such practice and the threat to individual liberties posed by such restriction. The freedom of religion is neither unlimited nor without restriction or constraint as the Constitution itself contains that restrictions can be imposed on freedom of religion on certain grounds. But there must be legitimate reasons for placing restrictions on the exercise of religious practice and religious groups have a right to due process legal protections.

611. However, how and in what manner puja or prayer to God or Namaz will be performed is not the concern of the government and priest is free to perform the same as this is no 'acts of state power' as being matters in which state ought not to interfere. The organization of puja in temples, Namaz in a mosque and church service are matters of the self-determination of the religious community and are exempt from state judicial review unless the religious community submits the matters voluntarily under such review. There is no review of internal procedures of religious communities as to whether and how elections are held or appointments of person in religious offices are conducted. However, in case of specific legislation like Wakfs Act, the procedure prescribed in the Act is to be followed and given effect.

Chapter 5. Professional Secrecy

612. Making confessions before a pastor who is expected to keep such confession secret is common and widely prevalent among Christians which has no identical parallel in any other religion. No such practice exists among Hindus or Muslims in India. Among Hindus pashchatap (repentance) and among Muslims Istaghfar is a matter between the individual and God and no person is there in between. In a 'recent case of a Kerala church where the father exploited a woman blackmailing her for the confessions she made to him led to a widespread demand for declaring the practice of confessions altogether illegal. 'Confessing in itself cannot be a criminal act, it's the misuse of confessions by select priests that needs to be checked. It's a far more progressive and sensible suggestion to eventually also include nuns are individuals who can hear confessions. This need not be enforced by law but the brought in through consensus building within communities. No legal change can satisfy all sections of the society but that does not mean that legislative changes should not be contemplated. However, it is important to separate the disease from the symptom of disease. The issue itself is not about religion for the individuals who indulged in such exploitation also do not have the patronage of any religion. Thus, such criminal cases cannot be seen as a problem with family law. The law already exists on the matter' (Consultation Paper on Reform in Family Law, Law Commission of India, p. 8, 31 August 2018).

§1. Practice among Christians

613. In modern confessional in the church, the penitent may kneel on the kneeler or sit in a chair facing the priest. In Catholic teaching, the Sacrament of Penance is the method of the church by which individual men and women may confess sins committed after baptism and have them absolved by a priest. Although it is not mandatory, the Catholic rite is usually conducted within a confessional box, booth or reconciliation room. This sacrament is known by many names, including penance, reconciliation and confession. While official church publications always refer to the sacrament as 'Penance', 'Reconciliation' or 'Penance and Reconciliation', many laypeople continue to use the term 'Confession' in reference to the sacrament.

614. For the Catholic Church, the intent of this sacrament is to provide healing for the soul as well as to regain the grace of God, lost by the sin of the individual. In theological terms, the priest acts in persona Christi and receives from the church the power of jurisdiction over the penitent. As per the Catholic Church, sacramental confession requires three 'acts' on the part of the penitent: contrition (sorrow of the soul for the sins committed), disclosure of the sins (the 'confession'), and satisfaction (the 'penance', i.e., doing something to make amends for the sins). The basic form of confession has not changed for centuries, although at one time confessions were made publicly.

615. Typically, the penitent begins sacramental confession by saying, 'Bless me Father, for I have sinned. It has been [time period] since my last confession.' The penitent must then confess what he/she believes to be grave and mortal sins, in both kind and number, in order to be reconciled with God and the church. The sinner may also confess venial sins; this is especially recommended if the penitent has no mortal sins to confess. According to the Catechism, 'without being strictly necessary, confession of everyday faults (venial sins) is nevertheless strongly recommended by the Church. Indeed the regular confession of venial sins helps form our conscience, fight against evil tendencies, let ourselves be healed by Christ and progress in the life of the Spirit'.

616. In general, Eastern Catholic and Orthodox Christians choose an individual to trust as his or her spiritual guide. In most cases this is the parish priest, but may be a starets (Elder, a monastic who is well known for his or her advancement in the spiritual life) or any individual, male or female, who has received permission from a bishop to hear confession. This person is often referred to as one's 'spiritual father' or 'spiritual mother'. Once chosen, the individual turns to his spiritual guide for advice on his or her spiritual development, confessing sins, and asking advice. Orthodox Christians tend to confess only to this individual and the closeness created by this bond makes the spiritual guide the most qualified in dealing with the person, so much so that no one can override what a spiritual guide tells his or her charges. What is confessed to one's spiritual guide is protected by the same seal as would be any priest hearing a confession. While one does not have to be a priest to hear confession, only an ordained priest may pronounce the absolution.

617. Confession takes place in the main part of the church itself, usually before an analogion (lectern) set up near the iconostasion. On the analogion is placed a Gospel Book and a blessing cross. The confession often takes place before an icon of Jesus Christ. Orthodox understand that the confession is not made to the priest, but to Christ, and the priest stands only as witness and guide. Before confessing, the penitent venerates the Gospel Book and cross, and places the thumb and first two fingers of his right hand on the feet of Christ as he is depicted on the cross. The confessor will often read an admonition warning the penitent to make a full confession, holding nothing back.

618. In general practice, after one confesses to one's spiritual guide, the parish priest (who may or may not have heard the confession) covers the head of the person with his Epitrachelion (Stole) and reads the Prayer of Absolution, asking God to forgive the transgression of the individual (the specific prayer differs between Greek and Slavic use). It is not uncommon for a person to confess his sins to his spiritual guide on a regular basis but only seek out the priest to read the prayer before receiving Holy Communion.

619. Eastern Christians practise a form of general confession, referred to as the rite of 'Mutual Forgiveness'. The rite involves an exchange between the priest and the congregation (or, in monasteries, between the superior and the brotherhood). The priest will make a prostration before all and ask their forgiveness for sins committed in act, word, deed, and thought. Those present ask that God may forgive him, and then they in turn all prostrate themselves and ask the priest's forgiveness. The priest then pronounces a blessing. The rite of Mutual Forgiveness does not replace the Mystery of Confession and Absolution, but is for the purpose of maintaining Christian charity and a humble and contrite spirit.

620. In the Anglican tradition, confession and absolution is usually a component part of corporate worship, particularly at services of the Holy Eucharist. The form involves an exhortation to repentance by the priest, a period of silent prayer during which believers may inwardly confess their sins, a form of general confession said together by all present and the pronouncement of general absolution by the priest, often accompanied by the sign of the cross. Private or auricular confession is also practised by Anglicans and is especially common among Anglo-Catholics. The venue for confessions is either in the traditional confessional, which is the common practice among Anglo-Catholics, or in a private meeting with the priest. Often a priest will sit in the sanctuary, just inside the communion rail, facing towards the altar and away from the penitent. Other times he will use a portable screen to divide himself and the penitent. Following the confession of sins and the assignment of penance, the priest makes the pronouncement of absolution.

621. There is no requirement for private confession, but a common understanding that it may be desirable depending on individual circumstances. An Anglican aphorism regarding the practice is 'All may; none must; some should'.

622. Most Protestant Churches believe that no intermediary except Christ is necessary between the Christian and God in order to be absolved from sins. Many mainline Protestant Churches include corporate confession in regular worship. For instance, the Presbyterian Church USA's Directory of Worship, in directing the components or worship, states, 'A prayer of confession of the reality of sin in personal and common life follows. In a declaration of pardon, the gospel is proclaimed and forgiveness is declared in the name of Jesus Christ. God's redemption and God's claim upon human life are remembered.'

623. Some Protestants confess their sins in private prayer before God, believing this suffices to gain God's pardon. However, confession to another is often encouraged and in some sects or denominations required when a wrong has been done to a person as well as to God. Confession is then made to the person wronged and also to God, and is part of the reconciliation process. In cases where sin has resulted in the exclusion of a person from church membership due to unrepentance, public confession is often a prerequisite to readmission. The sinner confesses to the church his or her repentance and is received back into fellowship.

624. The second form of confession and absolution is known as 'Holy Absolution', which is done privately to the pastor (commonly only upon request). Here the person confessing (known as the 'penitent') confesses individually his/her sins and makes an act of contrition as the pastor, acting in persona Christi, announces this following formula of absolution: 'In the stead and by the command of my Lord Jesus Christ I forgive you all your sins in the name of the Father and of the Son and of the Holy Spirit.' In the Lutheran Church, the pastor is bound by the Seal of the

Confessional (similar to the Roman Catholic tradition). Luther's Small Catechism says 'the pastor is pledged not to tell anyone else of sins to him in private confession, for those sins have been removed'.

625. In the nineteenth and twentieth centuries, the second form of confession and absolution fell into disuse; at the present time, it is, for example, expected before partaking of the Eucharist for the first time.

626. In the Methodist Church, as with the Anglican Communion, penance is defined by the Articles of Religion as one those 'Commonly called Sacraments but not to be counted for Sacraments of the Gospel', also known as the 'five lesser sacraments'. John Wesley, the founder of the Methodist Church, held 'the validity of Anglican practice in his day as reflected in the 1662 Book of Common Prayer', stating that 'We grant confession to men to be in many cases of use: public, in case of public scandal; private, to a spiritual guide for disburdening of the conscience, and as a help to repentance.' The Book of Worship of The United Methodist Church contains the rite for private confession in A Service of Healing II. Since Methodism holds the office of the keys to 'belong to all baptized persons', private confession does not necessarily need to be made to a pastor and therefore lay confession is permitted. Near the time of death, many Methodists confess their sins and receive absolution from an ordained minister, in addition to being anointed. As with Lutheranism, in the Methodist tradition, corporate confession is the most common practice, with the Methodist liturgy including 'prayers of confession, assurance and pardon'. The traditional confession of The Sunday Service, the first liturgical text used by Methodists, comes from the service of Morning Prayer in The Book of Common Prayer. The confession of one's sin is particularly important before receiving Holy Communion; the official United Methodist publication about the Eucharist titled This Holy Mystery states that:

> We respond to the invitation to the Table by immediately confessing our personal and corporate sin, trusting that, 'If we confess our sins, He who is faithful and just will forgive us our sins and cleanse us from all unrighteousness' (1 John 1:9). Our expression of repentance is answered by the absolution in which forgiveness is proclaimed: 'In the name of Jesus Christ, you are forgiven!'

627. Many Methodists, like other Protestants, regularly practise confession of their sin to God Himself, holding that 'When we do confess, our fellowship with the Father is restored. He extends His parental forgiveness. He cleanses us of all unrighteousness, thus removing the consequences of the previously un-confessed sin. We are back on track to realize the best plan that He has for our lives.'

628. The Church of Jesus Christ of Latter-day Saints teaches that 'Confession is a necessary requirement for complete forgiveness.' The sinner must confess both to those persons wronged by his sin and to God. Confession may also be required to an authorized priesthood leader: 'Those transgressions requiring confession to a bishop are adultery, fornication, other sexual transgressions and deviancies, and sins of a comparable seriousness.' The priesthood leader may counsel the sinner to submit to the authority of a disciplinary council, but does not have the authority to forgive sin. However, the confession must be held in strict confidence unless the sinner grants permission to disclose it to the disciplinary council.

§2. Practice among Buddhists

629. Buddhism has been from its inception primarily a renunciate and monastic tradition. Within the monastic framework (called the Vinaya) regular confession of wrongdoing to superiors (elders; Pali: Thera) is mandatory. In the sutras of the Pali Canon Bhikkhus confessed their wrongdoing to the Buddha himself. That part of the Pali Canon called the Vinaya requires that monks confess their individual sins before the biweekly convening for the recitation of the Patimokkha.

§3. Practice among Muslims: Istighfar

630. The act of seeking forgiveness from God for sins is called Istighfar. This act, generally done by repeating the Arabic words 'astaghfirullah', meaning 'I seek forgiveness from Allah', is considered one of the essential parts of seeking forgiveness of sins directly from God in Islam. Thus, confession of sins is made directly to God and not through man or priest except in asking for forgiveness from the victim of the sin. It is taught that sins are to be kept to oneself to seek individual forgiveness from God. God forgives those who seek his forgiveness and commit to themselves not to repeat the sin, although some sins in which another person is victimized are not forgiven unless that person forgives you, so they should also be asked for forgiveness.

631. The Prophet Muhammad (PBUH) said:

> 'When a servant commits a sin, a black stain is imprinted upon his heart. If he abandons that sin and embraces istigfar and inclines towards tawba, his heart is then polished. If he does not do so and turns back towards the sin, the black spots increase and consequently cover the entire heart. This is the situation that Allah Most High has mentioned in the Qur'an':
> 'No indeed! Rather what they have earned has rusted up their hearts' (Mutaffifin, 83:14) (Tirmidhi, Tafsir, 83/3334).

632. Whenever one commits a sin, which can happen to everyone as a result of being human, one must immediately repent and ask for forgiveness and turn back towards Allah. Almighty Allah praises his pious servants that he is pleased with as follows:

'Those who, when they act indecently or wrong themselves, remember Allah and ask forgiveness for their bad actions (and who can forgive bad actions except Allah?) and do not knowingly persist in what they were doing' (Al'i Imran, 3:135).
'The part of the night they spent asleep was small and they would seek forgiveness before the dawn' (Adh-Dhariyat, 51:17-18).

§4. Confession in Judaism

633. In Judaism, confession is an important part of attaining forgiveness for both sins against God and another man. Confessions to God are done communally in the plural. Jews confess that 'We have sinned.' In matters involving offences against a fellow man, private confession to the victim is a requirement to obtaining forgiveness from the victim, which is generally a requirement to obtaining forgiveness from God. If the victim refuses to forgive, the offender confesses publicly, before a larger and larger audience. Confession (viduy) is also performed on one's deathbed, if at all possible.

Chapter 6. Medical Deontology

634. Deontology is often associated with philosopher Immanuel Kant who believed that ethical actions follow universal moral laws, such as 'Don't lie. Don't steal. Don't cheat.' Deontology is an ethical theory using rules to distinguish right from wrong by believing that action must be justified. Deontology requires that people follow the rules and do their duty. Deontology requires the justification of actions and not of consequences. No doubt, following the rules makes deontology easy to apply. But it also means disregarding the possible consequences of actions when determining what is right and what is wrong. And sometimes consequences may be disastrous.

635. In this background, medical deontology is professional ethics of medical workers and principles of behaviour of medical personnel, directed towards maximum benefit of treatment. It includes problems of observing medical confidentiality, the problem of the extent of the medical worker's responsibility for the life and health of the patient, and problems of relationships of medical workers to each other. In accordance with medical deontology, in relation to the patient, the medical worker must pay maximum attention and apply all his knowledge so as to restore the patient to health and bring relief to him in his sufferings. The medical professionals must convey to the patient only information about his health that will be beneficial to him and establish contact between the patient and the physician. He must avoid in the presence of the patient conversations and discussions with colleagues, personnel, and with the patient himself concerning his illness.

636. In India, Charaka Samhita prescribes an elaborate code of conduct. The medical profession has to be motivated by compassion for living beings (bhuta-daya). Charaka's humanistic ideal becomes evident in his advice to the physicians. He who practices not for money nor for caprice but out of compassion for living beings (bhuta-daya), is the best among all physicians. Hard is it to find a conferor of religious blessings comparable to the physician who snaps the snares of death for his patients. The physician who regards compassion for living beings as the highest religion fulfils his mission (Siddhartha) and obtains the highest happiness.

§1. Informed Consent

637. There is a general belief among the doctors in India that in an emergency situation, it is not possible to get informed consent because of rampant illiteracy. They believe that the patients are unable to make a reasoned choice because they cannot appreciate the intricacies of alternative medical treatment, procedures or drug trials. Often a paternalistic view is taken: 'The doctor knows best.'

638. Charaka advises the physician to take into confidence the close relatives, the elders in the community and even the State officials, before undertaking procedures which might end in the death of the patient. The physician is then to proceed with the treatment. Can the doctor withhold treatment, if there is no informed consent? Can a man refrain from benefiting from medical treatment and forfeit saving his life? Will the doctor be assisting suicide? On the contrary, does not the patient have the right to control what shall be done to his/her body?

639. What is the status of informed consent when a patient is admitted to the hospital in a critical condition but in full possession of his/her senses? Can the surgeon who diagnosed the condition requiring immediate surgery refrain from operating on the sole ground that the patient had not given his/her consent for the operation? If the patient later dies, what is the liability of the doctor? An interesting case came up in the State of Kerala. A patient with acute abdominal pain was admitted to a district hospital. He was examined by the surgeon, who diagnosed perforated appendix with general peritonitis, which required an immediate operation. But the operation was not performed by the surgeon and the patient died the next day. The relations filed a petition in the court against the doctor personally and against the Kerala Government vicariously. The doctor's defence was that the operation was not performed as the patient did not consent to it. The court rejected this plea and granted a decree against the doctor. The decision was confirmed by the Kerala High Court in the appeal preferred by the doctor. Two specialist surgeon who were called as expert witnesses stated that they would have operated on the patient without the explicit consent.

640. In contrast is the view that every human being has a right to determine what shall be done with his or her own body. A surgeon who performs an operation without the patient's consent commits an assault for which he is liable? Indian physicians who are trained abroad or have imbibed this principle find themselves in a conflicting situation. The ancient teaching in such circumstances is that Charaka (Great Physician) advises the physician to take into confidence the close relatives, the elders in the community and even the State officials, before undertaking procedures which might end in the death of the patient. The physician is then to proceed with the treatment.

641. Everyone has the right to a standard of living adequate for the health and well-being of himself and of his family, including food, clothing, housing and medical care and necessary social services – Article 25 of the UDHR. If health is a fundamental human right, it becomes the responsibility of the State to protect and promote the health of all the people. The Alma-Ata Conference declared: 'Governments have a responsibility for the health of the people, which can be fulfilled only by adequate and equitably distributed health and social measures.'

642. All religions advocate the care of the poor and needy. Christ declared: 'When you have done this to the least of my brothers, you have done it to me.' Gandhiji said: 'I will give you a talisman. Whenever you are in doubt or when the self becomes too much with you, apply the following test: recall the face of the poorest and weakest man you have seen and ask yourself if the step you contemplated is going to be of any use to him. Will he gain anything by it?' Kabir said: 'The valiant fighter is only he who fights for justice to the poor.'

§2. ABORTION

643. Hindu medical ethics stem from the principle of ahimsa – of non-violence. When considering abortion, the Hindu way is to choose the action that will do the least harm to all involved: the mother and father, the foetus and society. Hinduism is therefore generally opposed to abortion except where it is necessary to save the mother's life. Classical Hindu texts are strongly opposed to abortion. One text compares abortion to the killing of a priest and another text considers abortion a worse sin than killing one's parents. Still, another text says that a woman who aborts her child will lose her caste. Traditional Hinduism and many modern Hindus also see abortion as a breach of the duty to produce children in order to continue the family and produce new members of society. Many Hindus regard the production of offspring as a 'public duty', not simply an 'individual expression of personal choice' (*see* Lipner, 'The classical Hindu view on abortion and the moral status of the unborn' 1989). In practice, however, abortion is practised in Hindu culture in India, because the religious ban on abortion is sometimes overruled by the cultural preference for sons. This can lead to abortion to prevent the birth of girl babies, which is called 'female foeticide'.

644. The soul and the matter which form the foetus are considered by many Hindus to be joined together from conception. According to the doctrine of reincarnation a foetus is not developing into a person, but is a person from a very early stage. It contains a reborn soul and should be treated appropriately. By the ninth month the foetus has achieved very substantial awareness. According to the Garbha Upanishad, the soul remembers its past lives during the last month the foetus spends in the womb (these memories are destroyed during the trauma of birth).

645. The Mahabharata refers to a child learning from its father while in the womb. The doctrine of reincarnation, which sees life as a repeating cycle of birth, death and rebirth, is basic to Hindu thinking. The doctrine of reincarnation can be used to make a strong case against abortion. If a foetus is aborted, the soul within it suffers a major karmic setback. It is deprived of the opportunities its potential human existence would have given it to earn good karma, and is returned immediately to the cycle of birth, death and rebirth. Thus, abortion hinders a soul's spiritual progress. Reincarnation can also be used to make a case that abortion should be permitted. Under the doctrine of reincarnation, abortion only deprives the soul of one of many births that it will have the consequences of abortion in the framework of reincarnation are therefore not as bad as they are in those religions where a soul gets only one chance to be born and where abortion deprives the soul of all possibility of life.

646. As a general rule, abortion is forbidden in Islam. However, in certain circumstances, Islam is considerably liberal concerning abortion like: (i) the threat of harm to mothers; (ii) the status of the pregnancy before or after ensoulment (on the 120th day of gestation); and (iii) the presence of foetal anomalies that are incompatible with life.

§3. Drinking of Alcohol

647. Drinking of Alcohol is prohibited in Islam and a large body of Muslims in India abstain from drinking.

With respect to alcohol, there is a consensus among Muslim scholars about the prohibition of using pure wine as medicine. In case it is part of some other medicines then it can be used when there is no other alternative. The Hanafis school of thought allowed the use of forbidden and filthy matters in treatment with the condition that: it is known to be a cure and there is no alternative. If alcohol was utilized in the preparation, but the final medicine is not intoxicant, this medicine will be halal to use.

Imam Ibn Taymiyyah said, 'If alcohol falls into water and is altered, then someone drinks it, he would not be drinking khamr and the hadd (penalty) shall not be warranted for him, since nothing of its taste, color or smell remained.'

648. Therefore, physician and pharmacist to use alternatives of alcohol whenever possible, if patient so desires. As for the patients, they may use medications in which alcohol was utilized in the preparation, as long as the medicine is not intoxicant, and it does not have alternatives. As there is a large population of non-drinkers in all the communities, the medical professionals sometimes find themselves in a dilemma if such susceptibilities are shared with them.

Chapter 7. Non-discrimination

§1. Caste System

649. In the post-Vedic times for several centuries caste-based social system occupied a dominant position among Hindus. There are about three thousand castes, with different social statuses. The caste is in the form of four varnas: the learned people, the warriors, traders and agriculturists and the service class. But verna (which means colour) is different from jati (caste). The verna refers to a national category based on the individuals' attributes; by contrast jati refers to a concrete category into which one is born. Castes conferred a social identity on their members. Marriage, property inheritance and peaceful pursuit of occupations were made possible under the aegis of caste framework. The negative aspect of caste is that it fixes permanently the status of an individual in the society and thereby guide or control exclusive attitude of other castes members. There are also ritual restrictions, which limit the psychological barriers in daily life. With modernization taking over the way of thinking and changing the way of living some of these restrictions are modified but within the closed circle of caste and particularly at village level they continue in one way or the other. All spheres of life like professions, services, political affiliations are influenced by castes in some way or other. When the candidates contest the elections for the assembly or the Parliament, caste and community consideration come into focus and considered to play a vital role.

650. Castes in India cut across the religion's barriers. In some form or the other, caste considerations are present among the Muslims, the Sikhs and the Christians as well. Among the non-Hindu groups, castes are not recognized in terms of doctrine or spiritual authority. But they exist as ground reality. Particularly marriages are solemnized within once own caste and not outside. Even the converts from upper castes to other religions prefer their own caste level, in choosing the marriage partners. In recent years, the lower castes have acquired some special status in the form of quotas for admission to colleges, jobs, etc. The sects which exist in India are in Principle different from castes but they too have some caste preferences.

651. In present times the castes are interacting in public places as never before. The old social isolation does not exist in the form in which it existed earlier particularly in cities. In buses and trains, people move together and take food in hotels without reference to their caste. But in villages still caste boundaries are followed even in sitting, interacting, taking food, marriages, etc. There are also instances of clashes between lower and upper-caste communities.

§2. Bhakti and Sufi Movements

652. Another important aspect with respect to non-discrimination was the Bhakti and Sufi movements among Hindus and Muslims, respectively. The rise of Bhakti, a devotional movement emphasized the common man's nearness to God through love, affection and goodwill. Guru Nanak in Punjab, Tulsidas and Kabir in the Hindi region of north India, Chaitanya Mahaprabhu in Bengal, Basaveswara in Karnataka, Shankardeva in Assam, Mira Bai in Rajasthan and Narsi Mehta in Gujarat were some of the prominent exponents of Bhakti movement. They came from diverse backgrounds. Tukaram who composed Marathi literature of high order came from a lower caste. The movement contributed to breaking the caste boundaries of Indian society by opening up the common channels of communication. Further, the social interactions among the people were not restricted to the caste background. In religious assemblies (Satsang) organized under the aegis of Bhakti men, women and children prayed together, ate the food served to them and also stayed in common shelters without distinction of caste, bringing elements of unity. Similarly, the Sufis of north India rallied people around them irrespective of their religious background. Both Bhakti and Sufi social gatherings ushered in widespread harmonious culture in India. The Hindu and Muslim groups shared many values by participating in devotional activities.

653. After independence, large sections of lower castes, including the most backward Dalits, have acquired a new sense of dignity and self-respect. They have used political mobilization and access to the state to assert and promote their interests at all levels of political life. There has been greater inclusion of the lower strata of the people at the local, state, and national levels in the transition of power from the upper castes to the lower castes with major political consequences. At the turn of the twenty-first century, lower-caste chief ministers were no longer rare, and the national cabinet had members from Dalit background. The logic of one person, one vote in free and fair elections has put power in the hands of the more numerous lower castes. The shift in political power has resulted in loosening of the grip of the caste system and the opening of religious places to that strata of society which was forcibly prevented from entering the temples.

654. Under the Constitution there are provisions for both secular and religious pursuits. The individuals and groups are free to follow their chosen way of life without curtailing each other's rights. B.R. Ambedkar, the main architect of the Constitution became a Buddhist and launched a social movement for the improvement of the underprivileged groups. The Constitution provides that the State shall not deny to any person equality before the law or the equal protection of the laws within the territory of India (Article 14). The State shall not discriminate against any citizen on grounds only of religion, race, caste, sex, place, or any of them either in general or in the matter of access to or use of general and public places and conveniences (Article 15). There shall be equality of opportunity for all citizens in the matter of employment or appointment under the state and no citizen shall on grounds only of religion be ineligible for or discriminated against in respect of any employment or office under the state (Article 16). The traditional religious concept of 'untouchability' stands abolished and its practice in any form is strictly forbidden (Article 17). If the State imposes compulsory service on citizens for public purposes no discrimination shall be made on the grounds of religion only (Article 23(2)).

§3. No Discrimination on the Basis of Sex: Entry of Women in Sabarimala Temple

655. In *Indian Young Lawyers Association and ors v. State of Kerala and ors* (WP Civil No. 373 of 2006) matter pertained to Sabarimala Sree Dharmasastha Temple which is dedicated to the Hindu celibate deity Ayyappan also known as Dharma Sastha. The deity is in the form of a Yogi or a Bramchari and this is the reason why young women aged 10 to 50 years are not permitted to offer prayers in the temple. The pilgrims have to observe celibacy for forty-one days before going to Sabarimala. They are also required to strictly follow a lacto-vegetarian diet, refrain from alcohol, not use any profanity and allow the hair and nails to grow without cutting. They are expected to bath twice a day and visit the local temples regularly. They wear black or blue clothes, do not shave until the completion of the pilgrimage, and smear vibhuti or sandal paste on their forehead.

656. The exclusion of (a class of) women from the Sabarimala Temple was justified on the basis of ancient custom, which was sanctioned by Rule 3(b), framed by the government under the authority of the 1965 Kerala Hindu Places of Worship (Authorisation of Entry) Act. Section 3 of the Act required that places of public worship be open to all sections and classes of Hindus, subject to special rules for religious denominations. Rule 3(b), however, provided for the exclusion of 'women at such time during which they are not by custom and usage allowed to enter a place of public worship'. These pieces of legislation, in turn, were examined in the light of constitutional provisions such as Article 25(1) (freedom of worship), Article 26 (freedom of religious denominations to regulate their own practices), and Articles 14 and 15(1) (equality and non-discrimination).

657. In response to a PIL filed in 1991, the Kerala High Court held that the restriction of entry of women ages 10–50 to the temple was in accordance with the usage prevalent from time immemorial, and it directed the Devaswom Board to uphold the customary traditions of the temple. However, on 28 September 2018, the Supreme Court of India overturned the restriction on the entry of women, declaring it unconstitutional and discriminatory. The Supreme Court had ruled that women, of all age groups, can enter Sabarimala Temple in Kerala. The Apex Court through a 4:1 majority said that the temple practice violates the rights of Hindu women and that banning entry of women to the shrine is gender discrimination.

658. So, on 28 September 2018, the Supreme Court had ended an age-old practice of keeping out women in their menstruating age from the temple and had called it discriminatory. Soon after the Apex Court's September 2018 ruling, when women below 50 years of age tried entering the temple, Kerala saw state wide protests that later turned violent. The temple town was virtually turned into a fortress with hundreds of police personnel, including armed commandos and women cops, deployed in large numbers.

659. Following the decision, as many as fifty-six review petitions and some fresh writ petitions were filed challenging the verdict. The five-judge bench of the

Supreme Court, with a 3:2 majority, referred Kerala's Sabarimala Temple case to a larger bench of seven judges. The Bench did not put any stay on the judgment passed on 28 September 2018 that had lifted the ban on entry of women between ages 10 and 50 to the temple. Women can still visit the shrine until the larger bench decides on the matter.

The Bench also said the issue is not only related to women entering the Sabrimala temple but also concerns the entry of Muslim women into mosques. The larger bench will look at all the issues of restriction imposed on women for entering religious places.

Chapter 8. Penal Law and Religion

660. Ancient India represented a distinct tradition of law and had a historically independent school of legal theory and practice. The Arthashastra, dating from 400 BC and the Manusmriti, from AD 100, were influential treatises in India, texts that were considered authoritative legal guidance. Manu's central philosophy was tolerance and pluralism and was cited across Southeast Asia. The appearance of similar fundamental institutions of international law in various parts of the world shows that they are inherent in international society, irrespective of culture and tradition. Inter-State relations in the pre-Islamic period resulted in clear-cut rules of warfare of a high humanitarian standard, in rules of neutrality, of treaty law, of customary law embodied in religious charters, in exchange for embassies of a temporary or semi-permanent character. With the advent of the British Raj, there was a break in tradition and Hindu and Islamic law were abolished in favour of British common law. As a result, the present legal system of the country derives largely from the British system and has few, if any, connections to Indian legal institutions of the pre-British era except the family law of different religious communities.

661. The IPC formulated by the British during the British Raj in 1860, forms the backbone of criminal law in India. The Code of Criminal Procedure, 1973 governs the procedural aspects of the criminal law. Jury trials were abolished by the government in 1960 on the grounds they would be susceptible to media and public influence. This decision was based on an 8-1 acquittal of *Kawas Nanavati in K. M. Nanavati v. State of Maharashtra*, which was overturned by higher courts. In February 2011, the Supreme Court of India ruled that criminal defendants have a constitutional right to counsel. Capital punishment in India is legal. The last execution was conducted on 30 July 2015, when Yakub Menon, a convict in the 1993 Mumbai Serial Blast case, was hanged in Nagpur Jail in the State of Maharashtra.

Part VIII. Financing of Religious Communities

662. The present-day Indian secularism has taken off from the past and as such retains the elements from previous times. Most of the rulers (foreign or Indian) adopted a policy of tolerance towards different faiths. The Greeks, Kushans, Muslims and British who ruled at different times in the form of small kingdoms or as a big empire usually gave grants and endowments to temples, mosques and churches.

663. The Government of West Bengal in April 2012 announced an allowance of INR 2,500 for each Imam, later also extending one to Muezzins, who say the Azaan, of INR 1,500 each. The decision of the government was challenged contending that India was a secular country and the allowance went against constitutional provisions ensuring equality of religion. It was also claimed that the allowance was not in the public interest. The State Government claimed it could lawfully extend the allowance and added that the assembly had okayed the expenditure. The Calcutta High Court rejected this allowance, ruling it to be unconstitutional and against the public interest. A Division Bench ruled that the allowance violated Articles 14 and 15 of the Constitution, which provide that the state shall not discriminate against any citizen on grounds only of religion, race, caste, sex, place of birth, or any of them. The court directed that the allowance be stopped immediately as it was in violation of the provisions of the Constitution (The Hindu, 2 September 2013).

Chapter 1. Direct Financing of Religious Communities

664. During the British period, Lord Curzon established Archaeological Survey of India (ASI) in the early part of the twentieth century for the protection and preservation of national monuments. This was a major step which led to protection, preservation and in some cases discovery of Hindu, Buddhist, Jaina, Sikh, Muslim and Christian monuments. The British government also established a muzarai (religious endowment department) in the government, to give grants for their upkeep. All these policies and practices have continued up to the present in free India. Today, major Hindu temples are managed by government offices.

665. Government make arrangements for the Kawad Yatra, Kailash Mansrower Yatra and pilgrimage to other religious places of the Hindus, Sikhs, Jains and Buddhists.

666. The grants by the Government to schools is another example of direct financing of religious communities. There are numerous schools and colleges run by Hindu, Sikh, Christian and Muslim groups imparting education and teaching general and secular courses and subjects which are not related to religion. There are also medical, engineering and management colleges run by the various trusts. These institutions help in the spread of education. These are not only recognized by the government but also receive grants. The examinations are conducted by various government agencies.

667. If one is a Hindu, Jain, Sikh or Buddhist, he can have a Hindu Undivided Family (HUF) as a separate tax entity and have tax benefits under wealth tax and income tax. The concept of HUF is based on the joint family system. This family comprises of male members that are blood relatives, female members who are either married, mothers, unmarried daughters or widows, etc., along with the children and grandchildren, sometimes extending to five generations, putting up under the same roof. This arrangement of HUF highlights that there is a separate entity called 'Family' that has its source of income, liabilities and assets and fall under the taxation slab. Formation of HUF gives an opportunity to save tax and gain tax benefits under income tax and wealth tax. One can form an HUF and get a Pan Card in the name of the HUF. The Manager of the HUF is generally the senior-most person of the family who is referred to as 'Karta'. The family members under HUF share business, properties, wealth, income and also hold common accounts which are managed by the 'Karta'. This means that 'Karta' becomes the authorized signatory of these accounts. The common corpus gets created when all family members pool in their incomes in the accounts. The 'Karta' manages this, and the division of corpus can be made on the basis of agreement between every coparcener of the family. Tax benefits can also be availed under various sections and heads by formation of an HUF.

668. The Karta of the family is entitled to receive remuneration from HUF in order to carry forth the expenditure and in interest of the family. One needs to be married for creating a HUF. Having children for this purpose is not mandatory.

Daughters are entitled to be a coparcener even after their wedding. Daughters also enjoy the right of being coparcener in two HUFs.

669. Dealing with the issue of abolition of HUF, the Law Commission in Consultation Paper, 2018 has said it is high time that it is understood that justifying the institution of HUF on the grounds of deep-rooted sentiments at the cost of the country revenues may not be judicious.

Chapter 2. Indirect Financing of Religious Communities

670. When the major festivals of different communities are held and large numbers of people participate in them, the state police and paramilitary forces make arrangements and control the crowds. One example is Kumbha Mela which is held in Hardwar, a town situated in north India; once in twelve years, millions of people participate in this event. Unless the state employs its security agencies, these events cannot remain free from mishaps. Therefore, it is quite clear that the government is actively engaged in protecting the people's religious interests. The central assumption is that even if the state does not believe in religion, most of the common citizens believe in it. Hence, the state extends its supports to the religious events. Another important policy is that the religious establishments controlled by the government are open to all people irrespective of their religious affiliation. If discrimination is reported, then the grants given by the government is suspended.

§1. Schemes for the Welfare of Minority Communities

671. To uplift minority communities a number of schemes are financed by the Government. On the basis of Census 2011 data, 870 Minority Concentration Blocks (MCBs), 321 Minority Concentration Towns (MCTs) and 109 Minority Concentration Districts HQs (MCD HQs) falling in 33 States/UTs have been identified.

I. Educational Empowerment Schemes

A. Pre-Matric Scholarship Scheme

672. It is a centrally funded scholarship scheme for students in all states, that aims to provide financial assistance to students from minority communities studying in classes 1 to 10. It helps cover educational expenses and encourages minority students to pursue education.

B. Post-Matric Scholarship Scheme

673. It is a Centrally Sponsored Scheme implemented through the State Government and UT administration and provides scholarships to minority students studying in classes 11 and 12 and pursuing undergraduate and postgraduate courses. It supports students in pursuing higher education and enhancing their career prospects.

C. National Means Cum-Merit Scholarship Scheme (NMMSS)

674. It is the Centrally Sponsored Scheme (CSS) launched in 2008 and focuses on providing financial assistance to meritorious minority students with limited financial resources. It encourages academic excellence and ensures equal opportunities for deserving students.

D. Education Loan Scheme by National Minorities Development & Finance Corporation (NMDFC)

675. NMDFC offers an Education Loan Scheme to students belonging to minority communities.

Concessional credit is provided for pursuing technical and professional courses with a maximum course duration of five years. Educational loans of up to INR 20 lakh are available for five-year courses in India and INR 30 lakh for five-year courses abroad.

II. Employment and Economic Empowerment Schemes

A. Pradhan Mantri Virasat Ka Samvardhan (PMVIKAS)

676. This scheme aims to preserve and promote the rich cultural heritage of minority communities and supports traditional crafts, art forms, and cultural practices to empower artisans and craftsmen.

B. NMDFC Scheme

677. This scheme provides concessional loans to minorities to support their economic ventures and entrepreneurship, enables economic self-reliance and promotes sustainable livelihoods.

III. Special Schemes

A. Jiyo Parsi

678. It is a unique scheme aimed at reversing the population decline of the Parsi community in India. It implements measures to encourage Parsi families to have more children and sustain their community's cultural legacy.

B. Qaumi Waqf Board Taraqqiati Scheme (QWBTS) and Shahari Waqf Sampatti Vikas Yojana (SWSVY)

679. It focuses on the development and utilization of Waqf properties for the welfare of minority communities. It enhances infrastructure and facilities in Waqf properties to serve the community better.

C. Infrastructure Development Schemes

Pradhan Mantri Jan Vikas Karyakram (PMJVK)

680. It aims at creating better infrastructure in minority-concentrated areas and provides improved amenities, healthcare facilities, education centres, and skill development opportunities.

§2. BUDGET ALLOCATION

681. The Budget estimate for the Ministry of Minority Affairs was INR 5,020.50 crore in 2022–2023. For 2023–2024, it has been reduced to INR 3,097 crore. The revised allocation of the funds to the Ministry in 2022–2023 was INR 2,612.66 crore. Several scholarship and skill development schemes got major fund cuts including the merit-cum means scholarship for professional and technical courses for students from minority communities. The schemes have been allotted funds of INR 44 crore this year, while the Budget for the same was INR 365 crore last year. The Finance Ministry has also slashed the funds for the pre-metric scholarship for minorities for the financial year 2023–2024 with over INR 900 crore. The scholarship funds in the last Budget were INR 1,425 crore, which is reduced to INR 433 crore for 2023–2024. The funds for post-metric scholarship, however, have been increased from INR 515 crore to INR 1,065 crore.

Schemes under the Ministry that provide support for students clearing Prelims conducted by UPSC, SSC, and State Public Service Commission got nothing in 2023–2024. The Budget for the same was INR 8 crore last year. Similarly, the free coaching and allied schemes for minorities too saw a Budget cut of around 60% this year. The same was INR 79 crore last year, while INR 30 crore has been allocated this year. The total allocation of the Budget for education empowerment for minorities which was INR 2,515 crore last year is reduced to INR 1,689 crore this year.

682. Skill development training like Nai Manzil, USTAD got a Budget of mere INR 10 lakh, the same was INR 235 crore and INR 7 crore in 2023–2024. The Budget for research schemes for minorities too has been slashed to INR 20 crore from INR 41 crore last year. The total funds for various skill development and livelihood schemes were INR 491 crore in 2022–2023 and the same is INR 64.40 crore this year. In a massive fund cut, the Education Scheme for Madrasas and Minorities has been allocated INR 10 crore for the financial year 2023–2024. The same is 93% less than the Budget allocation of 2022–23, which was INR 160 crore. Almost 50% cut is there in the special schemes for minorities which include research, studies, publicity, monitoring and evaluation of development schemes for minorities, for conservation protection of the heritage of minorities and schemes for containing population decline of minorities.

Meanwhile, a new addition, Prime Minister Virasat Ka Samvardhan (PMVIKAS) has been added to the Ministry of Minority Affairs' Budget for 2023–2024. A total of INR 540 crore has been allotted under the same.

683. The Budget allocation for the Pradhan Mantri Jan Vikas Karyakram (PMJVK), erstwhile Multi-Sectoral Development Programme (MsDP) launched in 2008 and restructured in June 2013, a Centrally Sponsored Scheme (CSS), is reduced massively this year. The Budget for PMJVK was INR 1,650 crore last year which is reduced to INR 600 crore in 2023–2024. The objective of the Scheme is to develop socio-economic infrastructure and basic amenities in the identified Minority Concentration Areas to improve the quality of life of the people in these areas and reduce imbalances as compared to the national average.

Part IX. Education

Chapter 1. Religious Education in Public and Private Schools

684. No religious instruction is to be imparted in the schools wholly maintained by State funding. Further, those attending any State-recognized or State-aided school cannot be required to take part in any religious instruction or services without, and if they are a minor, their guardian's consent (Article 28). However, some elements and governments of some states have tried and still trying to pass on majority religious practices in the name of national cultural heritage and practices like the introduction of learning of Gita in schools in Rajasthan, Surya Namaskar in Haryana, etc., which is being opposed by the minority religious communities like Muslims and Christians.

685. India is a country where religion plays an important role in the daily lives of the people. Four of the world's great religions namely Jainism, Hinduism, Buddhism and Sikhism originated in India as well as several other religions found in certain pockets like followers of Deen-e-Elahi (religion founded by Mughal Emperor Akbar), Kabir Panthis (Followers of Kabir, a Hindi poet). India also has the third-largest Muslim population in the world. While there was a period of widespread religious hatred at the independence of the country (1948–1949) and there have been communal violence and scattered terrorist attacks, still the various religious communities have managed to live in comparative harmony. The Muslim minority has for the most part found the country's democratic institutions offered adequate protections and have faith in the judiciary barring some stray incidents and exceptions. The government-run schools are generally secular. There are a large number of private schools as well imparting religious and/or secular education in the country.

686. In schools and colleges people of different faiths get education. For instance, the Banaras Hindu University is open to non-Hindus and Aligarh Muslim University for non-Muslims. Likewise, Catholic schools and colleges admit many non-Catholics. There is no such religious instruction in these institutions, which implies or amounts to indoctrination. The religious trust retains control over the selection of the staff members subject to the common qualification laid down by the educational boards of the government.

687. The government at the state and central level has embarked upon extensive spread of education. This effort is supplemented by private enterprise. In the early part of twentieth century Banaras Hindu University was brought into existence by the efforts of Annie Besant (an Irish person) who worked with the Indian nationalists and Madan Mohan Malaviya. Sir Syed Ahmad Khan established Muhammadan Anglo-Oriental College which later on became Aligarh Muslim University. The Christian missionaries spread education in south-central and south-eastern tribal areas on a large scale. Still there are large sections of people who are not educated.

688. Article 28(1) of the Constitution requires that religious instruction shall not be imparted in any educational institution wholly maintained out of State funds. Article 28 covers four types of educational institutions:

(a) Institutions wholly maintained by the State.
(b) Institutions recognized by the State.
(c) Institutions receiving aid out of the State fund.
(d) Institutions being administered by the State but have been established by some trust or endowment.

In the institutions of (a) type no religious instructions can be imparted. In (b) and (c) type of institutions, religious instructions may be imparted only with the consent of the individuals. In the (d) type institution, there is no restriction on religious instructions and these can be imparted to all.

689. The Kerala State Education Board in February 2008 recommended banning of religious worship and use of religious graffiti on the walls in private schools that receive assistance from the state. The numerous Christian schools in Kerala conduct regular prayers, including the mass, and their walls abound with verses from the Bible. School buildings are also used for religious conventions. Other recommendations included giving of religious instructions only to those students who have permission from their parents, substituting religious teachings with moral science classes and appointing teachers only from a list prepared by a free agency with statutory powers. Article 30 of the Constitution grants the right to religious and linguistic minorities to establish and administer educational institutions of their choice. However, Christians in Kerala allege that the government is 'interfering' in the administration of their institutions.

690. The educational rights of minorities under Article 30 of the Constitution have been the subject of a large number of judicial decisions of all kinds and implications. In Re Kerala Education Bill case, the Supreme Court held that the Constitution has guaranteed certain cherished rights to the minorities concerning their language, culture and religion. So long as the Constitution stands as it is and is not altered, it is, we conceive, the duty of this court to uphold the fundamental rights and thereby it is our sacred obligation to the minority communities who are of our own. The right guaranteed under Article 30(1) is a right that is absolute, and any law or executive direction which infringes the substance of that right is void to the extent of infringement.[139]

691. In the case of *St Xavier's College v. State of Gujarat*, the court observed that these provisions enshrined a befitting pledge to the minorities in the Constitution of the country whose greatest son had laid down his life for the protection of the minorities. As long as the Constitution stands as it is today, no tampering with those rights can be countenanced. Any attempt to do so would not only be an act of breach of faith but it would also be constitutionally impermissible.[140] In the case of *St Stephen's College v. University of Delhi*,[141] the Supreme Court decided that minority intake in minority institutions should, in the interest of national integration be limited to 50%.[142]

692. From 1997 onwards, larger Supreme Court Benches have looked into various aspects of the provision of Article 30, generally restricting its scope.[143] Some critics say that by judicial interpretation a right has been converted to the extent of percentage of admission into a duty or obligation of institution established by minorities to admit 50% students from other communities. It is also questionable as to how a strength of 50% students from the community will preserve their culture, which will always be threatened by the culture of equal number of students of the communities other than minorities. This seems on the face of it discriminatory, being applicable without casting a corresponding duty on institutes' run by majority or by the government to ensure any percentage of students of minority communities, which will better, protect and advance the cause of national integration. A relook is required as from this decision it seems that it is the duty of institutions established by minority community to work for national integration and no corresponding duty has been cast on institutions run by majority community to restrict the percentage of the majority community students or at least ensure that there are not to say 50% but the presence of even some percentage of minority community students.

139. AIR 1958 SC 956.
140. AIR 1974 SC 1389.
141. (1992) 1 SCC 558.
142. However, there is no law or judicial decision to ensure a reasonable presence of children from the minority communities in educational institutions established and run by the majority community.
143. *TMA Pai Foundation v. State of Karnataka* (2002) 8 SCC 481; *Islamic Academy of Education v. State of Karnataka* (2003) 6 SCC 697; *PA Inamdar v. State of Maharashtra*, AIR 2005 SC 3226.

Chapter 2. Religious School

693. Religion can affect a family's appreciation of the type of education parents want for their children. Various religious groups have also set up schools imparting religious as well as secular education and others imparting only religious education like gurukuls by Hindus, madarsas by Muslims, etc. The Christian Societies and Institutes have played a major role in the country's educational system. Most Indians attend secular state schools. The largest system of religious education has been the Islamic madrassas set up by Muslims and gurukuls set up by Hindus. During the British rule, Christian private schools were quite prominent and widely attended by both the UK (British) and Indian students. Many of the schools established during this era are still functioning and imparting education.

§1. Madarsas and Maktabs

694. In India madarsas and maktabs were originally started from Khanqas which taught Quran recitation and Islamic rituals. From the thirteenth to nineteenth centuries, the Muslim rulers of India built maktabs or madrasas alongside mosques to teach both religion and science. Thus, madrasas became the principal institutions in the education system. The syllabus of Madarsa known as Darse-Nizamia was first consolidated by Mulla Nizamuddin during the reign of Aurangzeb which has been static since then. At present there are a large number of madarsas in India, which are providing free education to the specially deprived section of the Muslim society. There are various estimates about the number of madarsas in India and different sources estimate different numbers and some sources exaggerate these numbers with some motives. In the state of Bihar, there are a number of madarsas under government control. Bihar government pays the salary of the teaching and non-teaching staff. There are 507 madarsas affiliated to the West Bengal Madarsa Board. The madarsas are mainly concentrated in the state of Assam, Bihar, Gujarat, Karnataka, Kerala, Madhya Pradesh, Rajasthan and UP. There are in fact many madrasas in India that would like to prepare Muslim children to be good Muslims and responsible, engaged, and productive members of society and these operate part-time from mosques with the time not in clash with regular schools. In India, generally Urdu is the medium of instruction in these madarsas.

§2. Gurukuls

695. In schools run by Hindu organizations, Hindu students are typically taught the Bhagavad Gita, which explains the ethics and duty of a person, as well as one's relationship with Krishna, the God. This is taught in Vaishnavism, the Hindu sect for which the Gita holds the most importance. Students are also taught the Sanskrit language and Vedic philosophy. Other Hindu religious texts, including the Upanishads and Itihasas (history), are studied in these contexts, in both religious and secular schools.

§3. Christian Societies and Education

696. In the Indian context, the Christian community has related itself to the multicultural and multireligious reality. Throughout the history of the Indian Church, it aimed its missionary goal as the preaching of the Gospel and the making of disciples. The Christian education along with making members aware of the total Christian heritage of the faith and witness also helps widen the horizons of understanding. In the present teaching, Christian education is limited to the imparting of the Bible and Christian tradition. Christian education is a process in which the learner is facilitated to look at his or her faith in relation to scripture, traditions of the church as well as to the Indian context and to the life situations. In Christian education, the Bible needs to be used as both the beginning point and a reliable way to interpret the meaning of God's liberative activity in human experience. Living within a modern, secular and pluralistic society, one is bound to be confronted with people of different faiths and life stances.

697. There are a number of Christian seminaries and theological colleges spread throughout India like Academy of Integrated Christian Studies; Andhra Christian Theological College; Bishop's College, Calcutta; Eva Rose York Bible Training and Technical School for Women; Kerala United Theological Seminary; South Asia Theological Research Institute; Trinity Theological College, Dimapur; Charis Bible College, Mumbai, etc. These Seminaries emphasize practical ministerial exposure. Students and faculty participate in annual Gospel Campaigns (camps at rural villages). A student will not graduate without completing the practical work assignments. After graduation, they work as pastors and evangelists in ministries throughout India. Some work in Bible Colleges as lecturers while others are involved in children's or church planting ministries. Many graduates continue their theological education in higher studies.

Part X. Matrimonial and Family Law

Chapter 1. Legal Position of Religious Marriage

698. India is a land of diversity with several religions and has the personal laws governing the Hindus, Muslims and others. The Hindu personal law has undergone changes by a continuous process of codification. The process of change in society has brought changes in law reflecting the changed social conditions and attempts to solve social problems by new methods in light of the experience of legislations in other countries of the world. The Muslim Personal Law has been comparatively left untouched by legislations.

699. The Indian Parliament and before that British Colonial Governments have enacted legislations covering family laws which are applicable to the religious communities defined in the respective enactments themselves. The main marriage law legislation in India applicable to the majority population, constituted of Hindus, is the HMA, 1955, which is an Act to amend and codify the law relating to marriage among Hindus. Ceremonial marriage or religious marriage is essential under this Act and registration is optional. It applies to any person who is a Hindu, Buddhist, Jaina or Sikh by religion and to any other person who is not a Muslim, Christian, Parsi or Jew by religion. The Act also applies to Hindus who reside outside India. Nothing contained in the Act shall be deemed to affect any right recognized by custom or conferred by any special enactment. So religious law arising out of the custom has been left untouched.

700. The Special Marriage Act, 1954, is another important enactment which provides for a special form of marriage in certain cases, for the registration of such and certain other marriages and for divorces under this Act. This enactment of solemnizing marriage by registration can be resorted to by Hindus, non-Hindus and foreigners marrying in India who opt out of the ceremonial marriage under their respective personal laws. Registration is compulsory under this enactment. This legislation governs people of all religions and communities in India, irrespective of their personal faith. Likewise, under the Foreign Marriage Act, 1969, a person has only to be a citizen of India to have a marriage solemnized under this Act outside the territorial limits of India.

§1. Jain Marriage Law

701. Werner Menski explored the role of Jain law under British rule as well as in post-independence India. He highlighted the fact that conciliatory offers by the British to ascertain 'Jain Law' through an examination of their sacred texts were largely rebuffed by Jains, and as a result, Jains, as a community distinct from Hindus, tended to become functionally invisible. In addition, Jains showed a marked reluctance to participate in the Anglo-Indian courts. Since the HMA of 1955–1956, in which Jains, Buddhists, and Sikhs were lumped together under Hindu law, this situation has not changed. Menski suggests, however, that an unofficial 'Jain Law' has functioned and continues to function in unreported lower court decisions and in extra-judicial arenas, but so little data has been collected thus far that the extent of application of any such unofficial Jain law in practice is still a matter of speculation.

702. Among the Jains, the main purpose of marriage is to maintain the continuity of human race by getting legitimate children. Here the institution of marriage is viewed clearly in its social aspect. There is no religious motive whatsoever in contracting a marriage as such. The necessity of marriage arises to provide a legitimate outlet to sexual feelings and to maintain the continuity of human race. Both purposes are served by regulating the sexual behaviour of people through the institution of marriage. That is why among the Jains, like Hindus, vivaha or marriage is generally considered obligatory for every person and it is included in the Sarirasamskaras (i.e., sacraments sanctifying the body) through which every man and woman must pass at the proper age and time.

703. Though Jains and Hindus regard marriage as obligatory for every person, however, there is a difference in their outlook. Jains look at it from a purely social point of view but Hindus treat it from a religion point of view. Among the Hindus, marriage is made compulsory for every person because the birth of a son is said to enable one to obtain Moksa. Again, it is believed by Hindus that one's progeny is considerably connected with and instrumental to happiness both in this world as well as hereafter. Moreover, the birth of a son is conceived by Hindus to be especially contributory towards helping the father to execute his obligations due to the departed ancestors – one of the three debts or obligations which every Hindu is bound to discharge. There is an intimate connection between marriage and the ultimate object in life viz., Moksa. As marriage is related to the emancipation of soul, marriage and religion are very closely connected with one another in Hindu society. Thus, the institution of marriage among Hindus loses its entirely social character, gets mixed up with religious behaviour of the people and considered a religious act as such. In the Jain religion, on the contrary, marriage is not treated as a religious duty but is considered a purely social act. It is regarded more in the nature of a civil contract than of a religious ceremony. Its object is to maintain the continuity of human race and not to obtain salvation by securing male offspring. Marriages are entered into for purely practical reasons and religion has nothing to order in this respect. When no offerings are to be made to the forefathers, the question of discharging obligations due to departed ancestors does not arise. Jain scriptures do not lay down elaborate rules and regulations regarding marriage. Marriage is completely based on the customs of people designed to adjust the life of persons in this world.

704. For Jains the ultimate object in life is the attainment of Moksa, i.e., liberation of soul from worldly bondage. The best way, according to Jainism, to achieve this aim is to perform right action along with right faith and right knowledge. The right action includes proper channelizing of sexual practices with a view to lead a useful life which serves as a stepping stone for getting salvation. Moreover, religion depends for its existence on the number of its followers. The strength of the followers can be rightfully maintained through the procreation of legitimate children. Taking into account these considerations it can be stated that the object of marriage in Jainism is twofold, viz.: (a) to give a legitimate outlet to sexual feelings; and (b) to promote the cause of dharma (Law) by generating righteous and chivalrous sons and daughters.

705. The Jain philosophy gives more importance to the policy of renunciation. The strict observance of celibacy throughout whole life is valued more than indulgence in sensual pleasures. But Jainism is not against marriage. Persons who lead a complete celebrate life are highly appreciated, yet those who cannot follow that path are not denounced. There are many people who cannot practice the strict life of renunciation and such persons are advised to get married as the next best course. That is why marriage has been included in the sacraments through which every Jain must pass at the proper age and time. This arrangement makes it obligatory for every householder to give of his own accord his daughters in marriage before they attain puberty. Further, it has been ordained that those persons who will keep their grown-up daughters in their homes without marrying them would fall from religion. In view of these injunctions, parents rush in to contract the marriages of their children.

§2. Parsi Marriage Law

706. The Parsi Marriage and Divorce Act, 1936 as amended in 1988, is an Act containing the law relating to marriage and divorce among the Parsis in India. The Christian Marriage Act, 1872, was enacted as an Act to consolidate and amend the law relating to the solemnization of the marriages of Christians in India and the Divorce Act, 1869 as amended in 2001, is an Act to amend the law relating to divorce and matrimonial causes relating to Christians in India.

§3. Muslim Marriage Law

707. The Muslim Personal Law (Shariat) Application Act, 1937, The Dissolution of Muslim Marriages Act, 1939, The Muslim Women (Protection of Rights on Divorce) Act, 1986 and the Muslim Women (Protection of Rights on Divorce)

Rules, 1986, apply to Muslims of India. The marriage is solemnized by the religious rituals and registration is not essential. The issue of registration of all marriages is being debated and is under active consideration for making a legislation. The Muslim Women (Protection of Rights on Divorce) Act, 1986 was brought to provide for maintenance to Muslim women and children on talaq. Recently the government has enacted the Muslim Women (Protection of Rights on Marriage) Act, 2019 which has been implemented retrospectively from 19 September 2018. This Act makes triple talaq in one sitting void and illegal and the husband shall be punished with imprisonment for a term which may extend to three years and shall also be liable to fine.

§4. Inter Caste Marriages

708. The Constitution of India guarantees the fundamental rights to equality, freedom and protection of life and personal liberty. Equality of laws and equal protection of laws is the touchstone and the spirit of these rights. Additionally, the Directive Principles of State Policy endeavour that the State shall strive to promote the welfare of the people in a social order in which justice, social, economic and political, shall inform all the institutions of national life. However, when young men and women marry outside their castes or community, strong sentiments are evoked in society, particularly in rural areas and even results in murders in the name of honour killings even though there is no bar to inter-caste marriages under any codified marriage law.

709. one such decision rendered by the Supreme Court, it was held that the caste system is a curse on the nation and needs to be destroyed for the better. Acts of violence and threats against such inter-caste couples are wholly illegal and those who commit them should be severely punished. The Supreme Court directed the administration and police authorities to ensure that no inter-caste couple is harassed by anyone or subjected to any threat or act of violence. Truly, the message of the court is clear: India of the twenty-first century cannot be built on the basis of casteism.

§5. Child Marriage

710. Child marriage existed historically in India; it is believed that child marriage was prevalent in the ancient as well as medieval times.[144] Some Indian scholars question the existence of child marriage in ancient India, but in most religious texts the father was urged to marry off his daughter at a very young age. Most religious texts recommend[145] ages between 8 to 10 as the ideal age for marriage. Sage Manu, in his Manusmriti has categorically written[146] that if a girl remains unmarried after reaching puberty, the father has failed in his duty towards her. Similarly,

144. J. Sagade, *Child Marriage in India* (Oxford University Press 2005).
145. M. Smriti, *The Constitution of Vedic Society.*
146. *Supra* n. 46.

another sage, Parasara, said that the parents or guardians of a girl who reaches puberty before marriage will definitely go to hell. Among the Yadavs, Guptas, Thahare, Kurmis, and Mourya it was believed that if a daughter was married before the start of her menstrual period the blessings that will accrue will be akin to the donation of 7,800 cows. However, if the marriage is solemnized after a daughter's menstrual period, it will have the same effect as killing 7,800 cows. One thing that must be kept in mind when tracing the religious and cultural roots of child marriage is that in 400 BC the average life span of a woman was between thirty-five and forty years; if this was a rationale for early marriage at one time, this is no longer an issue. According to Customary Muslim Law, child marriages are permitted. A person can enter into a valid marriage after reaching puberty, that is once he or she attains the age of 15.

711. The practice of child marriage was prevalent during the British period. Two significant cases in the nineteenth century brought the issue of child marriage into limelight. The *Rukhmabai* case[147] in Maharashtra and *Phulmonee* case[148] in Bengal as they are popularly known raised significant questions about the age and issue of consent in Hindu marriage. In the case of *Phulmonee* the girl child aged 11 years died because of a haemorrhage from a rupture of the vagina caused by her husband who had forcible sexual intercourse with her, but the court acquitted her husband as the girl was above 10 years and according to the law sexual intercourse with a wife who was above the age of 10 was not rape. This case galvanized public support for the Age of Consent Bill and in many ways silenced the opposition. Both the cases marked the tension between the Hindu orthodoxy on the one hand that upheld child marriage and perceived any opposition to it as an affront to tradition and social reformers opposing such religious bigotry on the other hand. For the latter such blind adherence to social norms meant the continuation of harmful practices in the name of tradition and therefore necessitated immediate challenge of such socially sanctioned practices including child marriage.

I. The Child Marriage Restraint Act, 1929

712. The issue of child marriage was first addressed in the 1860s when the IPC laid down provisions dealing with child marriage. The minimum age for marriage was not laid down; laws were made to punish those who had sexual intercourse with their wives below a particular age. The change was intended to give protection to young girls from sexual abuse within the institution of marriage. Section 375 of the IPC provided that sexual intercourse by a man with his wife who is under the age of 15 is considered rape. This was the first step taken in the direction of making child marriage illegal; however, this law could not be successfully implemented and the practice of child marriage continued all over the country. In 1929, the Child Marriage Restraint Act or the SARDA Act came into force with the objective of

147. Cited in Meera Kosambi, Gender Reform and Competing State Controls over Women: The Rakhmabai Case (1884–1888), p. 271.

148. *Supra* n. 49.

eliminating the practice of child marriage. The minimum age of marriage was raised to 14 years for girls by this Act; later it was amended in 1978 by which the minimum age was raised to 18 years for girls. However, this Act has several loopholes and weaknesses, and very few persons have been prosecuted under this Act.

II. The Prohibition of Child Marriage Act, 2006

713. The goal of this Act was to amend the laws in force in relation to child marriage and to abolish the evil practice. However, this legislation could not really abolish the practice of child marriage and merely discouraged it.

A. *The Main Provisions of the Act of 2006*

714. The following are the main provisions of the Act of 2006:

- Section 3 of the Act lays down that a petition can be filed for annulling a child marriage at the option of either party. The act states that a Child Marriage is voidable at the option of either party to the marriage.
- Section 4 contains a provision for maintenance and residence to the female contracting party to Child Marriage.
- Section 5 of the Act deals with the custody and maintenance of the children born out of Child Marriage.
- Section 6 of the Act lays down the rules for the legitimacy of Children born out of Child Marriage.
- Section 9 of the Act lays down the punishment of the male adult marrying a child.
- Section 10 of the act lays down punishment for solemnization of Child Marriages.
- Section 12 of the Act contains a provision as to when a Child Marriage shall be deemed to be void.
- Section 13 of the Act provides for the power of the court to issue an injunction prohibiting Child Marriage.
- Section 15 of the Act makes the offence of Child Marriage cognizable and non-bailable.
- Section 16 of the Act provides for the appointment of a Child Marriage prohibition officer by the state government.

III. The Legal Status of Child Marriage

715. One of the main reasons for the persistence and existence of child marriage after specific legislation is weak legislation and lack of strict implementation. This results in child marriages being conducted with impunity. The age of marriage is 18 for a female and 21 for a male.[149] Any marriage of a person below this age is punishable.

Under the Prohibition of Child Marriage Act, 2006 child marriages were not made void but voidable, that is the parties to an underage marriage could declare it void after attaining adulthood. However, the girl still had the right to maintenance from her husband even if the marriage was declared to be void, hence the right of the girl was protected. Another change that was brought about by the act is that the punishment for encouraging child marriage was increased. Before the passing of this Act, the punishment was a meagre simple imprisonment of up to three months and a fine. Under the new Act, a male adult marrying a child can be punished with rigorous imprisonment which can extend to two years and also liable to pay a fine up to INR 2 lakhs. Persons solemnizing the marriage, abetting the marriage or taking part in the marriage in any way can also be punished in a similar fashion. Under section 12 of the Prohibition of Child Marriage Act, 2006 certain marriages can also be declared to be void.[150] The marriage of a minor child is rendered to be void if the child:

(a) is taken or enticed out of the keeping of the lawful guardian;
(b) by force compelled, or by any deceitful means induced to go from any place; or
(c) is sold for the purpose of marriage; and made to go through a form of marriage or if the minor is married after which the minor is sold or trafficked or used for immoral purposes, such marriage shall be null and void.

716. The court has also been given more powers under this Act. Prevention is always better than cure; the Act envisions situations wherein conducting child marriages should be stopped. The court has the power to issue an injunction prohibiting child marriages.[151] If on an application of the Child Marriage Prohibition Officer or on receipt of information through a complaint or otherwise from any person, a Judicial Magistrate of the first class or a Metropolitan Magistrate is satisfied that a child marriage in contravention of this Act has been arranged or is about to be solemnized, such Magistrate can issue an injunction against any person including a member of an organization or an association of persons, prohibiting such marriage. Under this Act, provisions are made for the maintenance of the girl even if the marriage is annulled later, so the rights of the girl to get maintenance is protected. The children born out of such a marriage are also deemed to be legitimate for all purposes. At present, a child marriage is considered to be a valid marriage, although it can be annulled at the option of one or both parties.[152] Recently it was held[153] by the Delhi High Court that the marriage between an 18-year-old boy and a 16-year-old girl is valid since it is not declared to be void or voidable under any Act, and although both are underage for the purpose of marriage, the marriage is legal and

149. The Child Marriage Restraint Act, 1929.
150. Section 12, 'Prohibition of Child Marriage Act, 2006'.
151. Section 13, 'Prohibition of Child Marriage Act, 2006'.
152. Section 3, 'Prohibition of Child Marriage Act, 2006'.
153. *Supra* n. 71, at p. 27.

binding. After the passing of the Child Marriage Prohibition Act, such marriages are made voidable, but nobody other than a party to the marriage can file a petition for the annulment of the marriage. However, in another case, the same High Court has held a child marriage as a human rights violation, and a minor girl and her 40-year-old husband were restrained from consummating their marriage till she attained the age of majority. The girl was ordered to stay with her parents till attaining the age of majority. However, the court refused to declare the marriage void. Hence, the courts have given conflicting judgments and as a result, the legal position is not very clear, and in many cases, it has been seen that the offenders have gone unpunished in spite of committing the offence.

717. The Supreme Court interpreted section 9 of the Prohibition of Child Marriage Act, 2006, which says: 'whoever, being a male adult above 18 years of age, contracts a child marriage shall be punishable with rigorous imprisonment which may extend to two years or with fine which may extend to one lakh rupees or with both'. The court said neither does the provision punish a child for marrying a woman nor a woman for marrying a male child. The sole objective of the provision is to punish a man for marrying a minor girl. 'The intention behind punishing only male adults contracting child marriages is to protect minor girls', the court reasoned. The case concerned a boy who married a 21-year-old woman when he was 17 years old (The Hindu, 3 January 2020).

IV. Child Marriage Law and Other Statutes

718. The intention of the legislature to disapprove the validity of child marriage is evident in other enactments as well. It is distressing to note that the IPC, 1860 acquiesces child marriage.[154] The exception to section 375 specifically lays down that sexual intercourse of a man with his own wife, the wife not being under 15 years of age is not rape, thus ruling out the possibility of marital rape when the age of the wife is above 15 years.[155] However, if the girl is not the wife of the man, but is below 16, then the sexual intercourse even with the consent of the girl amounts to rape? It is rather shocking to note the specific relaxation given to a husband who rapes his wife when she happens to be between 15 and 16 years. This provision in the IPC, 1860 is a specific illustration of legislative endorsement and sanction to child marriages. Thus, by keeping a lower age of consent for marital intercourse, it seems that the legislature has legitimized the concept of child marriage. The Indian Majority Act, 1875 lays down 18 years as the age of majority, but the non-obstante clause[156] (notwithstanding anything contrary) excludes marriage, divorce, dower and adoption from the operation of the Act with the result that the age of majority

154. *See* s. *375* which defines rape. Though perfectly defined, the Code does not include sexual intercourse with a minor wife above the age of 15 with its purview.

155. Sexual intercourse by a man with his own wife, the wife not being under 15 years of age, is not rape. *See* s. 375 of the Indian Penal Code, 1860.

156. Section 2 of the Indian Majority Act, 1875 says: 'Nothing herein contained shall affect: (a) The capacity of any person to act in the following matters, namely marriage, dower, divorce and adoption. (b) The religion and religious rites and usages of any class of citizens of India.'

of an individual in these matters is governed by the personal law to which he is a subject. This saving clause silently approves of child marriage, which is in accordance with the personal law and customs of the religion.

719. Another glaring instance of legislative endorsement of child marriage can be seen in the Hindu Minority and Guardianship Act, 1956, which clearly says that the natural guardian[157] of a minor girl is her husband. This section does not envisage the impact when the husband of the minor girl also happens to be a minor himself. This acceptance of guardianship of the minor wife itself indicates the legislative intention of giving legitimacy to such marriages. It may be pointed out that legislations like the IPC and Indian Majority Act are pre-independence legislations whereas the Hindu Minority and Guardianship Act is one enacted in the post-independent era. Another post-independent social welfare legislation, the Dowry Prohibition Act, 1961, also contains provisions which give implied validity to minor's marriages. The words 'when the woman was minor' used in section 6(1)(c)[158] reflect the implied legislative acceptance of child marriage. Criminal Procedure Code, 1973 also contains the legislative endorsement of child marriage. The Code makes it obligatory for the father of the minor married female child to provide maintenance to her in case her husband lacks sufficient means to maintain her.[159] The insertion of option of puberty to Hindu law through an amendment in 1976 indicates the silent acceptance of child marriages. The option of puberty provides a special ground for divorce for a girl who gets married before attaining 15 years of age and who repudiates the marriage between 15 and 18 years. Legislative endorsement and acceptance which confers validity to minor's marriage in other statutes definitely tarnishes the very purpose and object of the Child Marriage Restraint Act, 1929 – to restrain and to prevent the solemnization of child marriage. These provisions containing legal validity provide an assurance to the parents and guardians that the legal rights of the married minors are secured. The acceptance and acknowledgement of such legal rights itself and providing a validity of child marriage defeats the legislative intention to curb the social evil of child marriage.

V. Judicial Trends Regarding Child Marriage

720. Solemnization of child marriage is an offence under the Child Marriage Restraint Act, 1929. The Act was simply designed to restrain solemnization of child

157. Section *G(c)* says that the natural guardian of a Hindu minor, in respect of the minor's person as well as in respect of minor's property – in case of a minor married girl is the husband.
158. It reads: 'when any dowry is received by anyone other than the woman in connection with whose marriage it is given, that person shall transfer it to the woman, (c) If the dowry was received when the woman was a minor within one year after she has attained the age of eighteen years and pending such transfer shall hold it in trust for the benefit of the woman'.
159. Section 125(l)(d) Proviso reads: 'Provided that the Magistrate may order the father of a minor female child referred to in clause (10) to make such allowance, until she attains her majority if the Magistrate is satisfied that the husband of such minor female child is married is not possessed of sufficient means.'

marriage without affecting the validity of marriage. The Preamble of the Act specifically states that the aim of the Act is 'to restrain' the solemnization of Child Marriage. How far this object has been achieved, poses a debatable issue. The word 'restrain' means to keep in check, under control, or within bounds and is different from 'prohibit – avoid or invalidate'. Hence, it is doubtful whether the validity or invalidity comes within the scope of the Act. Even before the enactment of the Act, the marriage of a minor duly solemnized had been considered valid. Marriage under Hindu law is a religious ceremony and a sacrament or sanskara. Hence when the marriage rituals are completed by saptapadi before the consecrated fire, it creates a religious tie, which once created cannot be undone. Thus, completion of the marriage ceremony with rituals is enough to confer validity to the marriage.

721. In *Venkatacharyula v. Rangacharyula,*[160] a Vaishnava Brahmin girl got married without the consent of her father. Her mother falsely informed the priest, that the father had given his consent. Accordingly, he performed the marriage with all the rituals. The validity of the marriage was questioned on the grounds of lack of consent of the father. Declaring the validity of that marriage, the Division Bench pointed out that the person married may be a minor or even of unsound mind, and yet if the marriage rituals are duly solemnized, it is a valid marriage. Thus, the duly solemnized marriage was valid even if the parties to marriage were incapacitated. A perusal of the provisions of the Child Marriage Restraint Act 1929 reveals that it is silent about the validity aspect of child marriage. It only penalizes the solemnization of child marriages.

722. In *Munshi Ram v. Emperor,*[161] the daughter of one Ram Chander was married to one Munshi Ram's minor son. The marriage ceremony was completed with the observance of all rituals connected with the marriage. The court pointed out that the gauna ceremony is not a part of the marriage ceremony, and the failure to perform it does not affect the completion or performance of the marriage. Considering the validity of child marriage, Justice Ganga Nath stressed his view in the following words:

> The Act aims at and deals with restraint of the performance of the marriage. It has nothing to do with the validity or invalidity of the marriage. The question of validity and invalidity of the marriage is beyond the scope of the Child Marriage Restraint Act, 1929.

Hence the judges are constrained by the limitations in the Act. Even if the judge feels the omission in the legislation he has no power to fill the gap. Judicial activism is restricted by the express words used in the statute or by necessary implication. If the omission of the legislature is intentional, the courts have nothing to do

160. I.L.R. 189 1 Madras, 316.
161. AIR 1 936 Allahabad, 111. The daughter of Ram Chander had been married to Munshi Ram's minor son. The parents of both the parties were prosecuted. They accepted the solemnization of marriage and hence were convicted under ss 5 and 6 of the Act. On appeal, the Sessions Court confirmed the sentence. An application for revision was filed before the High Court.

with it. The courts have to delve deep into the words to find out the true purpose and object of the Act at the time of enactment. In *Moti v. Beni,*[162] a complaint was made against one Chhotulal that he had kept Beni's daughter Chamelia in wrongful confinement. Chamelia was taken from the custody of Chhotulal and was given into the custody of the mother as per the request of Beni. During the proceedings, it was known that the girl was married to Moti. Then the Magistrate directed to produce the girl before the court and handed her over to the husband. Against this order, an application for revision was filed before the District Magistrate. The District Magistrate ordered Chamelia to the custody of the mother saying that she was yet a girl of 13 years and she cannot be legally married and therefore the proper guardian is the mother. The matter was referred to the High Court. While setting aside the order of the District Magistrate, Justice Thomobo observed that the court below acted without jurisdiction. He vehemently criticized the remark of the District Magistrate that the marriage of Chamelia with Moti was an illegal marriage. His words reflect the real status of the child marriage and the penal nature of the offence under the Act:

> It is true that celebration of this marriage may have contravened the provisions of the Child Marriage Restraint Act, 1929; but marriage of a child is not declared by the Child Marriage Restraint Act, 1929 to be an invalid marriage. The Act merely imposes certain penalties on persons bringing about such marriages.

723. In 1961, Justice S.P. Mohapatra strongly emphasized the indisputable aspect of the validity of marriage in *Birupnkshya Das v. Khujubehare.*[163] The Act does not invalidate the marriage even though it may be in contravention of the provisions of the Act.[164] The HMA was enacted in 1955 and contains the same age limit for the bridegroom at par with the Child Marriage Restraint Act, 1929.[165] The said Act remains silent about the legal validity of child marriage and continues the earlier penal policy adopted in the Child Marriage Restraint Act in case of violation.[166] The legislative policy adopted by the colonial government has been followed even after independence without any change. The judicial decisions also support the view that the validity of the marriage is not affected by the violation of age rule.

162. AIR 1936 Allahabad, 85.
163. AIR 1961 Orissa, 104.
164. In spite of the marriage being valid, it is transparent from the provisions of the Act that the marriage in contravention of its provisions is a criminal act, punishable under the law. The legislature no doubt disapproves all such marriages and makes the performance of such marriage punishable in law.
165. Section 5 of the Hindu Marriage Act deals with the conditions for a Hindu Marriage and clause (iii) says that, at the time of the marriage the bridegroom should have completed the age of 21 years and the bride, the age of 18 years.
166. According to s. 1 S(a) of the Hindu Marriage Act, 1955, a contravention of the condition specified in clause (iii) of s. 5 is punishable with simple imprisonment which may extend to fifteen days, or with fine which may extend to INR 1,000, or with both.

724. In *Kalawati v. Devi Ram*,[167] the Judicial Commissioner of Himachal Pradesh declared that the marriage in violation of the age rule prescribed under the HMA, 1955 would be neither void nor voidable. Further, the minority of the wife or of her guardian itself is not a ground for getting it declared null and void. He affirmed his view in his next decision *Naumi v. Narotam*.[168] Realizing the unnecessary hardship and consequences of making the child marriage void, the legislature may have intentionally omitted incorporating any provision dealing with invalidity of child marriage in the HMA.

725. In *Premi v. Dayararn*[169] the Shimla High Court held that it is not the duty of the court to fill the gaps intentionally left by the legislature. 'A marriage which contravenes the condition specified in clause (iii) of section 5 of the HMA, 1955 is not declared void by section 11 of the HMA, 1955 or any other section of the Act. The omission to declare such a marriage to be void by section 11 of the HMA, 1955 or any other section does not appear to be merely accidental. The legislature has provided punishment under section 18 of the Act, for the breach of the aforesaid conditions. It is not for the court to speculate upon the reasons for the aforesaid intentional omission. But it may not be that the legislature did not intend to declare child marriages contravening the condition about age, specified in clause (iii) of section *5* as void, as though such marriages are discouraged by society and Law, yet the evil is deep rooted and child marriages are not rare in the country and declaring such marriages as void must have resulted in unfortunate consequences and unnecessary hardship to the parties.'

726. In another case *Ma Hari v. Director of Consolidation*,[170] the Allahabad High Court observed that the solemnization of marriage in contravention of the provisions of the HMA may result in punishment, yet the marriage would not become null and void and the marriage would remain valid in Law and enforceable and recognizable in a court of law.

Justice S. Acharya of the Orissa High Court shared the same view in *Buda Sahu v. Laburani Sahuni*.[171] However, in *Budhan v. Manraj*,[172] the court adopted the opposite view while considering the issue of restitution of conjugal rights that the marriage may not be valid if performed in contravention of the age rule but the invalidity cannot be pleaded as an answer to a petition for restitution of conjugal rights. This judicial interpretation which was in sharp contrast to the earlier judicial

167. AIR 1961 Himachal Pradesh, 1.
168. AIR 1963 Himachal Pradesh, 15.
169. AIR 1965 Himachal Pradesh, 15.
170. AIR 1969 Allahabad, 623.
171. I.L.R. 1970 Cuttack, 1215. It is observed that clause (iii) of s. 5, providing for the age of bride and bridegroom is thus specifically excluded from the operation of the provisions of s. II of the Act. The conditions rendering a Hindu marriage null and void mentioned in s. II of the Act are exhaustive and it is only on those grounds a court can grant a decree of nullity under the Act.
172. 1970 P.L.R. 102.

trend was discussed in the 59th Report of the Law Commission[173] and the Commission emphasized the general understanding that child marriage is valid.

727. In *Mohindev Kaur v. Major Singh*[174] The Division Bench of the Punjab and Haryana High Court emphasized that the marriage in contravention of the age rule is not a nullity and hence such contravention cannot be pleaded as a defence to a petition for restitution of conjugal rights. It was further observed that the infringement of clause (iii) of section 5 did not affect the tie of marriage and render the marriage either void or voidable. While deciding a petition on the restitution of conjugal rights in *Gindan v. Barila*,[175] Justice Tankha affirmed the validity of the child marriage and the penal nature of the offence.[176]

728. In 1977, the Full Bench of Andhra High Court in *Venkata Ramana v. State*[177] overruled the earlier *Saramma's* case upheld the validity of child marriages in India. In this case, the wife had made a complaint against the husband under section 494[178] of the IPC as he contracted a second marriage. The age of the husband and wife at the time of marriage was 13 and 9 years, respectively. The defence of the husband was the first marriage as null and void, as it infringed the age rule required for a valid marriage and he relied on *Saramma's* case. The Full Bench observed that the violation of clauses (iv) and (v) of section 5 of the HMA renders the marriage null and void, whereas, it is silent about the effects of violation of clause (iii) of section 5 of the HMA, 1955. Neither section 11 nor section 12 makes any reference to the violation of conditions relating to age rule. The silence of the legislature about the legal effect of violation of clause (iii) except the penal liability clearly reveals the absence of legislative intention to invalidate child marriage. It may be noted that the position under the Child Marriage Restraint Act, 1929 is also the same. In both the statutes marriages in violation of the age rule cannot be considered invalid, but only punishable. So, it is clear that the intention of the legislature is only to punish the solemnization of marriage without touching the validity of the marriage. Further, by introducing the concept of option of puberty[179] in the

173. *See* the 59th Report of the Law Commission of India, on the Hindu Marriage Act 1955 and the Special Marriage Act 1954 (19741, Government of India).
174. AIR 1977 Andhra Pradesh, 43.
175. AIR 1976 Madhya Pradesh, 83.
176. It is observed that a marriage solemnized in violation of the age rule is neither void *ab initio* or even voidable and they do not find place in s. 11 and s. 12 of the Hindu Marriage Act. It is only punishable under s. 1 8 of the Act. However, such marriage is valid, enforceable and recognized by law.
177. AIR 1977 Andhra Pradesh, 43.
178. Section 494 of the IPC reads: 'Whoever, having a husband or wife living, marries in any case in which such marriage is void by reason of its taking place during the life of such husband or wife, shall be punished with imprisonment of either description for a term which may extend to seven years, and shall also be liable to fine.'
179. Option of puberty means the right of a girl to repudiation of the marriage if the marriage was solemnized before she attains the age of 15 years. After attaining the age of 15 years but before reaching 18 years she can exercise this right. This is a principle of Muslim law now incorporated in the HM Act. Whether the marriage is consummated or not she can exercise this right in Hindu law.

Marriage Laws (Amendment) Act, 1976[180] the legislature conferred implied validity on minor's marriages. The incorporation of option of puberty reflects the attitude of the legislature towards the decision of *Saramma.*

After considering the statutory provision and abundant case law supporting the recognition of the validity of child marriage, the Full Bench categorically decided that the marriage solemnized under clause (iii) of section 5 of the HMA is neither void nor voidable.

729. In *D. Pradhan v. Bengabali Dei*[181] Justice Acharya of Orissa High Court also dissented from *Saramma* and held that violation of clause (iii) of section 5 of the HMA does not vitiate the marriage. In this case the wife's petition for maintenance and separate residence was contested with the help of the ruling of *Saramma.* It is to be noted that the judgment, aimed at eradicating the evil of child marriage was thus being unscrupulously used to wriggle out of the consequences following the violation of other important principles. However, the decision of Venkitaramana[182] gives a severe blow to this undesirable and unintended result of *Saramma.*

730. From the study of above case law it is seen that the Indian Judiciary has been in a trend of upholding the child marriages which are being solemnized in contravention of the Prohibition of Child marriages Act, 2006.

VI. Defects in Child Marriage Law

731. Even after the passing of the Prohibition of Child Marriage Act 2006, certain loopholes remain in the law relating to child marriage, the legislation is weak as it does not actually prohibit child marriage. First, child marriages are made voidable at the option of the parties but not completely void. That means child marriages are still lawful. Making such marriages voidable does not really help matters in most cases as girls on attaining majority do not have the agency or adequate support from their families to approach the court and go for annulment of the marriage. The reason behind not making such marriages void probably is that child marriages once solemnized and consummated make it very difficult, if not impossible for girls, to deny and step out of those marriages. Therefore, it is in keeping with the social reality that such marriages are not declared void. If the social reality largely remains the same, the likelihood that young girls will now choose to nullify their marriages, which would probably be consummated by the time they attain maturity and decide to approach the courts, seems very unlikely. Second, the applicability of the Prohibition of Child Marriage Act, on various marriages of different communities and religions is unclear. Social customs and personal laws of different religious groups in India allow the marriage of minor girls and the Prohibition of Child Marriage Act, 2006 does not mention whether it prohibits all underage marriages that are sanctioned by religious laws. Further, registration of marriages has still not been made

180. Marriage Laws (Amendment) Act, 1976 (Act No. 68 of 1976).
181. AIR 1977 Orissa, 36.
182. *Supra* n. 21.

compulsory. Compulsory registration mandates that the age of the girl and the boy getting married have to be mentioned. If implemented properly, it would discourage parents from marrying off their minor children since a written document of their ages would prove the illegality of such marriages. This would probably be able to tackle the sensitive issue of minor marriages upheld by personal laws.

732. The legislature on the one hand declares child marriage to be illegal that is against the law and on the other hand it does not declare it to be void and the only remedy it provides to the affected parties to the marriage is that the marriage is voidable at the option of the party. There is also an urgent need to amend the laws related to sexual assault to address the issue of child marriages and to protect the rights and ensure the safety of young girls. IPC, 1860 states that sexual intercourse by a man with his wife who is not under 15 years of age is not rape. The punishment for rape in section 376 is a minimum term of seven years imprisonment that may also extend to life. However, the same provision incorporates that a man is liable to punishment of a maximum of two years and fine only if his wife is under 12 years of age. Marital rape is not acknowledged under the IPC, 1860 there is also an indirect approval of underage marriages by stating that a man is only liable for rape only if he has sexual intercourse with a girl who is aged less than 15 and not 18. Hence the success of Prohibition of Child Marriage Act, 2006 is bound to be extremely limited without commensurate changes in other related laws involving children. Therefore, it is clear that despite having a law prohibiting child marriage, the child marriages in India is still prevalent.

733. All the codified marriage legislations in India stipulate conditions of a valid marriage. The bone of contention in these stipulations hovers around two harsh realities – age at marriage and registration of marriages. The principal family law legislation in India, i.e., the HMA, 1955, does not render a marriage void or voidable in the event that the boy has not completed the age of 21 years or the girl has not completed the age of 18 years. Child marriages in practically all religious communities in India are accepted practices, which obviously cannot be registered due to non-fulfilment of minimum age of marriage. Therefore, the violation of the condition of minimum age at marriage does not entail nullity of marriage since registration is optional and not compulsory.

734. The lack of a law for compulsory registration of marriages has not gone unnoticed by the courts. The Supreme Court of India directed all states in India to enact rules for compulsory registration of marriages irrespective of religion, in a time-bound period. This reform, which has been spearheaded by the National Commission for Women, has struck a progressive blow to check child marriages, prevent marriages without the consent of parties, check bigamy/polygamy, enable women's rights of maintenance, inheritance and residence, deter men from deserting women, and for checking the selling of young girls under the guise of marriage. The Supreme Court of India in another unreported decision dated 27 March 2006 has stayed the legal validity of the marriages of minor girls below 18 years of age, which had been earlier upheld by the two High Courts' orders. At least seven states in India have a high incidence of child brides and the law does not take care of the anomaly to ban child marriages.

735. The issue of registration is apprehended to create problems for not only Hindus but also other minority religious communities. Even among Muslims, mere non-registration of a marriage will not make a marriage invalid. Codification of personal laws among some religious communities in India is itself a very debatable issue. Besides, as a consequence of the non-registration of marriages, a large number of abandoned spouses have been living in India who are deserted by NRIs habitually residing abroad.

VII. Prohibition of Child Marriage Amendment Bill, 2021

736. The Government has proposed to increase the age of marriage to 21 years. This increase in the minimum age of marriage for women to 21 years as provided in the Prohibition of Child Marriage Amendment Bill, 2021, would come into effect two years after the Bill is notified following its passage in Parliament. This gap would provide ample time for citizens to prepare for this reform. It has provisions to make consequential amendments relating to the age of marriage in the Indian Christian Marriage Act, 1872; the Parsi Marriage and Divorce Act, 1936; the Muslim Personal Law (Shariat) Application Act, 1937; the Special Marriage Act, 1954; the Hindu Marriage Act, 1955; and the Foreign Marriage Act, 1969.

737. A task force was constituted before the introduction of the Bill in Parliament which had examined the correlation of age of marriage and motherhood and some other related aspects. After holding wide consultations with all relevant stakeholders, it had recommended raising the age of marriage for women to 21 years at par with men to provide an effective impetus for greater gender equality in society, paving the way for a girl to join and complete education, professional training and vocational courses. The Bill remained with the Parliamentary Standing Committee and has now lapsed due to the dissolution of the 17th Lok Sabha.

Chapter 2. Legal Position of Religious Family Law

738. In India every major community has its own family law thereby preserving unity in diversity. The attempt made by the first Parliament after independence to bring a Hindu Code comprising the entire field of Hindu family law did not succeed.

§1. Historical Background

739. There is little evidence for the practice of law in India prior to about the eighteenth century. In some regions, such as Maharashtra, a kind of hybrid Hindu and Islamic legal system was fashioned under the Maratha kings. In other places, such as South India, temples were intimately involved in the administration of law. Law during the classical period was highly based upon the teachings of the Dharmasastra and the distinguished sources of dharma as dictated by those learned in the Vedas. Although theologically law was primarily derived from Vedic knowledge, in actual practice, the community norms of particular social groups determined the actually rulings. Law was therefore highly decentralized and quite particular in nature towards specific groups.

740. The court records are completely lacking for classical and medieval India. In lieu of such records, other kinds of evidence for legal practice has to be used to piecc together an outline of Classical Hindu Law in practice. Such evidence includes prominently the numerous inscriptions from this period that record a variety of legal transactions, gifts, contracts, decrees, etc., associated with political rulers, temples, corporate groups and others. Many aspects of the law were likely under the jurisdiction of castes or other corporate groups such as merchant guilds, military groups, traders, and religious orders. Beginning around the eighth century, Hindu legal traditions began to be imported into certain parts of Southeast Asia (Cambodia, Java, Bali, Malaysia, Thailand, and Burma) as part of a larger cultural influence mediated by trade and diplomatic relations. In each of these regions, Hindu law fused with local norms and practices, giving rise to legal texts (Agamas such as the Kutara-Manawa in Java, and the Buddhist-influenced Dhammasattas/ Dhammathats of Burma and Thailand) as well as legal records embodied (as in India) in stone and copper-plate inscriptions.

§2. Jain Family Law

741. The following facets of Jain law relating to their family law are described hereunder:

I. Jain Law of Adoption

742. Jain law written by Acharya Bhadrabahu, as given in Bhadrabahu Samhita and translated by J.L. Jaini enumerates more than 100 rules related to adoption, separation, property distribution, partition, etc., in Jain families. These are as follows in brief:

> In the world, the existence of a son is such a source of happiness that, in the absence of a son, one's birth is fruitless, and a son is taken in adoption by a man. If a man has many brothers, and if they are one mind, it is due to his great punya (religious merit). So the great Rishis (ascetics) have said 'Because of the decline in religious merit, those many brothers for greed of wealth entertain hostile feelings. To remove this trouble, this Law of Partition in undertaken. On the death of father and mother, all those brothers get together the patrimony and divide it equally among themselves'. But during the lifetime of the father (the brothers take only), according to the desire of the father. If a son dies in the life-time of his parents, his chaste wife has no right, like him, in the grand-father's property. If the husband's property is placed in the hands of the father-in-law and mother-in-law, the widow cannot claim it; she can only take what the late husband gave her. If the widow with this permission takes a boy in adoption, she must take one of the same families, younger than herself and possessed of all qualities. In the Jain sacred procession, in the image installation ceremony, and in similar religious deeds, and in the bringing up of the family, the widow has power to spend. But in nothing else she has the power to spend.

II. Succession

743. The leading case on succession is *Bhagawandas Tejmal v. Rajmal*, a succession dispute within a Marwari Jain Agrawal family involving a widow's right of adoption. Adjudicated by C. J. Westropp at the Bombay High Court, the decision was confirmed by the *Privy Council in Sheosingh Rain v. Dakho*. The final judgment distinguished between 'Jain law' and 'custom', but affirmed Westropp's view that the Jains come under Hindu law unless they are able to provide evidence for the prevalence of different customs. In *Bhagawandas Tejmal v. Rajmal,* it was held that 'But when among Hindus (and Jains are Hindu Dissenters) some custom, different from the normal Hindu law of the country, in which the property is located, and the parties resident, is alleged to exist, the burden of proving the antiquity and invariability of the custom is placed on the party averring its existence.'

744. If a Jain marries a Buddhist, Sikh or Hindu, whether by religious rites or as a civil marriage, succession to his property is governed (since 1976) by the Hindu Succession Act 1956. But if he marries a Christian, Muslim, Jew or Baha'i it is regulated by the Indian Succession Act 1925. A Jain Succession Act was enacted in the Madras State in 1930. After the reorganization of states, it became applicable to various areas of Andhra Pradesh, Karnataka, Kerala, and TN carved out of the former Madras State.

§3. Muslim Family Law

745. Indian Muslims' personal laws are based on the Sharia, which is partially applied in India. Despite being largely uncodified, Mohammedan law has the same legal status as other codified statutes. The development of the law is largely on the basis of judicial precedent, which in recent times has been subject to review by the courts.

§4. Christian Family Law

746. For Christians, a distinct branch of law known as Christian Law, mostly based on specific statutes, applies. Christian Law of Succession and Divorce in India have undergone changes in recent years. The Indian Divorce (Amendment) Act of 2001 has brought in considerable changes in the grounds available for divorce. By now Christian Law in India has emerged as a separate branch of law. It covers the entire spectrum of family law so far as it concerns Christians in India. Christian Law, to a great extent, is based on English law but there are laws that originated on the strength of customary practices and precedents.

§5. Parsi Family Law

747. The Parsis are a strictly monogamous and endogamous group. At one time there was an avoidance of marriage between priestly and non-priestly families. Given these restrictions and the small size of the community, it is not surprising that close consanguineal and affinal relatives are potential mates. Cross- and parallel-cousin marriages are permitted, as well as intergenerational marriages (e.g., between uncle and niece). The greatest problem faced by the community today is a decrease in the number of marriages and a decreasing fertility rate. Since the 1950s, deaths have consistently outnumbered births every year, leaving an ageing population. This decline has two causes. Since independence in 1947 many younger Parsis have emigrated from India, thus strengthening the sense of crisis. Further, Parsi women who marry non-Parsis are strictly excluded along with their offspring from the community. Parsi divorce rates are higher than those for other Indian communities because, when compared to Hindu law, Parsi law has always made divorce easier. The education and economic emancipation of females also contributed to the high divorce rate. Remarriage after the death of a spouse is permitted for both sexes. Adoption is also permitted and is common among Parsis.

748. A Bench of the Supreme Court comprising of Mr Justice Kurian Joseph and Mr Justice Amitava Roy has sought the Central Government's response on a plea by a Parsi woman challenging the Parsi Marriage and Divorce Act, 1936 that allows local Parsi community to act as jury in the grant of divorce to an estranged couple. The court wondered why such a law has not been challenged so far.

The petitioner has contended that the involvement of the local Parsi community in the matter of matrimonial dispute violated her fundamental rights (Indo-Asian News Service, 25 November 2017).

749. Both sons and daughters may inherit from both parents. Despite the fact that formal rules of inheritance exist, it is not uncommon for wealthy Parsis to leave their entire estates for charitable purposes: endowing schools, hospitals, fire temples, or the like. The stress on generosity and a sense of communal responsibility for the weak and needy fostered during childhood finds its expression in wills and trusts. Hence there has occurred a continuous redistribution of wealth from the rich to the poor.

§6. Hindu Family Law

750. Since ancient times the framing of all property laws under Hindu law has been exclusively for the benefit of the man, and the woman has been treated as subservient, and dependent on male support. The right to property is important for the freedom and development of any human being. Hindus were governed by Shastric and Customary laws which varied from region to region and sometimes it varied in the same region on a caste basis. The vastness and difficulty in communications and social interactions led to a regional diversity in the law. Consequently, in the succession, there were different schools, like Dayabhaga in Bengal and the adjoining areas; Mayukha in Bombay, Konkan and Gujarat and Marumakkattayam or Nambudri in Kerala and Mitakshara in other parts of India with slight variations.

751. The law of inheritance consists of rules which determine the mode of devolution of the property of the deceased on heirs solely on the basis of their relationship to the deceased, while laws of testamentary succession deal with the rules relating to devolution of property on relations as well as others. This is the main distinction between the two terms, succession and inheritance. Succession opens at the time of the death of the person whose estate is in question and is governed by the law in force at the time. A person who dies without making a will is known as intestate.

752. The multiplicity of succession laws, diverse in their nature, owing to their varied origin made the property laws even more complex. A woman in a joint Hindu family, consisting both of man and woman, had a right to sustenance, but the control and ownership of property did not vest in her. A female cannot be a member of the coparcenary in Mitakshara law and joint family property devolves by survivorship within the coparcenary. Therefore, with every birth or death of a male in the family, the share of every other surviving male either gets diminished or enlarged. The Mitakshara law also recognizes inheritance by succession but only to the property separately owned by an individual, male or female. Females are included as heirs to this kind of property by Mitakshara law. Before the Hindu Law of Inheritance (Amendment) Act 1929, the Bengal, Benares and Mithila sub schools of

Mitakshara recognized only five female relations as being entitled to inherit, namely widow, daughter, mother paternal grandmother, and paternal great-grandmother.

753. The Madras sub-school recognized the heritable capacity of a larger number of females heirs that is of the son's daughter, daughter's daughter and the sister, as heirs who are expressly named as heirs in Hindu Law of Inheritance (Amendment) Act, 1929. The son's daughter and the daughter's daughter ranked as bandhus in Bombay and Madras. The Bombay school which is most liberal to women, recognized a number of other female heirs, including a half-sister, father's sister and women married into the family such as stepmother, son's widow, brother's widow and also many other females classified as bandhus.

754. In inheritance matters, Hindus are governed by the Hindu Succession Act, 1956. The Hindu Minority and Guardianship Act, 1956 amends and codifies certain parts of the law relating to minority and guardianship among Hindus and the Hindu Adoptions and Maintenance Act, 1956 deals with the law relating to adoptions and maintenance among Hindus. The Hindu Succession Act of 1956 amends and codifies the law relating to intestate succession and brings about some fundamental and radical changes in the law of succession. The act lays down a uniform and comprehensive system of inheritance and applies, *inter alia,* to persons governed by Mitakshara and Dayabhaga schools as also to those in certain parts of southern India who were previously governed by the Murumakkattayam, Alyasanatana and Nambudro systems of Hindu law. The act was last amended in 2005 and has brought in major changes in the classical concept of coparcenary as also in the class I heirs to the property of a male intestate

I. Judicial Pronouncement on Succession

A. Partition of Coparcenary Property

755. In *Shivgonda Balgonda Patil v. Director of Resettlement,*[183] the contention of the petitioners that there was automatic partition among the heirs of the deceased Karta on his death has been negatived because it is only when the deceased had left his surviving female heirs as provided in the proviso to section 6 of the Act, a notional partition is deemed to have taken place in the joint family property for the purpose of ascertaining the share of the deceased in the joint family properties which comes to the share of the female heirs. If there are male heirs there is no automatic partition.

756. In *Rameshwari Devi v. State of Bihar,*[184] the dispute was concerning the payment of family pension and death-cum-retirement gratuity to two wives of Narain Lal, who died in 1987 while posted as Managing Director, Rural Development Authority of the State of Bihar. The appellant is the first wife. Narain Lal is

183. AIR 1992 Bom. 72.
184. AIR 2000 SC 735.

stated to have married a second time with Yogmaya Devi while the appellant was still alive. From the first marriage, he had one son and from the second marriage four sons born in 1964, 1971, 1972 and 1976. Learned single judge in his judgment held that children born to Narain Lal from the wedlock with Yogmaya Devi were entitled to share the family pension and death-cum-retirement gratuity and further that family pension would be admissible to the minor children only till they attained majority. It was also held that the second wife Yogmaya Devi was not entitled to anything. Appeal by the first wife Rameshwari Devi against the judgment was dismissed by the Division Bench. According to her, there was no marriage between Narain Lal and Yogmaya Devi and the children were, therefore, not legitimate. Aggrieved Rameshwari Devi has come to this Court.

757. The Supreme Court observed that 'we are concerned only with the question as to who is entitled to the family pension and death-cum-retirement gratuity on the death of Narain Lal. When there are two claimants to the pensionary benefits of a deceased employee and there is no nomination wherever required State Government has to hold an inquiry as to the rightful claimant. Disbursement of pension cannot wait till a civil court pronounces upon the respective rights of the parties. That would certainly be a long drawn affair. Doors of civil courts are always open to any party after and even before a decision are reached by the State Government as to who is entitled to pensionary benefits. Of course, inquiry conducted by the State Government cannot be a sham affair and it could also not be arbitrary. Decision has to be taken in a bona fide reasonable and rational manner. In the present case an inquiry was held which cannot be termed as sham. Result of the inquiry was that both lived as husband and wife since 1963. A presumption does arise, therefore, that marriage of Yogmaya Devi with Narain Lal was in accordance with Hindu rites and all ceremony cannot be disputed that the marriage between Narain Lal and Yogmaya Devi was in contravention of clause (i) of Section 5 of the Hindu Marriage Act and was a void marriage. Under Section 16 of this Act, children of void marriage are legitimate. Under the Hindu Succession Act, 1956, property of a male Hindu dying intestate devolves first on heirs in clause (1) which include widow and son. Among the widow and son, they all get shares (*see* Sections 8, 10 and the Schedule to the Hindu Succession Act, 1956). Yogmaya Devi cannot be described a widow of Narain Lal, her marriage with Narain Lal being void. Sons of the marriage between Narain Lal and Yogmaya Devi being the legitimate sons of Narain Lal would be entitled to the property of Narain Lal in equal shares along with that of Rameshwari Devi and the son born from the marriage of Rameshwari Devi with Narain Lal. That is, however, legal position when Hindu male dies intestate. Here, however, we are concerned with the family pension and death-cum-retirement Gratuity payments which is governed by the relevant rules. It is not disputed before us that if the legal position as aforesaid is correct, there is no error with the directions issued by the learned single Judge in the judgment which is upheld by the Division Bench in LPA by the impugned judgment. Rameshwari Devi has raised two principal objections: (1) marriage between Yogmaya Devi and Narain Lal has not been proved, meaning thereby that there is no witness to the actual performance of the marriage in accordance with the religious ceremonies required for a valid Hindu marriage and (2) without a civil court having pronounced upon the marriage between Yogmaya Devi and Narain Lal in accordance with Hindu rights, it cannot be held that the children of Yogmaya Devi with her marriage with Narain Lal would be legitimate under Section 16 of the Hindu Marriage Act. First objection we have discussed above and there is nothing said by Rameshwari Devi to rebut the presumption in favour of marriage duly performed between Yogmaya Devi and Narain Lal. On the second objection, it is correct that no civil court his pronounced if there was a marriage between Yogmaya Devi and Narain Lal in accordance with Hindu rights. That would, however, not debar the State Government from making an inquiry about the existence of such a marriage and act on that in order to grant pensionary and other benefits to the children of Yogmaya Devi. On this aspect we have already adverted to above. After the death of Narain Lal, inquiry was made by the State Government as to which of the wives of Narain Lal was his legal wife. This was on the basis of claims filed by Rameshwari Devi. Inquiry was quite detailed one and there are in fact two witnesses examined during the course of inquiry being (1) Sant Prasad Sharma, teacher, DAV High School, Danapur and (2) Sri Basukinath Sharma, Shahpur Maner who testified to the marriage between Yogmaya Devi and Narain Lal having witnessed the same. That both Narain Lal and Yogmaya Devi were living as husband and wife and four sons were born to Yogmaya Devi from this wedlock has also been testified during the course of inquiry by Chandra Shekhar Singh, Rtd District Judge, Bhagalpur, Smt. (Dr) Arun Prasad, Sheohar, Smt. S.N. Sinha, w/o Sri S.N. Sinha, ADM and others. Other documentary evidence were also collected which showed Yogmaya Devi and Narain Lal were living as husband and wife. Further, the sons of the marriage between Yogmaya Devi and Narain Lal were shown in records as sons of Narain Lal. But then it is not necessary for us to consider if Narain Lal could have been charged of misconduct having contracted a second marriage when his first wife was living as no disciplinary proceedings were held against him during his lifetime. In the present case, we are concerned only with the question as to who is entitled to the family pension and death-cum-retirement gratuity on the death of Narain Lal. When there are two claimants to the pensionary benefits of a deceased employee and there is no nomination wherever required State Government has to hold an inquiry as to the rightful claimant. Disbursement of pension cannot wait till a civil court pronounces upon the respective rights of the parties. That would certainly be a long drawn affair. Doors of civil courts are always open to any party after and even before a decision are reached by the State Government as to who is entitled to pensionary benefits. Of course, inquiry conducted by the State Government cannot be a sham affair and it could also not be arbitrary. Decision has to be taken in a bona fide reasonable and rational manner. In the present case an inquiry was held which cannot be termed as sham. Result of the inquiry was that Yogmaya Devi and Narain Lal lived as husband and wife since 1963. A presumption does arise, therefore, that marriage of Yogmaya Devi with Narain Lal was in accordance with Hindu rites and all ceremonies connected with a valid Hindu marriage were performed. This presumption Rameshwari Devi has been unable to rebut. Nevertheless, that, however, does not make the marriage between Yogmaya Devi and Narain Lal as legal. Of course, when there is a charge of bigamy under Section 494 IPC strict proof of solemnization of the second marriage with due observance of rituals and ceremonies has been insisted upon'.

758. Having considered all the facts of the case presented before us we do not find any error in the impugned judgment of the Division Bench of the Patna High Court upholding the judgment of the learned single judge referred to in the beginning of this judgment. The appeal was dismissed.

B. Right of Child in Womb

759. A child who was in the womb at the time of the death of an intestate and who is subsequently born alive has the same right to inherit the intestate as if he or she had been born before the death of the intestate, and the inheritance shall be deemed to vest in such a case with effect from the date of the death of the intestate.

C. Equal Rights to Daughter

760. In a joint Hindu family governed by Mitakshara law, the daughter of a coparcener shall by birth, become a coparcener in her own right in the same manner as the son and have the same rights in the coparcenary property as she would have had if she had been a son, inclusive of the right to claim by survivorship; and shall be subject to the same liabilities and disabilities in respect thereto as the son:

- at a partition in such a joint Hindu family the coparcenary property shall be so divided as to allot to a daughter the same share as allotted to a son;
- Provided that the share which a pre-deceased son or a pre-deceased daughter would have got at the partition if he or she had been alive at the time of the partition shall be allotted to the surviving child of such pre-deceased son or of such pre-deceased daughter;
- Provided further that the share allotted to the pre-deceased child of a pre-deceased son or of a pre-deceased daughter, if such child had been alive at the time of the partition, shall be allotted to the child of such pre-deceased child of the pre-deceased son or of the pre-deceased daughter as the case may be;
- any property to which a female Hindu becomes entitled by virtue of the provisions of clause (i) shall be held by her with the incidents of coparcenary ownership and shall be regarded, notwithstanding anything contained in this Act or any other law for the time being in force, as property capable of being disposed of by her by will or other testamentary disposition;
- Nothing in clause (ii) shall apply to a daughter married prior to or to a partition which had been effected before the commencement of the Hindu Succession (Andhra Pradesh Amendment) Act, 1986.

D. Testamentary Succession

761. Any Hindu may dispose of by will or other testamentary disposition any property, which is capable of being so disposed of by him or by her, in accordance with the provisions of the Indian Succession Act, 1925 (39 of 1925), or any other law for the time being in force and applicable to Hindus. The interest of a male Hindu in a Mitakshara coparcenary property or the interest of a member of a tarwad, tavazhi, illom, kutumba or kavaru in the property of the tarwad, tavazhi, illom, kutumba or kavaru shall notwithstanding anything contained in this Act or in any other law for the time being in force, be deemed to be property capable of being disposed of by him or by her.

E. Position of Will

762. A will permits a person, the testator, to make decisions on how his estate will be managed and distributed after his death. At common law, an instrument disposing of Personal Property was called a 'testament', whereas a will disposed of real property. Over time the distinction has disappeared so that a will, sometimes called a 'last will and testament', disposes of both real and personal property. If a person does not leave a will, or the will is declared invalid, the person will have died intestate, resulting in the distribution of the estate according to the laws of Descent and Distribution of the state in which the person resided. Because of the importance of a will, the law requires it to have certain elements to be valid. Apart from these elements, a will may be ruled invalid if the testator made the will as the result of undue influence, fraud, or mistake.

1. Requirement of a Will

763. A valid will cannot exist unless three essential elements are present. First, there must be a competent testator. Second, the document purporting to be a will must meet the execution requirements of statutes, often called the Statute of Wills, designed to ensure that the document is not a fraud but is the honest expression of the testator's intention. Third, it must be clear that the testator intended the document to have the legal effect of a will.

764. If a will does not satisfy these requirements, any person who would have a financial interest in the estate under the laws of descent and distribution can start an action in the probate court to challenge the validity of the will. The persons who inherit under the will are proponents of the will and defend it against such an attack. This proceeding is known as a will contest. If the people who oppose the admission of the will to probate are successful, the testator's estate will be distributed according to the laws of descent and distribution or the provisions of an earlier will, depending on the facts of the case.

765. The development of the country after independence has changed practices and lifestyles in urban India while rural setups are still struggling with adherence to customary practices in family law matters. Will society catch up with law or will the legislature enact a law on the asking of the courts to change societal practices? This remains to be seen. However, the fact remains that until the rural masses in India are educated and motivated to change for the better, any change in laws may not really help. True change is not likely to come until the local society concludes that the unhealthy social edifices of child marriage must be dismantled and that the exploitation of married women must cease. Awareness and motivation for change must come from within the community and cannot be enforced by any law.

Part XI. Religion and Culture

Chapter 1. Religion and Art

766. Indian art is religious inasmuch as it is largely dedicated to the service of one of several religions. The primary purpose may be to induce contemplation and thereby put the worshipper in communication with the divine. Not all Indian art, however, is purely religious, and some of it is only nominally so and deals with other aspects. For example, an image of Vishnu and an image of Buddha of the same period are stylistically the same, religion having little to do with the mode of artistic expression. The religious nature of Indian art accounts to some extent for its essentially symbolic and abstract nature. It scrupulously avoids illusionistic effects, evoked by imitation of the physical and ephemeral world of the senses; instead, objects are made in imitation of ideal, divine prototypes, whose source is the inner world of the mind.

767. Religion has, over the years, played a major role in Indian art. Religious beliefs, such as, Hinduism, Buddhism, Jainism and Islam have provided several themes which had enabled the variant art forms in India to flourish. In fact, it would not be completely wrong to state that in India art is religion and religion is art. At the very beginning Indian symbols of art voiced the same truth as Indian philosophy and myth. Religious texts of Hinduism and Buddhism specifically stated that making of images leads to heaven. Indian art in all periods is close to the lives of all creatures on earth.

The Mathura School of Art and Gandhara School of Art and Sculpture which flourished during the reign of Kanishka of the Kushana Empire has strong influence of Buddhism. But Buddhist art reached its zenith during the Gupta period. While the north Indian kingdoms showered their patronage on both Buddhist and Hindu forms of art, the scenario down south was quite different. The imperial Cholas, the kingdom of Vijayanagar Empire, Cheras and other dynasties encouraged the development of Dravidian art and sculpture. Built out of stone, the temples in South India narrate tales of the brilliant craftsmanship. One of the greatest instances of Indian art still available in the ancient village of Hampi.

768. The medieval era of Indian art was hugely influenced by the spread of Islam and Muslim rule. This period in turn was inspired by Persian art. The amalgamation of Indo-Islamic style was introduced in India by the Delhi Sultanate. This development brought rich innovative ideas into Indian art. The influence of Islamic art reached its peak under the Mughals and was spotted in all major forms of paintings, pottery, ceramics and miniatures. The influence of Hindu religion is greatly perceived in the Rajput art forms. But the Rajput paintings also reflect Mughal influence. The theme of the paintings revolves around the epics of Ramayana and the Mahabharata and the life of Lord Krishna. The Rajputs paintings of Amber and Jaipur bear Mughal influence because at that time the Mughals ruled the princely state of Rajasthan. Hinduism, during this era, has cast its influence on the temple architecture of southern India. The colossal structures and the sculptures engraved in these shrines speak volumes about the artistry that was predominant during that era. The rampant construction of Hindu temples continued under the Hoysala Empire, Chalukya Dynasty and Rastrakuta Dynasty in South India.

769. In Punjab and Haryana, the Music in Muslim Shrines Act, 1942 was brought to regulate activities of dancing which is against Islam. No doubt Qawwali takes place at the shrines which is a normal feature. The expression 'Muslim Shrine' has been defined as a shrine of a recognized Muslim saint and shall include the premises of the shrine and the premises owned by and attached to the shrine. If any woman or girl sings to the accompaniment of a musical instrument or dances with or without a musical instrument in a Muslim Shrine, she shall be guilty of an offence under this Act and shall be liable on conviction to be punished with fine not exceeding INR 500 or with imprisonment of either description for a term not exceeding six months or with both such fine and imprisonment.

If any person abets an offence punishable under the last preceding section, he shall, whether such offence be or be not committed in consequence of such abetment, and notwithstanding anything contained in section 116 of the IPC, be liable on conviction to be punished with the punishment, provided for the offence. An offence punishable under this Act shall be cognizable, bailable, non-compoundable and triable by a Judicial Magistrate of the first class.

770. With the advent of Christianity and start of British dominance, Indian works of sculpture, painting, and architecture were devoted to reveal the divine personality of the Gods and to increase the dignity of the church. Before the intrusion of Western influence, there was never in Indian art anything corresponding to the copying of nature. The sculpture and architecture of the colonial period varied from the early attempts to create the classical prototypes to the comparatively newer Indo-Saracenic style, which is a mixture of Hindu, Islamic and Western elements. The several religions which include Hinduism, Buddhism, Christianity, Islam and others at different times have immensely contributed in shaping the various styles of Indian art. The diverse spiritual inspiration and the religious beliefs added to the unique nature of Indian art.

Chapter 2. Religion and Media

771. The stories on religion, religious groups and its use in election politics occupy a substantial part of the media coverage. It is a well-known fact that ignorance and prejudices are the main obstacles to fair reporting of religious controversies. The reporter must know and have a basic understanding of the religion if that is not their religion and even if it is their religion and they are ignorant of the aspect being reported. For example, it has been seen many times that the journalists who report about Fatwa did not know that every moulvi or maulana or Hafiz or Imam of a mosque cannot issue a Fatwa unless he has been authorized as a qualified mufti. The reporter goes to the extent that if any bearded man with Muslim dress says something it is tried to be passed as Fatwa. Further, Fatwa is neither a religious dictat nor a ruling; it is just a jurist's opinion on specific facts and circumstances brought to the notice by one who wants to get a Fatwa. The facts and circumstances may be brought to the notice of the mufti by one party only and the other party is not consulted and such Fatwa is not binding on everyone. So even a properly issued Fatwa is only an opinion on the basis of, maybe, one-sided facts.

772. The aspect is that religion-related violence is reported by the media in such a way that sometimes it helps in the incitement, production and reproduction of violence. The media, which seek to classify and label communal incidents, often become part of the diversionary tactics of the organizers of violence to displace blame from themselves to others, says Paul R. Brass.[185] He exposes a lacuna in the study of collective violence saying that journalists and social scientists study the phenomena of violence 'to display their theoretical skills' rather than expose the dynamic processes that produce those phenomena.

773. As per certain studies, the violence or a 'riot' is incited in three phases: preparation or rehearsal, activation or enactment and explanation or interpretation, says Brass. In the sites where rioting is endemic, producers of violence continuously work to create an atmosphere of religious animosity as part of their preparation and rehearsal process, he says. The activation or enactment of a large-scale riot takes place under particular circumstances, often in a context of intense political mobilization or electoral competition in which riots are precipitated as a device to consolidate the support of ethnic, religious, or other culturally marked groups, by emphasizing the need for solidarity in face of the rival communal group. It is generally criminals and sometimes certain elements in society prone to incitement who are recruited and rewarded for enacting the violence. The third phase follows the violence in a broader struggle to control the explanation or interpretation of the causes of the violence. In this phase, even journalists, politicians, social scientists, and public opinion become involved. For, it is marked by a process of blame displacement, in which social scientists and journalists themselves become implicated,

185. Professor (Emeritus) of Political Science and International Studies at the University of Washington, Seattle, in his book, *Forms of Collective Violence: Riots, Pogroms, and Genocide in Modern India.*

a process that fails to isolate effectively those most responsible for the spread of violence, and instead diffuses blame widely, blurring responsibility, and thereby contributing to the perpetuation of the same cycle in future. The principal beneficiaries of this process of blame displacement are political leaders, who try to derive political capital out of it. Brass says politicians and the vernacular media, during the violence, and in its aftermath, draw attention away from the perpetrators of the violence by attributing it to the actions of an inflamed mass public. Ignorant of the diversionary tactics, researchers think they must know what they are studying or label an incident of violence before they can make the necessary generalizations. But, 'the producers of violence are themselves engaged in the same process and they continually outpace and outwit the civil society, producing new and varied forms of collective violence', Brass observes.

774. The producers of pogroms 'insist that the violence that has just occurred is nothing more than a riot'. They label genocide-like acts 'as merely spontaneous revenge and retaliation by justly and excusably outraged members of a group, acting spontaneously against an "other" group whose members have misbehaved'. Brass says there exist 'institutionalized riot systems' in several parts of the country. He concludes that the main job of researchers should not be to classify and label precisely such violence, as 'no hard and fast distinction can be made between these supposedly distinct forms of violence, since pogroms masquerade as riots and many, if not most, large-scale riots display features supposedly special to pogroms'. There are other forms of genocide than the likes of the Holocaust and which are 'particularly of the mutual and retributive type (which seem like riots between two communities), a form of violence that develops in stages that constitute clear danger signals'. The researchers, he suggests, should rather 'observe' the assignment of blame as part of the process of production of violence and seek 'to expose to view the dynamics of violence and the ways in which each new large event of collective violence is, in fact, different from all others that have preceded it because of the very fact that its producers know very well what it is that they do, what has happened before, how to displace blame from themselves to others'.

§1. Focus of Media on Politicians' Concerns

775. It is a general trend in the reporting of political affairs that journalists focus the most on politicians' concerns. There are numerous reports in newspapers, agencies, and magazines that deal primarily with how certain policies and moves by a political party are likely to affect the party itself – rather than how those developments will affect the people or democracy. The same trend is apparent in the reporting of religion and politics. For example, the Tehelka weekly featured a cover story on the Kashmir shrine land row issue in its 12 July (2008) edition. The cover line read: 'Kashmir, A Losing Hand: Will the Bungling of the Amarnath Issue Fan Communal Fires and Separatism and Prove Costly for the Congress in an Election Year?' Instead of laying the emphasis on how the government could have handled the conflict or exposing the misuse of religion in politics, the story focused on how it would affect the Congress in an election year.

§2. FOCUS OF MEDIA ON MUSLIMS AND CHRISTIANS

776. Muslims get the maximum attention of mainstream and social media. This is because not only are Muslims India's largest minority community but also the main target of certain organizations for polarization in the society. There is no dearth of coverage of issues related to Muslims, which is mainly negative in nature. There is little coverage of progress in the community taken place after independence and how they can be brought out of the backwardness. There is a narrative on mainstream and social media that has widened the gulf between the country's majority Hindus and the minorities. This narrative has directly or indirectly resulted in the rising incidence of lynching over cow slaughter, the questioning of Muslims for their allegiance and patriotism towards the country, the backlash against interfaith marriages, the anti-conversion attacks on Christians, etc. Further, there was labelling of those speaking out for communal harmony as 'terrorist sympathisers' on Twitter and Facebook. India has been recognized globally for its negligible indoctrination and recruitment to pan-Islamist terror groups like Islamic State of Iraq and Levant (ISIS) and Al-Qaeda. Even then, the discourse lends no space for a dialogue so as to understand each other on ways to end the violence. From time to time, political personalities come out with speeches and opinions which verge on hate speech and downgrading and blaming a particular community in general terms. Certain communities are used as whipping boy for various reasons like diverting the attention from real issues of bread and butter.

777. Besides, some Hindu organizations complain that problems related to their community are not adequately featured in the media, mainly the English language publications. One such problem they bring to the fore is the condition of Kashmiri Hindu pandits, who had to flee Kashmir due to a threat from Kashmiri and foreign militants in 1990. Till today, thousands of displaced Kashmiri pandits live in refugee camps.

Chapter 3. Religion and Civil Society

778. The civil society acts as the conscience keeper of the nation and takes up common causes. Civil society includes social institutions and networks which lie outside of the state and the market. Thus, it includes under its definition, NGOs, communities and local groups. Civil society may be defined as the space of interaction between the state and society. Today we talk mainly in terms of good governance in development and social science discourses. Good governance involves adopting initiatives that develop capacities, which in turn realize development and empower the poor and marginalized. Good governance involves the management of power and resources in a way that is participative, equitable, transparent and efficient.

779. In India a civil society based on rational thinking and reasonable approach is existing and further evolving. However, people are prompted to line up more on religious and caste basis rather than on merits of issues and/or matters. In elections these caste and religious sentiments are exploited. In the process, certain section of citizenry is alienated which is not desirable. In the interest of nation-building, there must not be communities or groups or regions that may feel alienated from the state or marginalized from the circles of power. Sometimes attempts to keep communication open with dissatisfied groups have been made and in some cases issue has been resolved successfully.

780. The inability to participate effectively in economic, social, political and cultural life of the mainstream society, implicating thereby alienation and distance is social exclusion. This concept of social exclusion which is sometimes intentionally used by majority, is employed specifically to try and understand the social, economic and political place of religious minorities in Modern India. What is attempted is the understanding of the ways in which discrimination and deprivation work and how through proactive policies, the law and democracy may protect rights, increase participation and enhance securities.

781. In India, some elements propagate an idea that Muslims constitute a fifth column and a threat which is sometimes voiced by certain leaders from time to time. Recently Christians have also been accused of conversion and a threat to the country. This idea has been unfortunately buttressed by the history of partition, the long battle over Kashmir with Pakistan and Hindu-Muslim violence in different parts of the country mainly after Independence.

782. While a genuine fear of terrorist activity cannot be dismissed, but the vilification of an entire community cannot aid understanding or contribute a solution to the problem. Terror activity can happen any time and is difficult to prevent. Efforts cannot focus solely on terror prevention through increasing security measures, rather efforts are to be made to establish more equitable and just social and political structures, responsive government. The grouping based on caste and communities must be empowered so as they may not feel suffocated and at the end of the road or cornered.

783. It is unfortunate that there have been many occurrences that have contributed to spreading fear and uncertainty among minorities. There has been public questioning of the idea of secularism and its value for the Indian nation by some political parties. This has contributed to a growing sense of unease among different communities. There has been increasing collective violence against minorities and the complicity of the state has been pointed out by scholarly and investigative reports and action is delayed and tardy.

784. India has more Muslims than Pakistan and Muslims qualify probably to be called India's second majority, rather than merely its largest minority. Even so, the average standard of living of Indian Muslims is below that of the Other Backward Classes and only slightly better than that of the Scheduled Castes.

785. Some political groups contend that secularism is a 'favour' to minorities and that secularism exists in India largely because of the presence of so many minority groups. But the fact remains that even if all Indians were of one religion, only secularism could protect the democratic framework. This is because, crucially, secularism not merely protects 'communities' from each other but also protects individuals from the tight confinement that communities sometimes seek to impose on them. The militancy and terror are best prevented and contained when communities have faith in the government and judicial system, the law and the police and are willing to work with them. Security is thus best ensured by ensuring the protection of life, property and livelihood.

786. Engaging with civil society prevents civic conflict and can help contain militancy and terrorism. The state is to work to flush out terrorists without alienating or incriminating whole communities. The police and army only cannot protect against terror; the active and continuous watchfulness of communities and the public is a must. Security cannot be assured by the display or employment of sophisticated weaponry. Security lies in the acts of vigilance of ordinary citizens, which can only be built on the mutual trust of all the communities without alienating any community.

787. The representatives of the state need to interact continuously with local-level committees (such as mohalla committees) and with other civic groups in society. It is of greater significance that quick and impartial actions are taken in times of civic and ethnic violence. The protection of all citizens must be taken as and ensured by the state being the state's primary duty. Justice needs to be done; even more than that, it needs to be seen to have been done.

Chapter 4. Religion and Public Debate

788. The public debate on religion has been focused on secularism, conversion, the Uniform Civil Code, Love Jehad, the role of Madarsas, etc. Certain States came out with their own Uniform Civil Code like the State of Uttarakhand.

§1. Secularism

789. The debate on secularism has gained importance and come into focus in past decades in India. Secularism is understood as mere tolerance of other people's religions. However, secularism is not necessarily the same as atheism. It is an attitude which actively seeks a rational understanding of life's phenomena and resists transcendental explanations or beliefs based on authority. The debate started heating up since the Ram Janmabhoomi-Babri masjid controversy leading up to the Babri masjid demolition (on 6th December 1992). The incident showed how powerful religion can be and this generated a debate on the existing theories of secularism in India. Thus, different shades of this debate became visible in the due course, with no proper long-term solution in sight. All that is visible is a name game, whereby a particular community blames the other for communal actions and likewise, political parties blame their counterparts for being communal or rather spreading communal tension.

790. Secularism, in India is understood as meaning equal respect to all religions, it should not mean equal encouragement to fundamentalism of all communities or political parties. Presently because of vote politics, secularism is under great threat in many countries, including India. There are multiple intervening forces at work the either slow down or hamper the successful functioning of a secular State. A strange combination of religious fundamentalism mixed with political conditions of the country is often seen which is mistaken for nationalism.

§2. Conversion

791. Almost all the countries in the world guarantee freedom of religion in some form or the other. Such a guarantee assumes importance in a multi-religion country like India which owes its religious diversity to history rather than any recent or contemporary phenomena. International instruments like the Universal Declaration of Human Rights (UDHR), European Convention on Human Rights (ECHR) and ICCPR (International Covenant on Civil and Political Rights) explicitly recognize that the right to conversion is implicit in the right to freedom of religion. Why people convert is a subject matter of many disciplines viz. psychology, sociology, and theology but not law as law is only concerned with the legality or illegality of the reasons but not the reasons per se. One of the most significant factors credited with motivating individuals to convert to other religions is relative deprivation and rights of individuals as set by the social system. The studies conducted on conversion reveal that economic, social, moral, spiritual, and psychological deprivation has been described as the key impetus behind a person's decision to alter their religious identities. Most importantly gravitation towards other religions may also be a consequence of brainwashing, or persuasion by way of coercion.

792. Religion is a volatile issue and religious conversions add more to the volatility of the issue therefore various state governments have enacted anti-conversion laws with the purported aim of preventing conversions brought about by coercion or inducements. Such laws have been a subject of intense debate and criticism and have been alleged as infringing on one's right to freedom of religion. Anti-conversion laws are promulgated on the premise that forced or induced conversions happen and need to be prevented. Such laws are controversial because they run the risk of being abused by certain sections in the country. Because legislative intent of such laws can be ascertained by reading the statute holistically with the aid of various tools of interpretation but no such tools exist to ascertain the intent behind an act of conversion, which is deeply personal or spiritual. So how one can distinguish between conversion as a sincere act of conscience from that of one brought about by corruptible means. The problem is further aggravated in case of mass conversions (as opposed to individual conversion) and a question is often debated regarding the genuineness of such acts because they are often done for a political agenda more and have little or nothing to do with faith or conscience. Conversion, by its very nature, defies any setting up of rational standards against which pronouncements regarding its genuineness can be made.

§3. Uniform Civil Code (UCC)

793. Every few years, the country engages in a furious debate on the Uniform Civil Code (UCC). It seeks to replace India's religious and customary laws governing marriage, divorce and inheritance with one code that applies to all communities. Opponents question the need for the code and argue that it would destroy the diversity of the country. The current debate started when the 22nd Law Commission issued a public notice seeking comments on the UCC. This came as a surprise given the 21st Law Commission, after public discussion, concluded that a UCC was 'neither necessary nor desirable at this stage'. The 22nd Law Commission's primary justification for the re-examination was that more than three years had passed since the previous report. The campaign for a UCC has been part of certain political party's agenda and has repeatedly featured in their manifestoes over the years. There is also demand for a UCC from certain sections of the women's rights movement. The tribal community and certain northeast states do not want UCC. They are excluded from statutory Hindu law which is a recognition of their special status under the Constitution. The Constitution accords special status to certain tribals and tribal-dominated northeastern states, exempting them from the application of personal laws made by Parliament.

794. The Hindu code preserves certain unique features of Hindu personal law, such as the concept of a 'joint family'. A Hindu has a share in the family's ancestral property as a birthright, which entitles them to maintenance through such property and to seek partition of the property in court. This right was only available to Hindu men but an amendment in 2006 expanded coverage to Hindu women. A Muslim does not have such type of right at birth. Further, Joint Family also has certain benefits under income tax laws which are not available to non-Hindus.

795. Any UCC will need to deal with the complexity of religious and tribal identities and answer some sensitive questions. Lawmakers will need to decide whether to abolish the unique features of Hindu law along with those of other legal systems. Can tribal communities be forced to follow a system of law against their age-old cultural traditions which they never asked for and do not want? These are difficult questions that any UCC draft will need to address and without a central draft currently available, it is unclear how a UCC will be acceptable. The supporters insist that uniformity will address these problems. In the absence of a comprehensive draft of a UCC from the Union Government, this debate will continue without any result.

Selected Bibliography

Brass Paul R, Professor (Emeritus) 'Forms of Collective Violence: Riots, Pogroms, and Genocide in Modern India', September 2006.

Cheema Karamat Iqtidar (Dr). 'Constitutional and Legal Challenges Faced by Religious Minorities in India', US Commission on International Religious Freedom, February 2017.

Consultation Paper on Reform of Family Law, Law Commission of India, Government of India, August 31, 2018: http://lawcommissionofindia.nic.in/reports/CPonReformFamilyLaw.pdf.

Diwan Paras. 'Family Law (Hindus, Muslims, Christians, Parsis and Jews)', Allahabad Law Agency, 2013.

Evaluation of the Implementation of the Scheme for Providing Quality Education in Madarsas (SPQEM) Report, January 2018, National Institute of Educational Planning and Administration.

'Genocide in Modern India' www.paulbrass.com.

International Religious Freedom Report, 2023 by US Commission International Religious Freedoms (USCIRF).

IOSR Journal of Humanities and Social Science (IOSR-JHSS) Volume 19, Issue 2, Ver. IV (February 2014), PP 08-19 e-ISSN: 2279-0837, p-ISSN: 2279-0845. www.iosrjournals.org.

Mahmood Tahir & Mahmood Saif. *Introduction to Muslim Law*, Delhi: Universal Law Publishing Co. Pvt. Ltd., 2013.

Mahmood Tahir. *Principles of Hindu Law-Personal Law of Hindus, Buddhists, Jains & Sikhs'*. Delhi: Universal Law Publishing Co. Pvt. Ltd., 2014.

Mustafa Faizan & Sahi Jagteshwar Singh. Freedom of Religion in India: Current Issues and Supreme Court Acting as Clergy;https//digitalcommonslaw.byu.edu/lawreview/vol2017/iss4/9.

Singh Rakesh Kumar Dr. *Text Book on Muslim Law*. Delhi: Universal Law Publishing Company, 2011.

Selected Bibliography

Index

The numbers here refer to paragraph numbers.

Index

Index

www.ingramcontent.com/pod-product-compliance
Lightning Source LLC
Chambersburg PA
CBHW070242030525
26096CB00033B/1228
* 9 7 8 9 4 0 3 5 1 1 7 9 5 *